Studies in Political Science

Edited by DR MALCOLM ANDERSON
University of Warwick

7

THE GAULLIST PHENOMENON
The Gaullist Movement in the Fifth Republic

THE GAULLIST PHENOMENON

The Gaullist Movement in the Fifth Republic

Jean Charlot

Translated by Monica Charlot and Marianne Neighbour

London
GEORGE ALLEN AND UNWIN LTD
RUSKIN HOUSE · MUSEUM STREET

This translation © George Allen & Unwin Ltd 1971

Le phénomène gaulliste first published
by Fayard, Paris, 1970

ISBN 0 04 320069 9 Cased
0 04 320070 2 Paper

Printed in Great Britain
in 10 point Plantin type
by The Aldine Press, Letchworth

To Monica

CONTENTS

PART THREE: PRESIDENTIAL GAULLISM

TABLES

ILLUSTRATIONS

TERMS AND ABBREVIATIONS

C.D.	*Centre démocrate*
C.D.P.	*Centre démocratie et progrès*
C.D.R.	*Comités de défense de la République*
C.F.E.I.	*Centre féminine d'études et d'information*
C.I.C.	*Centre d'information civique*
C.N.I.(P.)	*Centre national des indépendants (et paysans)*
C.R.R.	*Centre de la Réforme républicaine*
F.G.D.S.	*Fédération de la gauche démocrate et socialiste*
F.L.N.	*Front de libération national (Algeria)*
(F.N.)R.I.	*(Fédération nationale des) Républicains indépendants*
F.N.S.P.	*Fondation nationale des sciences politiques (Paris)*
I.F.O.P.	*Institut français d'opinion publique (opinion polls)*
J.R.I.	*Jeunes Républicains indépendants*
M.R.P.	*Mouvement républicain populaire (Christian Democratic Party)*
N.A.T.O.	*North Atlantic Treaty Organization*
O.A.S.	*Organisation armée secrète (Algerian European terrorists)*
P.C.(F.)	*Parti communiste (français)*
P.D.M.	*Progrès et démocratie moderne*
P.S.U.	*Parti socialiste unifié*
R.P.F.	*Rassemblement du peuple français (Gaullist party 1947–53)*
S.A.C.	*Service d'action civique*
S.F.I.O.	*Parti socialiste (section française de l'Internationale ouvrière)*
U.D.Ve	*Union des démocrates pour la Ve République (Gaullist party 1967–8)*
U.D.R.	*Union des démocrates pour la République (Gaullist party 1968–)*
U.D.T.	*Union démocratique du travail*
U.G.Ve	*Union de la gauche Ve République*
U.G.P.	*Union gaulliste populaire*
U.J.P.	*Union des jeunes pour le Progrès*
U.N.R.	*Union pour la nouvelle République (Gaullist party 1958–67)*

INTRODUCTION

A Political Transformation

Two-thirds of this work had been completed when the country was
thunderstruck by the final NO at the referendum on April 27, 1969.
General de Gaulle resigned a little more than ten years after having
become President in 1958. Gaullism was subjected to its supreme trial:
that of finding an answer to the question of the succession. Many had
forecast and still believed that the outcome would be fatal; but our
analysis had led us to the conclusion that since 1962 the political fate of
gaullism had no longer been bound up with the fate of its founder. The
morning after the referendum, we wrote an article for *Le Monde* on the
theme that the NO of April 27 probably marked 'the end of one particular gaullism' but not 'the end of gaullism'.[1] Needless to say, we
followed the opinion polls – long unfavourable towards Georges
Pompidou – with the intensity not of a supporter but of a scientist
poring over his apparatus, fearing the fatal moment when his whole
theory will collapse. Was it luck, or the accuracy of our analysis? The
factors at stake, numerous and inextricable, oblige the political theorist
to be more cautious and more modest than the scientist or the mathe-
matician. However that may be, Georges Pompidou succeeded General
de Gaulle to the Presidency on June 15, 1969, and we have been able to
finish the book by publishing what had already been drafted with the
addition of a supplementary chapter to the part on presidential gaullism
(Part Three).

Many systematic explanations of the gaullist phenomenon have been
offered since 1958, but they must have been either inadequate or
repugnant to common sense, for no explanation has provided the
opposition with a solid basis on which to build a political strategy. The
weaknesses of the interpretations of gaullism have in the event reinforced gaullism itself.

Most French people, if not the specialists in political sociology,
attributed the strength of gaullism to that of General de Gaulle himself.
'In short,' Jean Touchard wrote in his lectures of 1962–3 at the Institute of Political Studies, 'there are only two sorts of gaullism: the

gaullism of General de Gaulle and popular gaullism, or rather let us say there is only one: the gaullism of General de Gaulle hailed and supported by the plebiscite of the masses.' [2]

The France of M. Pinay, it was said, may still feel a thrill of grandeur when voting for de Gaulle, but basically nothing has changed. The people have not forgotten June 18, 1940; they are still under the spell of the General and would be disappointed if he were not to participate a little longer in the affairs of the country. But one day this heroic interlude will come to an end and French political life will once more follow its normal course. Such an analysis appears rather facile, but it was one which the General's admirers and opponents alike were pleased to accept. But in doing so they disregarded the opinion polls, which revealed that public opinion accepted some of the specific contributions of gaullism not necessarily associated with de Gaulle himself, namely the authority of the state, political stability based on an institutional regime far removed from the old French parliamentary tradition, a policy of independence in East-West relations, of modernism and of economic expansion. As far back as 1962, the image of the gaullist party, as revealed in public opinion polls, was no mere reflection of de Gaulle's image.

The graph of the popularity of de Gaulle shows a downward trend, whilst the graph of votes for the gaullist party at general elections rises sharply.

The view, widely held amongst both politicians and vast sectors of public opinion, that the gaullist phenomenon could be reduced to de Gaulle alone, was less widespread amongst the political scientists. They preferred, on the whole, the more elaborate thesis of a social and economic transformation of society.

The marxists explain gaullism as a transformation of French capitalism: 'The present constitution of France and the working of the regime set up by General de Gaulle,' states Roger Garaudy, 'are the exact political reflection of the economic demands of monopolistic state capitalism.' [3] What does this mean? Henri Claude offers an explanation in the *Cahiers du Communisme* in November 1956 and in a work entitled *Gaullisme et grand capital* (Gaullism and Big Business). The concentration of capital, business and industrial power in a France which is open to the competition of international capitalism and is modernizing its system of production, has rendered the traditional political system obsolete in France. 'The parliamentary capitalism that existed in France during the nineteenth century,' says Henri Claude, 'corresponded to the needs of a competitive capitalism founded on the existence of an enormous number of independent capitalists, for whom parliament was a guarantee against the encroachment of the state. Its function, in so far as it was a public forum for the confrontation of all the interests concerned, was to define a common policy in accordance with the main interests of their class, for there was nowhere else this could be done.' Given the monopolistic state capitalism, on the other hand, the power of the state and that of the monopolies form one single and direct mechanism. 'The traditional parliament,' comments Henri Claude, 'is a body that is out-of-date in the present political situation. It is cumbersome and even harmful. It is a burden in that parliamentary debate delays decisions and harmful in that parliament reflects public opinion and interprets the reactions of the victims of its own exploitation and brigandage. . . . The development of a monopolistic state capitalism demands the presence of an executive power held firmly in hand by big business and entails the decline of parliament reduced to a secondary role.'[4]

It is no longer a matter of preserving a precarious balance between the various strata of the bourgeoisie, but of arbitrating between a limited number of industrial and financial groups, at the expense of the lower middle and middle classes as well as that of the masses. Thus authoritarianism comes into its own. We have here the classic marxist thesis relating to the infrastructure of society, which postulates that man, events and politics have, in practice, no impact on the course of economic and social history, which by definition is regulated by the relationship of production. This is an over-simplified pattern of analysis whose essential postulates have been contradicted by experience; the theory of a single causal factor, that of the exclusive influence of the economic structure on politics, that of the common interests and identical political behaviour of all financial groups, the postulate of the servile dependence of the politicians and administrators upon the 'bankers' and so on. Historical criticism alone is sufficient to reveal the limits of the marxist thesis. If the gaullist regime was to be so favourable to big business, why then did the employers as a whole give so little support to General de Gaulle in the days of the R.P.F., at the presidential election of 1965 and at the referendum of April 1969? In December 1965, the sympathies of most business men lay with Pinay or Lecanuet rather than with de Gaulle, and in June 1969 they hoped that Alain Poher would be elected to the Presidency in preference to the former director-general of Rothschilds, Georges Pompidou.

Some sociologists, like Serge Mallet,[5] without reaching the extreme conclusions of the marxists, also offer an explanation on economic lines centring on the 'infrastructure'. The Fourth Republic had, in a way, dug its own grave when it transformed the old liberal capitalism (almost a poverty-stricken family affair under the Third Republic) into a modern economic system, with a certain amount of planning, and more outward-looking. For from then on, France needed a large, modern party of the right and an authoritative political regime which could give the state the means of controlling the new economic forces which were far more powerful than the mythical 'two hundred families' of the inter-war years, and the strength to arbitrate between its own economic interests and those of the big private monopolies. Gaullism and political modernism, the personalization of power, depolitization, new forces, a new working class, technocracy and the rise of the white-collar worker, the decline of the peasant class, mass culture and television: these elements of wide and far-reaching discussions – more ideological than scientific – are gradually being linked together at a time when, curiously, it is the fashion to talk about 'the end of ideology'.

The French National Foundation of Political Science (F.N.S.P.) launched, in June 1966, a vast research programme directed towards determining, objectively and comparatively, the precise influence of the social and economic changes in France on the political attitudes of Frenchmen. So far only the study on voting behaviour by François Goguel has been published.[6] The work aims at comparing the way electoral voting has evolved in two series of stagnant and economically progressive cantons in nine politically representative 'departments' in France, from April 1928 to June 1968.[7] The hypothesis that the political behaviour of the citizens has been modified by the economic modernization of their environment can thus be tested. The conclusions of François Goguel hold a double interest for us. First of all, in regard to gaullism and communism, the study brings out notable differences in the electoral evolution of stagnant and economically progressive cantons in the same 'department'. The results are less clear in regard to the non-communist left and the moderates. In all cases, however, 'the nature of the traditional political trends of the various departments still constitutes today a very important factor in their voting behaviour, a factor whose effect tends to be weakened by the existence of economic change and reinforced by economic stagnation. This is possibly the result of the mobility, or absence of mobility, of the population. Tradition is weakened in those areas where newcomers from all regions are concentrated, but strengthened and hardened where only a small and increasingly ageing group of the native population remains.'[8] The second conclusion drawn by François Goguel related to gaullism: unlike communism, it finds a more favourable milieu in the progressive cantons of those departments whose traditional orientation is to the left; but it is still more successful in the stagnant cantons of traditionally 'moderate' departments.[9]

Hence, the gaullist phenomenon does not apply merely to the economically 'dynamic' areas of France, since it has made increasing progress in the 'static' areas which by tradition have been politically moderate. The political and economic elements overlap closely and are both shaped by the slow rhythm of social and cultural evolution.

Without wishing to underestimate the value of the above study or the importance of the complex relationship between the socio-economic and political systems, and while awaiting the results of further research in this field, we have studied the gaullist phenomenon from a political standpoint alone and tried to show that at this level anyway a change has definitely occurred.

In an earlier work on the *Union pour la nouvelle République*, we were struck by the fact that the gaullist party based its organization and its discipline on its function in the new political system of the Fifth Republic, and by which it justified itself. This function was to pave the way for the establishment of a majority parliamentary system in a country where the multiparty system and the strength of ideological barriers have created a long tradition of government by assembly.[10]

Many historians and constitutionalists, whilst not denying the originality of the gaullist Republic, limited its implications and above all its life-span by relating it to the cyclical return of authoritarianism – French institutional history is a succession of authoritarian periods spaced out by long periods of anarchic liberalism. René Rémond, for instance, underlined the similarities between gaullism and bonapartism, both founded on the personal authority of an exceptional leader, directly based on popular support, without the intervention of intermediaries.[11] This brilliant analysis, however attractive, only takes into account the gaullism of de Gaulle. Nicholas Wahl spoke of the Fifth Republic as a return to the French 'administrative tradition', which would in its turn be replaced by the 'representative tradition': 'Mixed government has never existed in France because the aristocratic principle of command and the democratic principle of consent, instead of becoming blended within each institution and thus assuring balance and co-operation among them, individually becomes *fully* embodied in *different* and ultimately antagonistic institutions.' [12]

By analysing election results and opinion polls, by using the methods of political science, in particular the systems analysis, we have tried to show that the gaullist phenomenon was not merely a period in an ever-revolving cycle but, on the contrary, the basis of a real change in the French political system: a change from a multiparty to a dominant-party system, with perhaps eventually, as Maurice Duverger foresaw a few years ago, the prospect of a two-party system, and the birth of a 'voter-oriented' party based on the electors and not on activists or notabilities, as are the mass and cadre parties. This transformation of French politics would probably not have occurred but for General de Gaulle, but it was soon to elude him and in part at least to spoil his plans.

Notes to the Introduction

1. Cf. *Le Monde*, May 2, 1969.
2. Jean Touchard, *Cours sur les idées politiques dans la France contemporaine*, I.E.P., Paris, 1962–3, Multigr., pp. 189–91.
3. Roger Garaudy, *Pour un modèle français du socialisme*, Gallimard, Paris, 1968, p. 257 (Collection idées).
4. Henri Claude, 'Constitution gaulliste et monopoles capitalistes', in *Cahiers du Communisme*, November 1969.
5. Cf. in particular *La nouvelle classe ouvrière*, ed. du Seuil, Paris, 1963, or *Le gaullisme et la gauche*, ed. du Seuil, Paris, 1965.
6. François Goguel, *Modernisation économique et comportement politique*, A. Colin, Paris, 1969, p. 88. (F.N.S.P. – Travaux et recherches de Science politique, I).
7. The nine departments taken in this sample are: Calvados, l'Ille-et-Vilaine, le Haut-Rhin, and les Vosges – dominated in 1928 by the moderates; la Drôme and le Gard – dominated by the left in the same period; le Cher, le Lot-et-Garonne and la Haute-Vienne, where the left was again victorious but was already marked by communism. The 103 cantons examined in this study represent 3.30 per cent of the votes cast in 1928 and 3.46 per cent in 1968 in relation to the whole of Metropolitan France. The distinction between stagnant and economically progressive cantons is based on the results of censuses in 1954 and 1962 – increase and rejuvenation of the population, expansion and variation of employment for some, restriction and demographic ageing, less opportunity for varied employment (especially in the peasant group) for others; the distinction is also based on the evidence of local notabilities.
8. François Goguel, op. cit., pp. 87–8.
9. Ibid., p. 86.
10. Jean Charlot, *L'U.N.R., étude du pouvoir au sein d'un parti politique*, A. Colin, Paris, 1967, general conclusion p. 306.
11. René Rémond, *La droite en France*, Aubier-Montaigne, Paris, new edition brought up to date and published 1969. Cf. in particular the last chapter.
12. Cf. Nicholas Wahl, *The Fifth Republic. France's New Political System*, Random House, New York, 1959; see also the same author's work on France in Beer and Ulam, *Patterns of Government: The Major Political Systems of Europe*, Random House, New York, 1959.

PART ONE

THE GAULLISM OF THE ELECTORATE

CHAPTER I

The Strength of Gaullism

ON STRATEGY IN POLITICS

It is never good strategy to 'forget' one's opponents. As Maurice Thorez remarked, 'He is a poor strategist who thinks it is enough to have drawn up detailed plans, to have mapped out the battle order and given the troops marching orders for everything to be settled and for one victory to lead to the next.' [1] The remark is full of good sense, but it is easier said than put into practice, for it requires self-control and objectiveness as well as the ability to analyse the situation.

Moreover, if the enemy is of a new type, if he uses unusual methods, things become even more complicated. The enemy no longer seems to be playing the game, because in fact he is playing *another* game; this was the advantage the armies of the French Revolution had in 1793 when they invented total war, mass conscription and the economic mobilization of the nation; the generals of the Ancient Regime found it incomprehensible that victories could be won by those vagabonds who ignored all the rules of war. It took them twenty years to reverse the situation and admit they had to forget what they had learned in their Military Academies.

Gaullism is like a foreign body within the French political system, and from 1946 to 1958 the system resisted it successfully. Had the Algerian problem in May 1958 not been so acute, de Gaulle would probably never have been transplanted to Matignon. The political notabilities, the traditional parties, the press and force of habit all converged to isolate him, to limit the effects of his presence on the French constitution. But in October 1962 the situation was fundamentally different because universal suffrage had helped surmount the first problem.

The great temptation of the French opposition parties was to await the return of a more normal political life – especially since the gaullist movement seemed fragile and 'post-gaullism' barely credible. The electors, according to the opinion polls, were not convinced of the durability of the movement. Prior to September 1962 not one Frenchman out of five thought it would last.

TABLE I: *The chances of gaullism according to opinion polls*

Opinion Polls I.F.O.P. (%)	February 1959[1]	September 1962[2]	Opinion Polls I.F.O.P. (%)	November 1962[3]	February 1967[4]	June 1968[5]	Opinion Polls I.F.O.P. (%)	March 1966[6]
Lasting success	17	19	Will win votes remain the same	27 —	14 24 } 38	34 —	Once de Gaulle has left, the U.N.R. will still have a part to play	31
Temporary success	48	37	Will lose votes	34	32	26	U.N.R. would cease to be important	46
Don't knows	35	44	Don't knows	39	30	40	Don't knows	23

1. 'Is the success of the U.N.R. temporary or lasting, in your opinion?' *Sondages* 1959, 2, pp. 45–6.
2. 'In the 1958 general election the U.N.R. won a great victory; do you think that this success was temporary, or that it will be confirmed by the next election?' *Sondages* 1963, 2, p. 71 and p. 74.
3. 'Without taking into account your personal preferences, do you think that the following political families will win or lose votes at the next election? U.N.R. . . .?' *Sondages* 1963, 2, p. 105.
4. 'In the next general election, do you think that the gaullists will win or lose ground? Or neither?' *Sondages* 1967, 3, pp. 41–2.
5. 'For each of the following political families, can you say whether, in the next election, you think they will win or lose votes in relation to 1967? . . . U.D.R.?'
6. 'Do you think that if General de Gaulle were to retire or to pass away, the U.N.R.-U.D.T. would continue to play an important part in French political life?' *Sondages* 1966, 1, p. 42.

Even the gaullist voters lacked confidence. In September 1962, 33 per cent of them refused to give their opinion as to the future of the U.N.R., 12 per cent thought its success would be short-lived, and only 55 per cent thought it would be confirmed by the next general election. As it went from victory to victory, the 'credibility' of the gaullist party became stronger, although still leaving the sceptics and the waverers with a comfortable two-thirds majority.

A more careful examination of these polls, however, shows that it was above all those who were against gaullism who saw it as condemned; its partisans, on the contrary, gradually became more sure of themselves. On the eve of the referendum in October 1962, 55 per cent believed that the success of November 1958 would be repeated; on the eve of the general election in March 1967, despite the victory won in November 1962 and the all-but absolute gaullist majority in the National Assembly, 25 per cent of the gaullist electors thought that the U.N.R.-U.D.T. party would do even better and 31 per cent that it would do as well. The next step – belief in the survival of gaullism after de Gaulle – had already been taken in March 1967 by 61 per cent of the gaullist electors. But these points easily escaped those who had no wish to see them. All the more so as public opinion as a whole expected socialists and communists to advance, gaullists to decline. It was not until the general election in June 1968 that the expectations of the electors were reversed, and they then foresaw the failure of the Federation of the Left and the success of the U.D.R.

The gaullists probably gained from their apparent weakness. In fact their presumed vulnerability further convinced their enemies that nothing irrevocable had occurred and that in time things would return to normal. In fact it is always difficult to perceive the transformation of a system when one is part of it and wishes to remain so. The opponents of gaullism have continually been the prisoners of purely defensive delaying tactics, completely lacking in strategy. '. . . It is not enough to evoke the myth of the chief and the bewitching power of propaganda,' Jacques Fauvet wrote after the gaullist success on March 5, 1967. 'Over and above the man and the circumstances, there is without doubt an evolution in the opinion of the public, a deep change. . . .' [2]

This hypothesis never entered into the calculations of those who were opposed to gaullism. By refusing to believe in it, the opposition lessened their own 'credibility' for a great number of Frenchmen.

1958: THE COMMUNISTS

General de Gaulle's return to power was viewed by the communists with a mixture of hostility, anxiety and misplaced confidence. Maurice Thorez thought his party would 'come out of the trial all the greater . . . it is united as never before round its central committee . . . new cadres have come into being . . . the circulation of *L'Humanité* has doubled . . . many new members have been enrolled.' [3] On the eve of the referendum on the Constitution in the autumn of 1958 the communists were convinced that the NO could win at least in France. 'Victory is possible,' stated the editorial of the *Cahiers du Communisme*, 'and the issue is exalting.' [4] The Communist Party appealed to its activists to give up their holidays and devote themselves entirely to the campaign.

The morning after the results was all the more difficult to stomach. The French Communist Party, in the general election of 1956, had obtained some 5,600,000 votes; on September 28, 1958 the NO to the referendum obtained only 4,600,000 votes. If one takes into account the contribution of the dissident socialists, the mendesists and the other left wing voters who had voted NO, then, as Marcel Servin admitted, 'about a million and a half communists voted YES'. An analysis of the different constituencies shows losses among the regular communist electors even in the working-class districts. 'It is the first time since the Liberation that such a phenomenon has occurred.' [5] In November 1958 the general election confirmed the phenomenon; over a million and a half communist electors, that is one in five, did not follow the party line.

1962: THE OTHER OPPOSITION PARTIES

In December 1958 the Socialist Party, the S.F.I.O., which had reaped little reward for coming out in favour of the Fifth Republic,[6] discreetly changed its approbation into 'constructive' opposition. But the turning point for the non-communist opposition came in November 1962. The Algerian affair had been finally brought to an end by the referendum of April 8, 1962 which showed massive approval of the Evian agreement with the Algerian National Front (F.L.N.). De Gaulle clearly saw that the traditional parties were becoming more restive and defiant and he preferred to attack first. Although it was contrary to the procedure set out in the constitution, he organized a referendum on the election of the President of the Republic by universal suffrage. George Pompidou's government was overthrown by the National Assembly; the referendum was pronounced illegal by the *Conseil d'Etat* and, in private, by the majority of the members of the *Conseil Constitutionnel*, which in public declared that the affair was not within its competence. The majority of the political notabilities and all the traditional parties recommended their electors to vote NO.

In fact thirteen million people voted YES, roughly 62.25 per cent of those who voted, 46.6 per cent of the electorate. In view of this latter figure the opposition claimed a partial victory.

The gaullists were expected to poll less votes at the general election; the radicals foresaw that the U.N.R. would be obliged to unite with other parties if it really wanted to govern, for it had, in their opinion, no hope of winning an absolute majority. The C.N.I. believed that its own strength and organization would give it the advantage in the election contest. As for the M.R.P., it counted its unhatched eggs before millions of TV viewers. 'Everyone', its general secretary declared, 'says that the M.R.P. will be one of the great victors in the next election.' Guy Mollet, the S.F.I.O. leader, was less enthusiastic and more concerned with seeing that the greatest possible number of gaullists were defeated. To this end he sought the help of the communists.

Nor on the whole did the political commentators give much encouragement to the gaullists. 'It is already very tempting,' Jacques Fauvet wrote in *Le Monde*, 'for the gaullists to compensate for middling referendum results by good election results and for them to urge the General to take an active part in the election to this end. But . . . if he loses . . . he will be entangled in an endless war. If he wins (*but how can he expect to if the coalition against him lasts until the election*), he will become the leader of a party.' [7]

In fact in the general election of November 1962 the gaullists won an absolute majority of the seats in the National Assembly, the independents lost two-thirds of their seats, the M.R.P. one-third, the communists and socialists won some fifty more seats than in 1958, thanks largely to their tacit agreement on the second ballot, which in many cases left the gaullist candidate facing a *single* representative of the left. The regime had reached a turning-point.

DEFEAT AND ITS REPERCUSSIONS

In 1958 the communists had attributed their defeat in the election to the mistakes made by the other left-wing parties and to the 'great mystification' exercised by gaullism. 'Must I stress,' Maurice Thorez had declared, 'that the policy of the party is right and that a fraction of our electors may have left us without it being evidence against the party or the party line?' At best the party recognized that it had not always listened to the masses with enough attention.[8]

In Marcel Servin's opinion the left had been discounted by public opinion on account of its internal divisions, and many republicans 'have seen in de Gaulle not the incarnation of personal power but a bulwark against the rebellious colonels in Algeria . . .'. Many had believed that de Gaulle 'was capable of solving at long last [the Algerian problem]. . . . For millions of Frenchmen whose national pride was humiliated by the servility of former governments, de Gaulle appeared as the custodian of national greatness and independence.' [9] Apart from the conclusion – that the gaullist hoaxes would be exploded by the constraints of everyday life – the analysis was accurate. But its author was soon to be stripped of all his functions within the Communist Party because of his 'revisionism'.

By 1962 all the opposition parties had found the same simple explanation for the unexpected U.N.R. victory. Political apathy was at the bottom of it, reinforced by the 'scandalous' propaganda of the party in power and the 'official' nature of the candidature. 'Political apathy in France helps gaullsim' read the headline of *Le Populaire* on November

19, 1962; and Claude Fuzier went on to explain that the gaullist regime had led to a falling off of the civic virtues and thus to an increase in the number of non-voters.[10] Political science could have afforded a more satisfactory, less over-simplified explanation of the abnormally low participation in the 1962 election: non-voting was a means of solving the cross-pressures resulting from a traditional attachment to one of the parties that had advised voting NO in the referendum and the fact that the elector had voted YES. But Claude Fuzier went further. Political apathy not only explained the increase in non-voters, but also the very victory of gaullism because to vote gaullist is to withdraw as it were from politics, to shift one's responsibilities; 'The gaullist candidates . . . represent in the eyes of a part of the population General de Gaulle's personal delegates.' The launching of this myth of political apathy and its reinforcement can be measured against the yardstick of gaullist successes and failures; when the former prevail then apathy is undeniable, but when times are happier for the opposition then 'the ballot radically destroys the myth of a politically apathetic France, which', Ernest Cazelles, the socialist, declared after de Gaulle had failed to obtain an absolute majority on the first ballot in 1965, 'the U.N.R. has entertained for the last seven years'.[11]

The 'absolute' weapon of the majority, propaganda and in particular television propaganda, is evaluated in a similar way. 'The strength of the gaullist majority,' the F.G.D.S. stated at the beginning of its election manifesto in 1967, 'is its propaganda.' Since they had been virtually alone in opposition in September 1958 the communists had been the first to incriminate 'the haunting campaign in favour of the YES due to the fact that the government of de Gaulle has the state machine at its service. The press, the radio, the cinema were all of gaullist persuasion.' [12] For François Mitterrand the gaullist victory in November 1958 'was only possible because of the mistakes made by the Fourth Republic and above all because of the massive propaganda peculiar to dictatorial regimes'; therefore it is an 'artificial' victory.[13] 'I had been a Member of Parliament for Flanders for the last sixteen years,' Paul Reynaud declared after his defeat in the 1962 election. 'No inhabitant of my constituency had ever stood against me. A man came from without, a friend of the President of the Republic. . . . His best election agent was the Head of State who, abandoning his role of arbiter above the parties, intervened thanks to the all-powerful television screen and allowed his ministers to declare that he would resign if the electors did not return to parliament a deferential majority. The electors thus made up their minds under pressure. . . .' [14] How then can one explain that de Gaulle was not elected on the first ballot in December 1965? For Paul Reynaud the explanation was obvious: 'for a month a few men have been able to speak freely on television, and therefore the

French people have been able to recover.' [15] 'Public opinion has been aroused,' Maurice Faure added; 'it will not sleep again.' [16] Alas, after the hopes of December 1965 and March 1967 came June 1968 and gaullism emerged still stronger. Yet again there was a ready explanation. 'The gaullist government has played on fear and has thus managed to rally to itself all the reactionary forces, and to deceive many Frenchmen of varying opinions' (Waldeck Rochet): 'Great fear is responsible' (Guy Mollet); 'General de Gaulle and Pompidou have launched a campaign of political and psychological trickery since they have virtually invited the French to choose between the terrorists we are supposed to be and the good people they are supposed to be' (François Mitterrand); 'a swing to the right which corresponds to a mood of fear among the mass of moderate electors' (Jean Lecanuet).[17] The people, as in 1958, as in 1962, as in 1965, as in 1967, had once again let themselves be 'taken advantage of'. 'Because we are democrats,' wrote the socialist editorialist Claude Fuzier, '. . . our task will be to explain, persuade and convince.' [18] Of introspection or internal reform no mention was made.

DISARRAY

In fact these attitudes bore witness to the deep confusion of the opposition faced with a phenomenon the very nature of which escaped them. The communists clung to proportional representation and to the Assembly regime which gave them, at least, an opportunity to apply pressure and to obstruct. They were accused in September 1958 of seeming to defend the 1946 Constitution. Maurice Thorez protested energetically, 'But it is not that we seemed to, we did defend it! This constitution, which was not the one we would have liked but that to which we rallied in the second Constituent Assembly . . . ensured the rights and gave guarantees and opportunities to the working class. . . .' [19] The communists will long remain conservative as regards the constitution.[20] They do not welcome the majority phenomenon which either weakens them or obliges them to become part of a counter majority. 'The fact that a single party, the gaullist party, is going to have a monopoly of power constitutes a great danger for democratic freedom. It is a step nearer fascism,' Waldeck Rochet declared on the evening of June 30, 1968. Guy Mollet also hesitated, faced with the regroupings necessary to form a new left wing 'majority' party, and this drew him nearer to Waldeck Rochet. In 1962 the General Secretary of the Socialist Party refused to sink the S.F.I.O. in a 'democratic constellation'. With more stubbornness than realism he waged a long rearguard battle against the increase in the powers of the President, even though this had been legitimated by the referendum of October 1962. Only after the abortive candidature of Gaston Defferre in 1964-5 and the continued skilful actions of François Mitterrand would Guy Mollet give up his attempts to render the presidential election hollow by supporting as a candidate some noble old man little connected with politics. Even the centrists, from Maurice Faure to Jean Lecanuet and Paul Raynaud, and later Alain Poher, preferred, as did Mendès-France, the automatic dissolution of parliament and the 'contrat de legislature' (the forming of a majority by concluding an agreement to last throughout the whole legislature) and a model which would be nearer to traditional French political life than was the power of a President supported by a majority party.

All that is logical in a majority system was denounced by all the oppositions. For example, after 1962 the fact that the gaullists and their allies were given the key posts in the National Assembly and in the government was stigmatized by the Democratic Centre (this 'extraordinary appetite for posts and prebends') and the Socialist Party was disquieted by 'the inextinguishable thirst for power which . . . will not soon be quenched'.[21] In June 1969 Alain Poher presented himself as the champion of the freedom of the state, colonized, in his opinion, by the gaullist 'clan'. The interventions of the Head of State in favour of the gaullist candidates at elections after 1958 were equally frowned upon: they were 'scandalous', an 'unacceptable pressure', the return to the 'official candidature' of the beginning of the Third Republic. Implicitly the perfect presidential model was incarnate in President René Coty at the end of the Fourth Republic. Disciplined party voting was derided in such terms as 'the unconditionals' or 'the general's boots'. The opposition dreamed of the impossible: the separation of de Gaulle from the gaullism of the M.P.s and the voters. The M.R.P., for instance, while noting in 1962 that the intervention of General de Gaulle in favour of the candidates who were for the referendum was a 'turning point' in the regime, nonetheless immediately stated: 'Whatever the result of the election, General de Gaulle will draw no conclusions from it as to his maintenance in power. The electors may therefore feel quite free to choose their M.P.s. . . .'[22] In the April 1969 referendum, Jacques Medecin, P.D.M. deputy and mayor of Nice, explained that to vote NO was to vote Pompidou, and then actively supported Alain Poher.

The oppositions dreamed of the post-de Gaulle era and their impatient generals regularly declared that the regime was on its last lap: on October 28, 1962, because the YES was not backed by the majority of the electorate, the P.S.U. diagnosed 'a mortal blow' and 'the beginning of the end'. In December 1965, since de Gaulle was not elected on the first ballot of the presidential election, his opponents had no doubt as to their victory in the third round, the general election of March 1967. 'Everything has changed,' the Radical Party proclaimed, 'gaullism, deeply wounded, will probably never recover.' The election 'can and

must establish the defeat of the U.N.R. and of gaullism', Waldeck
Rochet declared. 'The left will win soon,' Edouard Depreux averred.
'The hour is at hand when the Republic will win,' François Mitterrand
asserted. 'The French . . . will gather in the centre,' proclaimed Jean
Lecanuet.[23] But it was not to be, either this time or the next. 'We are
not far from our goal,' were François Mitterrand's words of comfort.
'For the right, it is the beginning of the end,' Guy Mollet said in his
turn. 'There is already a left-wing majority in this country,' declared
Pierre Mendès-France, and Jean Lecanuet went on believing 'that deep
down France is centrist'.[24] Thus they reasoned before the great hopes of
the referendum of April 1969 and the terrible disappointment of the
presidential election of June 1st and 15th that followed.

These superficial reactions clearly illustrate the delaying tactics of an
opposition thrown out of its course by the gaullist phenomenon.

THE TACTICS AND STRATEGY OF THE COMMUNIST PARTY

Until now only the Communist Party had managed to plan a strategy
against gaullism and had not been content to react to events as they
occurred. It is not often realized, so slight did its hope of success appear
at the time, that this strategy was fully defined by the party in 1958, at
its Ivry Central Committee on June 9th–10th. The communist speakers
compared the happy days of the Popular Front ('it is not surprising,'
declared Maurice Thorez, 'that in days like these, the memory of 1936
remains alive in the hearts of the workers and of all republicans' [25]) –
with the 'policy of war and poverty pursued by *all* the governments that
have come and gone over the last eleven years [that is since 1947]' [26]
From then on the aim is clear, to give 'the working class and its party,
side by side with the others, the position that is theirs by right in
parliament and *in the government*. The French Communist Party asks
no favours, it only asks the parties calling themselves democratic to
apply their principles and programmes. The choice is not between
fascism and communism. It is between a personal dictatorship founded
on reaction and militarism leading to fascism and a democratic regime
which will carry out the policy the majority of the French want.' [27] In
other words, the Communist Party's first objective is to escape from the
political ghetto into which the cold war and the socialists have driven
them since May 4, 1947 and to participate in a coalition left-wing
government for the realization of a limited programme, common to the
left. A strategy based essentially on elections, parliament and the
government, in no way revolutionary, even though it was defined at the
very moment when, according to an analysis of the party, 'a government which is fundamentally illegitimate, born of violence and reactionary threats' [28] was in power.

The Communist Party has not for a single moment swerved from this strategy in over twelve years of gaullism. It has, nonetheless, shown itself very pliable as far as tactics are concerned. From 1958 to 1962 the communists first retreated in good order: more time was needed for the other political groups and for the masses themselves to realize the nature of gaullism. The party adopted the classical attitude of its periods of isolation: tactics of 'The united front . . . orientated towards the rank and file',[29] of vigilance, 'Keep a look out on the right and on the left. For we may see, on the right signs of opportunism, on the left signs of sectarianism, which might cut us off from the masses.' [30]

The first change in tactics came in the autumn of 1962 with the referendum on the election of the President of the Republic by direct universal suffrage. On September 9th, during the annual fair organized by *L'Humanité*, Waldeck Rochet restored to honour the old slogan, 'Put to one side all that divides, only take into account that which unites.'

Any show of sectarianism among party activists, during the senatorial election of September 24, 1962, was publicly condemned by Roland Leroy in his report to the Central Committee on October 5th in Ivry. 'The criticism of the socialist leaders,' he declared, 'is not an end in itself. We criticize what harms the democratic combat, but we uphold fully any step forward. For the first time since the gaullist government came into being,' he underlined, 'all the non-gaullist parties by replying NO to the referendum have taken an identical stand on a fundamental question.' 'The situation is pregnant with democratic possibilities,' concluded Maurice Thorez. The united front was not as yet the order of the day, but already it was good to 'walk side by side and hit out together'. In the November 1962 election, by virtue of a tacit agreement of withdrawals in certain constituencies, the communists helped to elect at least 35 of the 65 socialists, 10 of the 23 radicals and at least 2 M.R.P. and 2 anti-gaullist moderates; they won for themselves some 30 seats thanks to these 'popular front' withdrawals. In December the central committee of the party went a step further. It declared that the Atlantic alliance was not an obstacle to reconciliation with the S.F.I.O. More than ever, the main danger was not revisionism but dogmatism, sectarianism. In May 1963 Maurice Thorez condemned the 'theory of the single party in socialist regimes' and considered it one of Stalin's mistakes. Once the centrist danger had been provisionally put aside – with the failure of the great federation of Gaston Defferre and the withdrawal of his first candidature as President of the Republic in June 1965 [31] – the union of the left was strengthened by an electoral alliance of the left from the radicals to the communists, to support François Mitterrand in the presidential election of December 1965, by an electoral pact between the Federation of the Left and the Communist Party, on December 20, 1966, for the second ballot of the general election on March 1967; and last but not least, on February 24, 1968 the Communist Party and the Federation of the Left, in a common declaration, recorded their wide agreement on the institutions and on economic and social policy – while noting their differences of opinion on foreign policy.

Until May to June 1968 the strategy of the Communist Party seemed a success, for it had managed to free itself from the political ghetto where it had been shut away since 1947. Radical, socialist and communist leaders put their heads together, published common communiqués, united their strengths in elections; the Communist Party was less of a bogey, the discipline of candidates and electors in following instructions was a surprise, though no doubt the unity of the left has been exaggerated and the number of centrist electors voting against the gaullists not sufficiently taken into account. The Communist Party, fighting alone in November 1958, gained the meagre total of 11 parliamentary seats; reintegrated with the left it won 41 in 1962, 72 in 1967, and even in 1968, 33.

TABLE 2: *Votes cast in favour of the left in general elections (France)*

Dates	Communist Left			Non-Communist Left*			Total 'Left'		
A. *Fourth Republic*	Votes cast	% of elec-torate	% of votes cast	Votes cast	% of elec-torate	% of votes cast	Votes cast	% of elec-torate	% of votes cast
1. Nov. 10, 1946	5,489,288	21.9	28.6	5,813,338	23.1	30.3	11,302,626	45.0	58.9
2. June 17, 1951	5,056,605	20.6	26.4	4,670,818	18.8	24.3	9,727,423	39.4	50.7
3. Jan. 2, 1956	5,514,403	20.5	25.6	6,474,915	24.5	30.1	11,989,318	45.0	55.7
B. *Fifth Republic*									
4. Nov. 23, 1958	3,907,763	14.3	19.0	4,959,311	18.1	24.0	8,867,074	32.4	43.0
5. Nov. 18, 1962	4,010,463	14.5	21.8	3,773,035	13.6	20.4	7,783,498	28.1	42.2
6. March 5, 1967	5,039,032	17.8	22.5	4,719,522	16.6	21.1	9,758,554	34.4	43.6
7. June 23, 1968	4,435,357	15.7	20.0	4,528,215	16.1	20.4	8,963,572	31.8	40.4

* Radicals, socialists of the S.F.I.O. and the 'new left' (P.S.U., P.S.A., U.F.D., U.G.S., etc.). *Source:* statistics of the F.N.S.P. established by A. Lancelot and J. Ranger.

Nonetheless, the essential aim has not been realized: gaullism is still in power, it has even been reinforced. Moreover the left has not managed to agree on a programme of government despite the objurgations of the Communist Party, the P.S.U. and Pierre Mendès-France. Worse still, united or not, since 1924 the left had always had more than half the total number of votes cast in general elections; the 'political' left – from the radicals to the communists – formed a majority in France and most of the time, had it reached an agreement, it could have governed. This has no longer been the case since gaullism came to power in 1958. Divided, the left represented 43 per cent of the votes cast in 1958; forming a coalition it did no better: 42 per cent on November 18, 1962, 43.6 per cent on March 5, 1967, 40.4 per cent on June 23, 1968 and only 32.23 per cent – for François Mitterrand's name – on December 5, 1965.

The 'shattered left' with its four candidates, all hostile to one another – Jacques Duclos, Gaston Defferre, Michel Rocard and Alain Krivine – fared little worse: 31.31 per cent of the votes cast on June 1, 1969, when the radicals deserted the left to rally to the centre.

The highest score of the Communist Party under the Fifth Republic in a general election – 22.5 per cent of the votes cast on March 5, 1967 – was less than its weakest result under the Fourth Republic: 25.6 per cent on January 2, 1956; similarly the non-communist left, once it rejoined the opposition in 1962, had as its highest score 21.1 per cent in March 1964 – 3.2 per cent less than its lowest Fourth Republic score of 24.3 per cent in June 1951. And 1951 was a poor year for the left anyway, a gaullist year; faced with the gaullist phenomenon, the 'dynamic' element which unity is supposed to secrete was not in evidence.[32]

THE DEFFERRE AFFAIR

Since despite union the percentage of left wing votes did not rise between 1962 and 1968, the left finally split again in 1969. The left was incapable of carrying a majority of parliamentary seats even if the gaullists lost them, and this seemed to condemn the left wing coalition to perpetual opposition against the union of gaullists and centrists or to rupture, leading to the constitution of a third force, with gaullism on its right and communism on its left. This analysis had inspired the Jean Moulin Club to produce an original strategy, revealed in *Un parti pour la gauche* (*A Party for the Left*) (Seuil) in 1965. Based on the election of November 1962, which they wisely refused to consider as abnormal, the study showed that the left was a minority, even with the inclusion of the communists and the radicals. It therefore proposed to create, without the communists, a great centre-left federation, grouping in a single political party the S.F.I.O. and the greater part of the centrist elements, in particular the Christian democrats. The Jean Moulin Club recognized that 'there would be no immediate transformation; on the contrary, such a strategy would ensure the stability of the present majority. In any case for the moment nothing seemed to endanger their security; and such a solution would prevent the U.N.R. from brandishing the bogey of "collusion" between communists and socialists.' (p. 31). The creation of such a 'great party of action' directed towards the mass of citizens and electors, open and inviting, based on the 'living forces' of the nation, in particular on the trade unions instead of on the old parties closed in on themselves, would create a psychological shock among the public and would enable the new group to compete with and overtake the Communist Party and throw out gaullism.

'In the last resort,' the Jean Moulin Club declared, 'the project rests on a double hypothesis. First that the Communist Party will progressively lose parts of its electorate and its activist strength and, secondly, that there are potential sources of agreement within the non-communist left which is capable of finding means of increasing its numbers.' The idea was tempting in its novelty, but it had come into being outside the partisan framework. A leader had to be found and above all the Socialist Party and the M.R.P. had to be convinced. The leader was found on May 8, 1965 when the mayor of Marseilles, Gaston Defferre, a socialist activist of long standing, and a candidate for the presidential election in December, announced that he would stand only if a socialist democratic federation were founded to group together all 'men of progress' from the socialists to the Christian democrats.

But on June 18, 1965 the representatives of the Socialist Party and those of the M.R.P., under pressure from Guy Mollet, Joseph Fontanet and Jean Lecanuet, caused the plan to founder and on June 25th Gaston Defferre withdrew from the presidential election. The strategists in the clubs had underestimated the power of resistance of the party machines.

THE DELAYING TACTICS OF THE NON-COMMUNIST LEFT

The non-communist left and the centre were thus condemned to a defensive attitude, since they had no alternative strategy.

Guy Mollet, with no illusions, set the Socialist Party on the road to union with the left. His first step in that direction, on November 12, 1962, had been merely tactical: '. . . In the ten or twelve constituencies, I don't know exactly how many, very few in any case,' he declared over the waves of *Europe No. 1*, 'in which in the second ballot we are faced with only a communist and a U.N.R. candidate, then, mark this . . . my party is used to realizing the imminence and the hierarchy of danger. . . . Today in this limited hypothesis in which we place ourselves, an additional communist in the National Assembly will change nothing: I prefer to have the U.N.R. candidate beaten.' [33] 'What exactly is the situation? Is this unity of action? Is it a 1962 Popular Front? Not at all,' declared *Le Populaire* on November 15th; and in his editorial of November 26th, on the day after the second ballot, Claude Fuzier recalled the 'deep-seated reasons for the division of the left'. After the presidential election in December 1965 and the creation of the 'little' federation of the democratic and socialist left (socialist S.F.I.O., radicals and some of the 'clubs') under the propulsion of François

Mitterrand, the union of the left was to go further, as we have seen, but no real platform was to be elaborated.

In fact, Guy Mollet was not convinced that the votes of the left alone would suffice to defeat gaullism; his preference was for a more subtle plan of election pacts, on the right or on the left according to the constituencies. The communists were bitterly against such tactics. The general secretary of the Socialist Party therefore merely 'saved' the greatest possible number of seats and waited, until he – like François Mitterrand – was obliged to withdraw after the failure of June 1968. With the 'small' federation on its last lap, and the 'big' federation still-born, the non-communist left was in total disarray and even before the April referendum and the presidential election of June 1969 it seemed unlikely that a new Socialist Party would solve the left's problems.

It is not surprising that under these conditions the replacement of General de Gaulle, necessitated by the NO to the referendum of April 27, 1969, did more harm to the left than to the gaullists, even though in the past the latter had frequently been told that it would toll their knell. Rapidly, so as to cut the grass from under Alain Poher's feet and oblige his political friends to support him despite the open hostility of Guy Mollet, Gaston Defferre announced that he was standing for the Presidency. He hoped to force the Communist Party into supporting him or, if they refused, to show them clearly the numerical superiority of the centre left (the S.F.I.O. and Christian democrats) over the communist left. He met with complete failure. The communists showed a certain political courage and decided to put up their own candidate, Jacques Duclos; the P.S.U. decided likewise and put up Michel Rocard; Alain Krivine, a trotskyist, was yet another left-wing candidate. The centre, full of illusions, pushed Alain Poher into the arena, for the first opinion polls showed him hot on George Pompidou's heels, 38 per cent to 40 per cent. The radicals immediately rushed to support the centre, just as they had rushed to support the left in 1965.

Gaston Defferre thus saw his political electorate reduced to the modest dimension of the S.F.I.O. socialist electorate. But he did not manage to stabilize even this electorate; half of the socialist electors deserted him to vote either further left or, more often, for the centre. The backing of Pierre Mendès-France was not sufficient to avert the catastrophe. Far from proving the superiority of the centre left and the fragility of communism, Gaston Defferre merely succeeded in breaking the 'new socialist party' at the very moment of its birth.

THE CENTRE COMES BACK TO EARTH

As for the centrists, they had been waiting since 1962 to have enough votes and, above all, enough seats in the National Assembly to play the part of a 'hinge-group' and the 'axis' of a majority which could not afford to dispense with it. In November 1962 the M.R.P. thought its transformation would bring success and called for 'the participation of the major social and professional forces in the essential decisions and choices affecting the nation . . . a participation it has already organized within its own framework'.[34] However, its NO to the referendum lost it over 800,000 electors, 35 per cent of its 1958 electorate and a third of the deputies it had at that time. The Républicains populaires drew the lesson from this failure at their annual conference in La Baule in May 1963. The M.R.P. agreed to destroy itself in order to promote a new political force capable of becoming a majority force. The results obtained in the presidential election of December 1965 by the M.R.P.'s former president, Jean Lecanuet, 15.9 per cent of the votes cast,[35] were considered encouraging and the Centre Démocrate was born, uniting under the presidency of Jean Lecanuet the moderates from the C.N.I. and the Républicains populaires.

In April 1966, after the Centre Démocrate had been launched, Jean Lecanuet had declared, 'It must be remembered that even a slight shift in the votes will destroy the present majority and hence enable the Centre Démocrate to become the axis of French political life.' In March 1967, he was certain that he would be an arbiter in the new Assembly. But he was to be disappointed: the new movement obtained only 12.6 per cent of the votes cast on the first ballot, 3.3 per cent less than Jean Lecanuet in the presidential election, and what was even more significant 7.9 per cent less than the non-gaullist moderates and the Républicains populaires in November 1962. Far from being able to arbitrate in the Palais-Bourbon, the Centre Démocrate was unable to form a parliamentary group of its own. In June 1968 the president of the group *Progrès et démocratie moderne*, Jacques Duhamel, eclipsed Jean Lecanuet, but the aim of the centrists remained the same: they wanted to have enough deputies to be able to dictate to the majority. Once again hopes ran high before polling day: 'I don't know whether we may speak of a miracle, but I can forecast a surprise,' promised Jacques Duhamel in his press conference on June 20, 1968. '. . . the impetus which is gathering will upset the experts' forecasts.' On June 21st the *Centre d'informations Jacques Duhamel* declared, 'Some polls taken by the P.D.M. group and other opposition parties show a considerable swing to the centrists, a swing of such magnitude that no government will be able to govern without their agreement.' But the C.P.D.M. fared even worse than the Centre Démocrate sixteen months earlier, gaining 10.3 per cent of the votes cast as against 12.6 per cent. The strategy of the centrists was based on the illusion that France refused to be divided into two rival blocks and that the centre, before directly exercising power itself, would oblige the gaullists to modify their policies. But the centre, in the end, was not even capable of arbitrating among its own factions, of choosing between Jacques Duhamel, who favoured alliance with the gaullists, and the more intransigent Jean Lecanuet. The centre was in the uncomfortable position of the English Liberals in the 1930s: the choice lay between absorption by the Conservatives in the hope of having some part in the government or continuing in opposition in the hope of a miracle which became more and more improbable as the years went by.

The problem was solved in 1969. Just as the National Liberals joined the Conservatives in England, so a certain number of centrists led by Jacques Duhamel and René Pleven supported Georges Pompidou in the presidential election. The victory of the gaullist candidate on June 15th marked the end of the hope that most of the centrists had put in Alain Poher and reinforced the integration of the centre in the majority. At the same time, some of the centrist ideas were assimilated by gaullism and from an ideological point of view this justified the integration. The first article of the centrist credo – the intrinsically harmful nature of a division of France in two blocks – was abandoned when faced with the reality of the majority phenomenon.

GAULLISM MISTAKEN

The failure of the various oppositions to assess gaullism, although they took General de Gaulle into account, can be attributed to their contempt for or underestimation of the political party supporting him – successively the U.N.R., the U.D.V^e, then the U.D.R.

For a long time, apart from the communists and the socialistes unifiés, the opposition parties treated General de Gaulle kindly. The Socialist Party S.F.I.O. kept in its 'campaign guide' until June 1968, the following article on de Gaulle, written in April 1962: 'Since we are democrats, we do not wish to attack the President of the Republic. And yet he does not play the part of an arbiter. . . . All too often General de Gaulle acts as leader of the majority – even as the leader of a party. . . .' Not until May 1968 did the centrists dare openly to express their hope for the departure of General de Gaulle: '. . . By his methods, his solitary exercise of power, his style, at his age, and after what has happened, the Head of State no longer appears as the man capable of instigating the new departures the nation hopes for.' But they are careful to add: 'It is up to General de Gaulle to tell us if he wants to leave. . . . It would be best for us all if he knew how to depart early enough, leaving behind him a great name in history.' [36] In March 1967 Jean Lecanuet was careful to say that he wanted to modify gaullist policies without affecting either the boat or its captain.

The gaullist party, however, is not in itself an object of respect, or fear, or needful of careful handling. Without de Gaulle it is nothing. In *A Party for the Left* the Jean Moulin Club spoke of the U.N.R. as 'a number of deputies . . . kept in hand by the head of the government'; gaullism, according to the Club, will leave a certain heritage, namely a lessening of the relative influence of parliamentarians, a taste for a leader not strictly affiliated to a party and the difficulty of succeeding to de Gaulle; but after de Gaulle gaullism will cease to be a political force. The M.R.P. in its last annual conference at La Baule in 1963 and in Le Touquet in 1964 insisted on the 'precariousness of the system'. 'The Gaullist regime is an exceptional regime, linked to the existence of one man; it has no future,' Jean Lecanuet declared at Le Touquet. 'The R.P.F. did not survive de Gaulle,' the Radical Party recalled in its campaign guide in 1962. 'Even if this time the U.N.R. lasts as long as the General, what will happen to it after the General has gone? Will it be left a programme? What other de Gaulle will the last will and testament propose? Debré? Chaban? Frey? Are these men capable of assembling 80 per cent of the votes? or even 40? They are not even lesser de Gaulles.' At the same time in its campaign guide the S.F.I.O. declared: 'This brilliant team has only one thing in common – idolatry of de Gaulle, and this will only last as long as the superman lasts.' In the *Tribune Socialiste* on January 19, 1967 the *Parti socialiste unifié* for its part declared: 'The Fifth Republic rests on the systematic attachment of the crowds to one man.'

This view made the future seem clear. De Gaulle was not young and his power was wearing thin. Time worked in favour of the opposition. The opposition watched the approach of old age: 'How are you feeling, General?' de Gaulle was asked on February 4, 1965 at a press conference. 'Not too bad. But have no fear, one day I shall die,' he replied mockingly. The oppositions scrutinized the election statistics that showed gaullism gradually becoming weaker: 80 per cent YES in September 1958; 62 per cent in October 1958, less than half of the potential electorate; only 44 per cent of the votes cast on December 5, 1967 when de Gaulle was obliged to submit to a second ballot; 38 per cent of the votes cast for the Fifth Republic on March 5, 1967 – the figures went steadily down.

But these proofs are scarcely conclusive for they rest on the comparison of figures which cannot really be compared, for they group referendums, presidential elections and general elections. 'It is not satisfactory,' Jacques Fauvet wrote in *Le Monde* on March 7th, 'to compare the general election of Sunday and the last presidential election and to draw from the comparison evidence of a decline in gaullism.'

The oppositions saw clearly the decline of gaullian gaullism, that is, of the idea of national unity inspired by the person of General de Gaulle, but they were so hypnotized by this aspect of things that they did not perceive the constant and parallel increase in another type of gaullism, that of the gaullist party. And it was precisely this legislative gaullism that was to come into its own after the departure of de Gaulle.

TABLE 3: *Votes cast in favour of the gaullists in general elections (France)*

Date	Votes cast	Percentages of the electorate	votes cast
A. *Fourth Republic*			
1. November 10, 1946 (Union gaulliste)	312,635	1.2	1.6
2. June 17, 1951 (R.P.F.)	4,058,336	16.5	21.2
3. January 2, 1956 (Républicains sociaux)	842,351	3.1	3.9
B. *Fifth Republic*			
4. November 23, 1958 (U.N.R.)	4,010,787	14.7	19.5
5. November 18, 1962 (U.N.R.-U.D.T.)	6,580,606	23.6	35.4
6. March 5, 1957 (U.D.V^e)	8,448,982	29.9	37.7
7. June 23, 1968 (U.D.R.)	9,663,605	34.3	43.6

Source: statistics of the F.N.S.P. calculated by A. Lancelot and J. Ranger.

From November 1958 to March 1967, the gaullist party doubled its electorate, going from 4 to 8.5 million votes cast; in June 1968 it had nearly 10 million – for every three potential electors, one effectively voted gaullist. The rise has been so great and so steady that one may well wonder whether the party system in France has not been qualitatively, *structurally* modified. *Figure 1* enables us to explore this important problem. The Fourth Republic, like the Third and the beginning of the Fifth, was characterized by a multi-party system in which the electoral strength of the parties was unequal, changing but never very much; no party obtained 30 per cent of the votes cast. In the French political test tube each general election resembled the brownian movement of suspended political particles. Only the Communist Party to the extreme left of the tube managed to rise slightly above this haphazard zigzag movement, and even then only for a time, for in November 1958 it was to be drawn back into the movement. On the contrary, from 1962 onwards one particle rose above the 30 per cent line; its rise cannot be explained by an exceptional short-lived shock, for in 1967 it moved further upwards, and in 1968 further still. The phenomenon had an immediate result: other particles joined together; the situation remained fundamentally the same, but the content of the test tube became simplified. This change in marketing terms can be analysed, according to certain experts [37] as the passage from an 'open', 'atomized' or

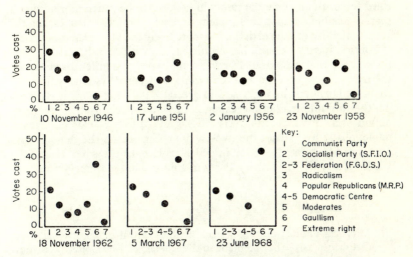

Fig. 1. The party system in France (general elections: 1946 to 1968).

'brownian' market in which no brand predominates, to a 'closed' market in which one brand, thanks to a successful move, has managed to rid itself of the small local or specialized potentates and has acquired a superior position over the whole market. If this is truly the case for gaullism on the French political market since 1962 and if political structures react much as commercial structures do, the consequences of this phenomenon would be considerable, for once the market is 'closed' it becomes very difficult and extremely expensive even for a new dynamic brand to break through in turn and rival the dominant product. The only strategy that can hope for success, it appears, is one which tries to create a sort of counter-image of the successful brand, while differentiating itself clearly from the successful brand, so that those who have never been satisfied by the latter, or have become disappointed by it, may rally to the new brand. If this strategy is successful, the monopoly of the first brand gives way to a sort of duopoly – very frequent on the commercial market (as in Philips-Remington, electric razors or Printemps-Galeries Lafayette, the French stores). At this point the market becomes 'saturated' and the only way of acquiring a major place on the market is to manage – although it is exceptionally difficult – to replace one of the two major brands.[38]

If all this applies to politics, the gaullist party has since 1962 enjoyed a monopoly; the best strategy for its adversaries would be to try to transform this monopoly into a duopoly by offering a sharp contrast to gaullism, and this obviously would condemn any attempt to create a third force. In any case the task will henceforth be much more difficult than it was before 1962 in a system of small political particles, for the smaller the size of the particles, the more lively the brownian movement.

Politics, it may be said, has nothing to do with soap-brands. Nevertheless, the rigorous parallel between the types of market discussed by the marketing specialists and the typology of party systems defined by Maurice Duverger in 1951, and in greater detail in 1960,[39] is striking. To the multiple market corresponds the multi-party system; the very notion of a 'dominant' party is closely linked to the 'closed' market, monopolistic by nature; the two-party system recalls the duopoly and occurs in a 'saturated' market in which replacements such as that of the Liberal Party by the Labour Party in England are extremely rare.

Notes to Chapter 1

1. Maurice Thorez, closing speech at the Central Committee at Ivry, October 4, 1958. Supplement to the *Cahiers du communisme*, November 11, 1958, p. 25.
2. *Le Monde*, March 7, 1967.
3. Closing speech at the Central Committee at Ivry, June 10, 1958, p. 22.
4. Editorial, 'Allons à la victoire de la République', *Cahiers du communisme*, September 3, 1958, p. 1275.
5. Marcel Servin, Report to the Central Committee at Ivry, October 3–4, 1958, op. cit. p. 4 and p. 15.
6. 11.7 per cent of those enrolled on November 23, 1958 as against 12.1 per cent on January 2, 1956. 'Betrayal does not pay', René Andrieu wrote in *L'Humanité* following the second ballot in 1958.
7. *Le Monde*, October 30, 1962, 'No conquerors, no conquered'. My italics.
8. Report, id., p. 15.
9. Marcel Servin, Report, pp. 6–7 and p. 12.
10. Claude Fuzier, *le Populaire*, November 19, 1962.
11. *Le Monde*, December 7, 1965.
12. Marcel Servin, Report, op. cit., p. 6.
13. *Le Monde*, December 2, 1958.

14. *Le Monde*, October 30, 1962.
15. *Le Monde*, December 7, 1965.
16. Ibid.
17. *Le Monde*, June 25 and July 2, 1968.
18. Ibid.
19. Closing speech, Central Committee at Ivry, October 4, 1958, op. cit., p. 21.
20. The French Communist Party now contents itself with demanding, within the perspective of a 'popular government', the revision of the articles in the constitution relating to 'personal power'.
21. Centre Démocrate, Dossier du candidat, March 1967. Supplement to the documents on the problems of France. No. 5: 'U.N.R. et ses satellites', p. 22. Socialist Party S.F.I.O. Dossier du candidat, November 1962, titled 'Et après lui?'
22. Dossier du candidat, circular to the federations, November 9, 1962, signed by M. R. Simonnet, General Secretary.
23. *Le Monde*, December 7 and 21, 1965.
24. *Le Monde*, March 7 and 14, 1967.
25. Closing speech, op. cit., p. 20.
26. Resolution, ibid., p. 23.
27. Ibid, p. 24. The official programme of the party at the elections of November 1958 ('Que proposent les communistes?' Supplement to No. 19 of the *Bulletin de propagande et d'informations du P.C.F.*) takes up the same themes: 'It is a fact that for the past twenty-five years all the great social victories have been won when the communists were in the government or in the governing majority . . . the only complete solution. . . . is socialism. . . . Nevertheless, it is possible, in the immediate future, to achieve a policy answering the demands of the workers and the nation. . . .' To the victories of 1936 and 1944–7 were opposed 'eleven years of government without the communists . . . the pernicious work of Pinay, Pflimlin, Guy Mollet, Gaillard, etc.'
28. Maurice Thorez, Closing speech, op. cit., p. 10.
29. Maurice Thorez, Closing speech, Central Committee at Ivry, October 4, 1958, op. cit., p. 35.
30. Marcel Servin, Report, ibid., p. 14.
31. 'This is good news,' Waldeck Rochet declared when he heard of the withdrawal on June 25th.
32. François Goguel was the first to draw attention to this fact. Cf. in particular his article on 'les élections législatives des 5 et 12 mars 1967', *Revue française de science politique*, XVII, June 3, 1967, pp. 457–8.
33. We have shown elsewhere (François Goguel, et alia – *Le Référendum d'octobre et les élections de novembre 1962*, A. Colin, Paris, 1965, pp. 79–84) the process in which Guy Mollet became involved on November 9th when he declared at Sanchez, in his constituency in the Pas-de-Calais: 'You will vote at the first ballot for the party you wish to be in power but never, neither at the first nor at the second ballot, for a yes

man.' On the following morning, the press weighed the consequences of this declaration: is Guy Mollet asking us to vote communist in the event of a straight U.N.R. – P.C.F. fight? On November 12th, on *Europe no. 1*, Maurice Schumann did not lose the opportunity to attack Guy Mollet on this question. The general secretary of the S.F.I.O. began by stating: 'I was speaking in the Pas-de-Calais where you know that the hypothesis of two candidates, one communist and one U.N.R., facing one another on the second ballot is highly unlikely.' In fact, in November 1958, no such instance was found in this department. Thus Guy Mollet had not originally envisaged the possibility of this kind of encounter nor, consequently, the transfer of the socialist votes to a communist candidate. But he agreed to consider this and to recommend that the votes should be transferred in favour of the communist candidate, though he thought that the case would arise only in a dozen constituencies at the most. In actual fact, fifty constituencies were involved. But the electoral realism of the socialist leader pressed him to continue on a path which had been, as it were, opened up by mistake.

34. Circular to the federations, November 9, 1962, signed: M. R. Simonnet, General Secretary.

35. His moderate support and that of the M.R.P., however, had totalled 20.5 per cent of the votes cast on November 18, 1962, in an election generally considered as catastrophic for them. But the comparison between the general and presidential elections is not convincing.

36. 'Dossier politique' of the C.P.D.M. candidate in June 1968. Reply to the question: 'Do you accept that General de Gaulle should remain President of the Republic?'

37. This analysis of ours was inspired by the extremely interesting and suggestive studies of Roland Muraz, 'Qu'est-ce que la publimétrie?' *Les Cahiers de la publicité*, March 19, 1968, p. 92–103.

38. Roland Muraz quotes the example of scouring-powders where the duopoly AJAX-VIM was formed, between 1954–6, after a cross-fire with NAB-AJAX. This latter brand, it is true, had the technical and financial backing of CADUM in its offensive against NAB.

39. From *Les Partis politiques*, A. Colin, Paris, 1951 (2nd part), then in 'Sociologie des partis politiques', Chapter 2, Volume 2 of the *Traité de Sociologie* published by P.U.F. in 1960, under the direction of Georges Gurvitch.

CHAPTER II

The Attraction of Gaullism

CHARISMA AS AN EXPLANATION

The electoral and political strength of gaullism came, according to many, from the charisma of General de Gaulle. 'The Fifth Republic was the fruit of charismatic leadership,' Raymond Aron wrote in 1959.[1] Ten years later Jean Jacques Servan-Schreiber was to declare, 'There he is, a legendary figure, truly fabulous, holding this country under the spell of his presence – but he no longer has anything to offer.' [2] In other words the gaullism of the majority of the French, regularly shown by opinion polls and elections, relied above all on a simple belief in an exceptional man. Gaullism was thus essentially personal and fragile, for it was linked to the life of an ageing man. That was the theory generally held until June 15, 1969.

The concept of charismatic power is relatively clear and neutral as accepted by Max Weber, but the term is now currently used in a far less precise way. For the German sociologist, the charismatic leader is opposed to the patriarch, the landed lord of former times, and to the servant of the modern state, because he is obeyed not by virtue of a custom or a law, but by virtue of the faith he inspires. One 'gives way' to the charisma of the prophet, the warrior, the demagogue, on account of their personal, exceptional merits. But the traditional leader, the charismatic leader and the legal leader are, for Max Weber, 'ideal types', rarely met with in reality. Moreover, after having analysed the birth of modern parties in Great Britain and in Germany, Max Weber concluded: 'When parties are directed and led by their plebiscitary leaders, the result is a "loss of soul" [*Entseelung*] . . . among their partisans. The partisans grouped in an organization of this kind can only be useful to the leaders if they are, as in America, enrolled in a machine which is not upset by the vanity of notabilities or a pretension to personal originality. The election of Lincoln was only possible because the organization of his party was of this sort; the same phenomenon occurred, as we have seen, with the caucus in favour of Gladstone. This is the exact price that must be paid for the installing of real leaders at the head of a party. The choice is simple: either a democracy accepts at its head a real leader – thus accepting the existence of a machine – or else it repudiates leaders and thus falls under the domination of "professional politicians" with no vocation who have not the deep charismatic qualities that make leaders.' [3]

This long quotation demonstrates the problem clearly. The French political system is in mutation owing to the apparition of what is for France a new type of party, already well known in Great Britain and the United States. In this respect, the controversy about the regime is a repetition, under the Fifth Republic, of the debates that occurred fifty years ago in Great Britain and the United States.[4] The problem of the charisma of General de Gaulle and of the nature of the gaullist party is thus a problem which cannot be limited to the person of the General and the U.D.R. group.

Let us try to clarify the controversy by distinguishing the different levels of the analysis. It is obvious that for General de Gaulle himself his power is of a charismatic nature. The leader finds in himself the sources of his action, and in his action his legitimacy. It is neither the function nor the stripes that make leaders, but their character translated into action. Nonetheless, from the beginning, General de Gaulle has held his personal legitimacy as insufficient. The leader must be anointed by the people, who are the fountain of legitimacy necessary to democratic regimes. The source of power, according to de Gaulle, is – to use Max Weber's categories – both charismatic and legal. The leader of June 18th declared in 1947 as in 1968 that it has never been his wish to impose himself on the people with the help of the army.[5] On June 1, 1958, before the National Assembly which was about to invest him again, he declared solemnly: 'Universal suffrage is the source of all power.' [6] On January 29, 1960, in the dramatic circumstances created by the barricades in Algiers, General de Gaulle summed up his doctrine of two-fold legitimacy: 'In virtue of the mandate that the people have given me and the national legitimacy in which I have been incarnate over the last twenty years, I ask all of you – men and women – to support me whatever may happen.' [7] 'With de Gaulle, for France,' said the gaullist posters; 'With the people, for France,' General de Gaulle returned. 'The new Republic has its President. I am the man. Here I am, as I am. I do not pretend that I am perfect nor that I am not the age I am. I do not pretend to know everything, nor to be able to do everything. . . . But with the French people I have been granted by history the privilege of succeeding in certain ventures. It is with the French people that I am at present working. . . .' [8] That is why he withdrew without hesitation on April 27, 1969, when the people's votes no longer supported him.

Let us leave to one side the Companions, the gaullist partisans. We shall see later that some are blindly gaullist, others have a more political attitude. But what did public opinion, what did the electorate, what did the French expect from de Gaulle between 1958 and 1969? Did those who voted for him do so on account of his charisma? The opinion polls give us precise, objective replies to this question, and it is sufficiently important for us to consider it with figures in hand.

The vulgar charismatic explanation – that of the mystification, the bewitching of the masses by the national hero – comes up against a major objection: the eclipses in the popularity of General de Gaulle. The French let him retire to Colombey in January 1946, less than a year after the victory; they did not follow his advice in October 1946, or in June 1951, or in the referendum of April 1969. After the political adventure of the R.P.F., the French opinion poll (I.F.O.P.) in December 1955 found only one Frenchman in a hundred who wanted de Gaulle to head a government. But in April 1956 there were 5 per cent, in July 9 per cent, in September 1957 11 per cent, and finally in January 1958 13 per cent – as many as the partisans of the Prime Minister of the day, Félix Gaillard, more than any other pretender, be he Pierre Mendès-France (10 per cent), Antoine Pinay (10 per cent), Guy Mollet (9 per cent), a communist (8 per cent) or Field-Marshal Juin (4 per cent). The popularity of General de Gaulle before he returned to power varied with the political situation; the rise in his popularity at the beginning of 1958 is due less to his charisma than to the failure of the Fourth Republic.[9]

After his return to power in June 1958, General de Gaulle's popularity rose sharply but it still varied – though at a higher level – with the political situation (see *Figure 2*). The highest point was reached in February 1960, just after the affair of the 'barricades' in Algiers, when 74 per cent of the French declared themselves 'satisfied' with General de Gaulle as President of the Republic. The lowest ebb occurred in March 1963, during the miners' strike when the number of 'dissatisfied' equalled the 'satisfied' – 42 per cent.[10] Even if one tries to minimize the exceptional periods by calculating annual averages, the variations remain clearly perceptible. 'Satisfaction' oscillates between 50 per cent in 1963 and 68 per cent in 1960, 'dissatisfaction' between 21 per cent in 1959 and 34 per cent in 1963. Two periods can be clearly distinguished (and all the other curves and statistics confirm this division), the 'Algerian' period of gaullism – from 1958 to April 1962 – during which General de Gaulle, the leader personifying national unity, was regularly supported by six or seven Frenchmen out of every ten, and contested by two; and the following period which ended with his departure and during which de Gaulle appeared more and more as the leader not of all but of the majority; he lost some 10 per cent of his partisans and his adversaries increased by as much. The two curves draw nearer to one another, whilst preserving a very characteristic symmetry.

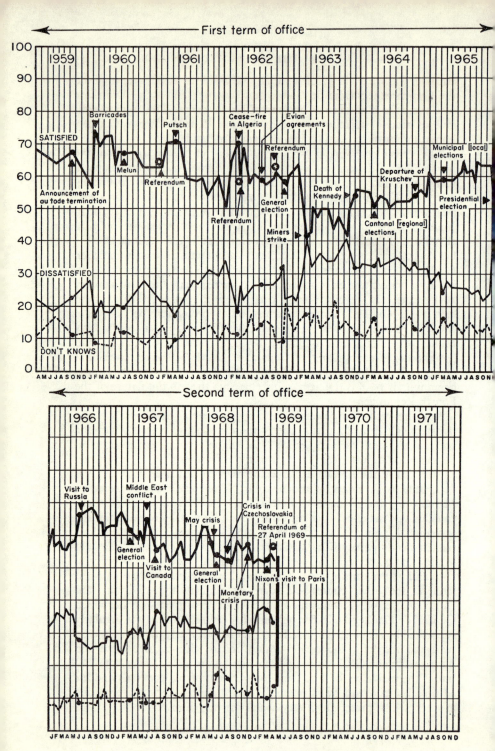

Fig. 2. The popularity of General de Gaulle. (I.F.O.P.)

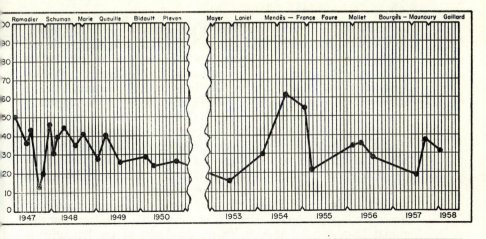

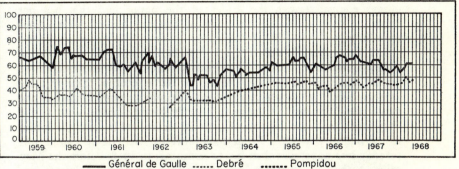

——— Général de Gaulle ...... Debré .... Pompidou

Fig. 3. The popularity of the Presidents of the Council (Fourth Republic), of the Prime Ministers and of the President of the Republic (Fifth Republic). (I.F.O.P.)

It may however be objected that General de Gaulle's level of popularity – even since 1962, even if it varied with the political situation – was too high to be 'normal'. During the Fourth Republic, only Pierre Mendès-France in the second part of his Premiership reached a similar level of popularity (see *Figure 3*).[11] Some consider Pierre Mendès-France as the de Gaulle of the left and see in this popularity a confirmation of the 'charisma' thesis. But one may say that in both cases public opinion took into account services rendered – peace in Indochina in 1954, peace in Algeria in 1962 – and that there was therefore a very similar system of relationships between government and governed which satisfied them: as did de Gaulle, Pierre Mendès-France sought the support of the people rather than that of the National Assembly, contrary to all the traditions of French parliamentarianism. In a regime in which the head of the Executive is in fact chosen by the people and not by Parliament, in which consequently the elector is more important than the parliamentarian, and is constantly solicited, the level of popularity of de Gaulle and Pierre Mendés-France is not 'abnormal'. In fact at the end of 1970 Georges Pompidou's and Jacques Chaban-Delmas's levels of popularity were in the region of 65–70 per cent according to the I.F.O.P. opinion polls. We can compare these figures with those of British Prime Ministers: in 1960, for instance, the average level of Harold Macmillan's popularity was 67.8 per cent – reaching on occasion 74, even 79 per cent; in 1965 Harold Wilson's average level was 57 per cent with a peak of 66 per cent.[12] The only difference with France is that the level of the British Prime Minister's popularity has sometimes been lower – 30–40 per cent – than that of the French President. But this results from the fact that in Britain the leader of the Executive is always compared with the leader of the opposition; this has not been the case in France, for want of a strong leader and a united opposition.

In this context, the differences in popularity up to 1968 of the Prime Minister and the President of the Fifth Republic can be explained more by the functions of the two leaders of the Executive than by their personalities. This distinction between the relative unpopularity of the two leaders became less sharp and finally disappeared as soon as the President abandoned his role of national leader and became the leader of the majority in 1962. From 1962 onwards, General de Gaulle was scarcely less unpopular than his government; in 1968, before the May crisis, he had become more unpopular than the Prime Minister (see *Figure 4*).

Among the partisans of gaullism a distinction remained: under General de Gaulle's leadership the President, further removed from day-to-day economic and social problems, preserved a certain advantage over his government; his popularity was, however, more subject to fluctuation whenever the international situation changed or when internal or external crises endangered the authority of the state and the stability of the regime. Political explanations account for the variations in popularity and there seems no need to have recourse to 'charisma' to explain them. Moreover, charisma supposes a certain intensity in support. Had it been possible to find among those 'satisfied' with General de Gaulle between 1958 and 1969 a hard, resistant core of 'very' satisfied, the charisma hypothesis would have been singularly reinforced. But in fact it is the other way round: those 'on the whole' satisfied always make up at least two-thirds of the satisfied, whereas the hard core of the 'very' satisfied is far from constant and varied with all those 'satisfied', diminishing or increasing with it. Gaullist or anti-

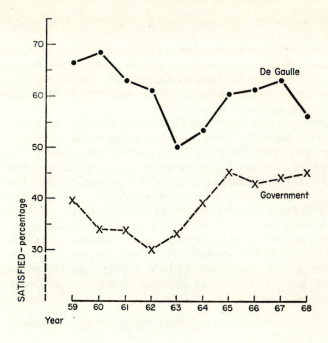

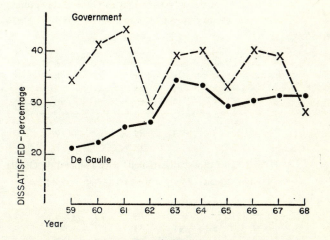

Fig. 4. Popularity and unpopularity of General de Gaulle and of the government of the Fifth Republic (annual averages). (I.F.O.P.)

gaullist fanaticism may exist among politicians; it is insignificant among electors (see *Table 4*).[13]

Figure 5 shows moreover, that since the end of the Algerian war and the passage of gaullism from a movement of national union to a majority party, anti-gaullism has been constantly more intense than gaullism. The unconditionals of anti-gaullism are proportionally more numerous than the unconditionals of gaullism.[14]

A few weeks after General de Gaulle's return to power, 63 per cent of the French found the future 'more encouraging than a year ago'; only 17 per cent saw it as 'darker'. The reasons for the optimism of the vast majority tell us something of the nature of their gaullism: 18 per cent said they felt confident in de Gaulle as a political leader: 'I trust de Gaulle – the reins of the state are in good hands – someone capable at last – de Gaulle is a strong leader – de Gaulle is honest . . .'; 17 per cent thought something had changed: 'We've got out of our mess – we are no longer on the edge of the precipice – there's more law and order – we can see things are going to work . . .'; 25 per cent gave details as to what had changed: for 15 per cent the Fifth Republic had brought political stability, for 4 per cent it had increased French prestige abroad, for 3

TABLE 4: *The degree of popularity and unpopularity of General de Gaulle as President of the Republic*

Satisfied % of 'very satisfied'	Total % of those 'satisfied' with General de Gaulle							*Total number of polls*
	40–44	45–49	50–54	55–59	60–64	65–69	70–74	
25–29	—	—	—	—	—	1	4	*5*
20–24	—	—	—	1	4	6	3	*14*
15–19	—	—	1	15	22	8	—	*46*
10–14	—	2	21	23	4	1	—	*51*
5–9	4	1	2	—	—	—	—	*7*
Total number of opinion polls	*4*	*3*	*24*	*39*	*30*	*16*	*7*	*123*

Dissatisfied % of 'very dissatisfied'	Total % of those 'dissatisfied' with General de Gaulle						*Total number of polls*
	15–19	20–24	25–29	30–34	35–39	40–44	
10–14	—	—	1	13	13	3	*30*
5–9	2	15	41	23	7	—	*88*
0–4	4	1	—	—	—	—	*5*
Total number of opinion polls	*6*	*16*	*42*	*36*	*20*	*3*	*123*

Source: Statistics from 123 I.F.O.P. opinion polls.

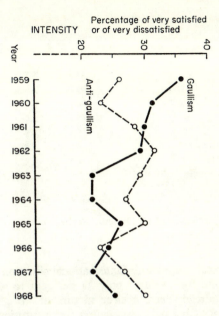

INTENSITY

Percentage of very satisfied
or of very dissatisfied

Year

Anti-gaullism

Gaullism

Fig. 5. Intensity of gaullism and anti-gaullism in relation to General de Gaulle (annual averages). (I.F.O.P.)

per cent it had put the economy on its feet, for 3 per cent it represented a chance of a settlement of the Algerian affair.[15] Georges Dupeux and Philip Converse have studied the replies given by a representative sample of the French electorate to the same 'open' question in the autumn of 1958: 'What do you like or dislike in General de Gaulle?' Their detailed classification of the replies sheds light on our discussion (see *Table 5*). At first it seems obvious that de Gaulle is a charismatic leader: 47.5 per cent of the gaullist supporters stress the personal qualities of the General; but, the authors remark, 'Sixty per cent of the references to the personality of de Gaulle concern the "public" qualities that are assigned to him': his patriotism, his disinterestedness, his honesty – whereas American electors supporting Eisenhower, for example, stress his 'private' qualities – intelligence, physique, education, religious beliefs – or content themselves with vague declarations of approval.[16] The confidence in de Gaulle, even if it is personal, is also political. Nor is it blind confidence: in August 1958, according to the I.F.O.P., 83 per cent of the French trusted him to make the army obey; 70 per cent to reform the Constitution; 68 per cent to settle the Algerian

TABLE 5: *The image of General de Gaulle*

	In favour		Against	
	Number	%	Number	%
Replies in general	118	8.5	11	3.2
Qualities (defects) as a private person	652	47.5	116	34
Qualities (defects) as a leader	241	17.5	45	13.2
His past	198	14.5	45	13.2
Recent activities	62	4.5	17	5
Hopes (fears) for the future	50	3.5	50	14.7
Political standpoints	46	3.5	50	14.7
Replies of a social nature	7	0.5	7	2
Total	*1,374*	*100*	*341*	*100*

Source: Philippe Converse and G. Dupeux, *Revue française de science politique*, XII, March 1, 1962, p. 59.

affair; 67 per cent to improve the international situation of France; 61 per cent to reunite the country; only 44 per cent to settle economic problems.[17] We already have a clear picture of the gaullism of the public – approval of his policy regarding the institutions and foreign policy – but also a lack of confidence in economic and social policy.

GAULLISM – ON BALANCE

One evening in 1967, during one of the television party political broadcasts for the general election, Valéry Giscard d'Estaing, who is not averse to theatrics, took a piece of paper and in front of the viewers wrote in two columns the negative and positive sides of gaullism in power. Public opinion also constantly weighs the two, and opinion polls enable us to know from time to time why the positive side continues to be greater than the negative (see *Table 6*). Concerning General de Gaulle's own personal action, the result is clear: negative on balance in internal affairs and increasingly so as discontent with the economic, financial and social policy grows; positive on balance regarding the overseas policy, with this field assuming less importance as the problems already settled become distant memories; clearly favourable on balance, and increasingly so in the field of foreign policy – the 'domaine réservé'.*

The years of power, with the combined action of the President of the Republic and of his government and the correlative behaviour of the different oppositions have drawn relatively clear images of gaullism, of the centre and of the left and have contrasted their respective attitudes

* Translator's note: the field of policy reserved for the President.

TABLE 6: *Appreciation of General de Gaulle's actions when in power* (I.F.O.P.)

Passive/Active (in percentages)	PASSIVE			ACTIVE		
	(1) 1962	(2) 1965	(3) 1967	(1) 1962	(2) 1965	(3) 1967
A. 1. Recovery, law and order	—	—	—	11 } 22	9 } 36	5 } 15
2. Single-handed power/stability	9	4	4	11	27	10
3. Economic and financial policy	3	21	10	8	8	6
4. Social policy	19	18	28	—	4	4
Total: domestic policy	*31*	*43*	*42*	*30*	*48*	*25*
B. 1. Abandonment of Algeria, of the colonies/peace in Algeria, decolonization	6	8 } 5		41	15	13
2. Aid to the developing countries	—	—		—	—	—
3. Did not fight against the O.A.S.	12	—	—	—	—	—
Total: overseas policy	*18*	*8*	*5*	*41*	*15*	*13*
C. 1. Peace	—	—	—	—	—	11
2. Policy of grandeur/increase in the prestige of France	—	—	—	7 }	} 13	} 20
3. European policy	3	4	2	6		
4. Rest of foreign policy	—	6	11	—		
5. Nuclear deterrent, military expenditure	—	4	1	—	1	—
Total: foreign policy	*3*	*14*	*14*	*13*	*14*	*31*

N.B. The classification of the answers was done by us, not by I.F.O.P. The question was of the kind: 'General de Gaulle has been President of the Republic since 1958. For you, what have been the best and worst things that he has done?'

(see *Figure 6*). The centre lacks originality and in public opinion its contribution to the unification of Europe is hardly recognized; in the end it is nearer to gaullism than to the left, with the reservation that the electorate is not sure that it can guarantee political stability in France, and this is one of the winning cards of gaullism.

But what is striking is the contrast between the image of gaullism and that of the left; so clear is it that one is almost the exact opposite of the other. The strong features of gaullism correspond to the weak spots of the left: foreign policy (make France respected, contribute to the lessening of international tension, and to the unification of Europe); the political regime (ensure in France political stability and the democratic working of the institutions); and lastly, prosperity and economic expansion, all of which are attitudes generally associated with the right –

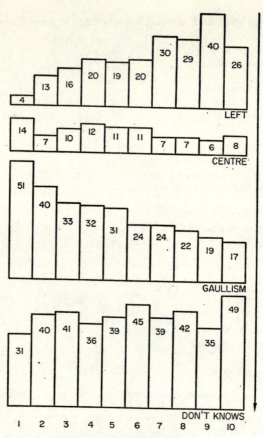

LEFT

CENTRE

GAULLISM

DON'T KNOWS

1   2   3   4   5   6   7   8   9   10

1   To make France respected throughout the world
2   To ensure political stability in France
3   To contribute to international understanding
4   To contribute to the unification of Europe
5   To ensure the prosperity of France
6   To ensure the democratic functioning of the institutions
7   To ensure the development of your region
8   To solve the housing problem
9   To fight against unemployment
10   To ensure a fair distribution of wealth amongst the French

Fig. 6. Confidence in the various political families . . . (I.F.O.P. Feb.–March 1967)

in England for example. Conversely, the strong features of the left constitute the weak points of gaullism: the defence of the weak against the strong (regional development opposed to Paris centralization, housing, struggle against unemployment), in short mercy and justice (bring about a just redistribution of wealth) rather than efficiency at any price.[18]

If one looks not at the whole French adult population but at the supporters of each political family, the contrast is even more striking: 73 per cent of the partisans of the gaullist majority think it is the best equipped to guarantee political stability, 67 per cent to ensure the prosperity of France, 64 per cent to contribute to the lessening of international tension. The electors of the left are less convinced of the capabilities of their own political family in these fields: 55 per cent think the left best equipped to ensure the prosperity of France, 45 per cent that it would help to reduce international tension, and only 40 per cent that it would be the best guarantee of political stability in France. Conversely, 63 per cent of the supporters of the left believe in the capacity of the left to redistribute wealth whereas only 41 per cent of the gaullists believe their party capable of doing so.[19] It would seem that, for their own supporters and *a fortiori* for the French population as a whole, gaullism and the left have different vocations, fulfil different functions. Immediately certain psychoanalytical interpretations spring to mind associating the right with the father figure – authority, security, order, efficiency – and the left with the mother – warmth, refuge, justice, humanity. This might explain why women vote more to the right and men more to the left!

However that may be, it is clear from this image of gaullism as seen by public opinion that the oppositions by attacking gaullism on its policy regarding the institutions, Europe and foreign affairs have chosen their domains very badly, for these are the strong points of gaullism.

GAULLISM AND STABILITY

Although separated by more than fifteen years, the results of the referendum of October 1962 and those of the second question of the referendum of October 1945 show, as François Goguel has demonstrated, an astonishing similarity, both numerical and geographical. Both consultations aimed at limiting parliamentary sovereignty organically: 'The convergence between what the electors have wanted for seventeen years and what General de Gaulle offers them is,' François Goguel concludes, 'the fundamental explanation of the result of these two consultations.' [20] The archives of the French Institute of Public Opinion (I.F.O.P.) confirm this idea that as far as the institutions and foreign policy are concerned, 'gaullism constitutes', as Michel Brulé

and Jeanne Labrousse have written, 'a response to certain expectations'.[21] If it changes the values and the habits of the political elite, it
gives public opinion the means of realizing a certain number of deep
aspirations.

The election of the President of the Republic by direct universal
suffrage and the recourse to the referendum – both major elements of
the new regime set up by the Fifth Republic – were already favoured
by public opinion in 1945: half the French already wanted to elect their
President (as against 40 per cent in favour of the election of the President
by parliament), 66 per cent were in favour of the referendum (20 per
cent against). The dissolution of the National Assembly by Edgar Faure
at the end of 1955 was badly received in political circles and well
received by the public: 42 per cent of the French wanted it, 17 per cent
were against (see *Table 7*).

TABLE 7: *Public opinion and the institutions of the Fifth Republic: the mechanisms*
(I.F.O.P.)

1. The election of the President of the Republic by direct universal suffrage

↓ %	Nov. 1945	Nov. 1961	Dec. 1962	May 1964	Nov. 1965	May 1969
favourable	50	52	46	74	78	81
unfavourable	40	17	23	10	6	8
don't knows	10	31	31	16	16	11

2. Use of the referendum

↓ %	July 1945	Sept. 1962	Oct. 1962	April 1969
favourable	66	51	45	45
unfavourable	20	24	32	35
don't knows	14	25	23	20

3. Right to dissolve the National Assembly

↓ %	Nov. 1955	Jan. 1958	Paris, May 31, 1968
favourable	42	46	75
unfavourable	17	17	11
don't knows	41	37	14

By adopting the direct election of the President and by facilitating
dissolution, the Fifth Republic reinforced its legitimacy but, by using it
too often, it slightly reduced that of the referendum.

Most of the public seem to have become used to the redistribution of
power between the President and parliament: the partisans of a diminu-
tion of the President's power represent only a third, even a quarter, of
the French, even if they are a majority – but only just – on the left (see
Table 8). In November 1970, a year and a half after Georges Pompidou

had replaced General de Gaulle at the Elysée, they represented only 13 per cent. The weakening of parliament, on the other hand, is more under attack since the major part of the centrists join with the left to ask for a certain reinforcement of parliament's role. One may imagine that if the President of the Republic were to show the Fifth Republic Parliament a respect such as that the British Prime Minister traditionally shows to the House of Commons, the problem would be solved without the new balance of powers between the Executive and the Legislative being threatened.

Nonetheless, by and large, the French are satisfied with the regime. In November 1961, 26 per cent thought France better governed than under the Fourth Republic, as against 21 per cent who thought it less well governed; in September 1962, those satisfied were 44 per cent as against 12 per cent. The U.N.R. electors at that time thought themselves better governed in a ratio of 80 : 1 – which is not surprising – but so did the M.R.P. electors, 62 : 5; the moderates 50 : 7; the radicals 39 : 17; the socialists 35 : 16; only the communist electors preferred the Fourth

TABLE 8: *Public opinion and the institutions of the Fifth Republic: the distribution of power* (I.F.O.P.)

Role of the President of the Republic

% Would like it to be	March 1946*	Feb. 1962	Dec. 1962	Nov. 1963	Oct. 1965	Jan. 1967	Nov. 1968
the same or greater	48	45	56	44	65	53	60
less great	37	26	33	33	20	31	25
don't knows	15	29	11	23	15	16	15

*Important political role: 48 per cent – the exercise of honorary functions: 37 per cent.

Role of parliament

% Would like it to be ...	Feb. 1962	Dec. 1962	Nov. 1963	April 1964	Oct. 1965	Jan. 1967	Nov. 1968
the same or less great	28	36	32	36	45	37	36
greater	38	40	40	36	32	41	36
don't knows	34	24	28	28	23	22	28

Attitude of the political families to the role of the President and of parliament

	September–December 1962		January 1967	
resident: maintenance : reinforcement as ainst weakening of s role.			Fifth Republic Centrists Left	77 against 13 53 against 39 37 against 51
arliament: weakening : maintenance as ainst reinforcement : its role.	U.N.R. M.R.P. Independents Radicals S.F.I.O. P.C.F.	59 against 19 39 against 36 38 against 37 30 against 50 21 against 58 12 against 66	Fifth Republic Centrists Left	52 against 29 37 against 49 26 against 57

Republic, by 45 : 11.[22] In January 1958, under the Fourth Republic, 52 per cent of the French considered that the French regime worked less well than that of Western Germany, 39 per cent that it worked less well than that of Great Britain; under the Fifth Republic, a maximum of 21 per cent – in May 1967 – of the French considered themselves less fortunate than the West Germans or the English.[23] The main defect of the Fourth Republic is, for the major part of French opinion, governmental instability and the division of the parties.

GAULLISM AND A CERTAIN FOREIGN POLICY

As far as foreign policy is concerned there is also agreement between gaullism and French opinion. From 1952 onwards, we find rather more Frenchmen favourably disposed towards a neutral force between East and West than committed towards America or, *a fortiori*, towards Russia (see *Table 9*). Gaullism in 1964 and 1965 increased this neutralist

TABLE 9: *Public opinion and the international role of France* (I.F.O.P.)

1. Neutrality towards East and West

↓ % France ought to be . . .	Sept. 1952	Nov. 1954	June 1955	Dec. 1955	May 1957	Dec. 1957	Nov. 1959	May 1960	May 1965	April 1966
on the side of the United States, of the West	42	36	18	25	28	21	24	30	14	19
on the side of Russia, of the East	4	2	3	5	4	3	4	7	7	9
neither on one side, nor on the other	43	43	57	45	39	51	48	51	62	57
don't knows	11	19	22	25	29	25	24	12	17	15

2. A united Europe independent of the United States

↓ %	June 1962	October 1964	May 1967
favourable	51	44	49
unfavourable	13	23	23
don't knows	36	33	28

3. The independence of France

↓ % Independence		September 1965	January 1968
a. political:	possible	46	34
	impossible	29	33
	don't knows	25	33
b. economic:	possible	41	26
	impossible	40	47
	don't knows	19	27
c. military:	possible	31	28
	impossible	41	42
	don't knows	28	30

trend. Most French people, including General de Gaulle, would like to see a united Europe independent of the United States, a third force between East and West. On the other hand, scepticism increased between 1965 and 1968 as to the chances of a politically independent France and even more independence in the economic and military fields. But this was of slight importance as more and more Frenchmen – 49 per cent in 1962, 58 per cent in April 1958 – came to consider de Gaulle as a decided partisan of European unification, and finally let themselves be convinced by the idea of a French deterrent (see *Table 10*). All things considered, despite the 'Free Quebec' speech and the embargo on arms for Israel, the majority of the French seem satisfied with the role of gaullist France in the concert of nations.

TABLE 10: *Public opinion and gaullist international policy* (I.F.O.P.)

1. General appreciation

↓ % The international role of France	Feb. 1963	Nov. 1963	Feb. 1965	Mar. 1968
satisfied	36	40	44	56
dissatisfied	17	21	16	25
don't knows	47	39	40	19

2. De Gaulle and Europe

↓ % Think of de Gaulle as . . .	June 1962	June 1965	Feb. 1966	July–Aug. 1966	April 1968
a decided partisan of European unification	49	61	51	66	58

3. The French nuclear deterrent

↓ % The French nuclear deterrent	Dec. 1957	July 1962	July 1963	April 1964	April 1966
favourable	41	39	37	39	46
unfavourable	28	27	38	40	42

GAULLISM AND PROSPERITY

There will come a day when the future of gaullism will depend on the prosperity of the French, or rather on their own evaluation of their prosperity. Questions of foreign policy mean little to the electorate, unless there is an exceptional crisis which is endangering world peace. Political and institutional stability is without doubt important, but is not sufficient to ensure a constant majority especially if the opposition refrains from attacking or counter-attacking on this problem, to its disadvantage, and if it manages to give a more united image of itself and to appear as a 'possible' solution.

The appreciation of one's standard of living is closely linked to political options as *Table 11* shows, although it is not easy to know whether economics colour one's view of politics or vice-versa. The evolution of the situation since 1958 contains elements favourable to gaullism and other less favourable elements. In its favour is the fact that in 7 196 fewer people than in 1962 believed that the standard of living was falling. Those who believed the latter in 1967 were less than half of each political party. In 1962, 58 per cent of the communist electors thought their standard of living had gone down since 1958; in January 1967 only 44 per cent held this opinion. On the other hand, if absolute pessimism is no longer the rule, neither is absolute optimism – among all shades of opinion, including gaullists, the number of those who thought their standard of living had risen fell sharply between 1962 and 1967.[24] The great majority of the French thought their standard of living was marking time. The social claims of May 1968 were at hand.

TABLE 11: *Gaullism and the standard of living (subjective appreciation of the standard of living by each political family)* (I.F.O.P.)

% —→	September–October 1962	January 1967
Your standard of living has been stable or has risen VERSUS: has lowered since . . .	**U.N.R.:** 63 (24 'risen') *versus*: 32%	**Fifth Republic:** 72 (18 'risen') *versus*: 27%
	M.R.P.: 63 (18 'risen') *versus*: 33%	**Centre démocrate:** 65 (14 'risen') *versus*: 34%
	Radicals: 60 (17 'risen') *versus*: 37%	**Fédération:** 63 (14 'risen') *versus*: 36%
	Independents: 55 (16 'risen') *versus*: 41%	**Communists:** 55 (11 'risen') *versus*: 44%
	Socialists S.F.I.O.: 54 (16 'risen') *versus*: 43%	
	Communists: 37 (9 'risen') *versus*: 58%	

The political system gaullism has founded, the policies it adopts, the personal value of its leaders are all fused in the public's feeling of general satisfaction or discontent. Does charisma play a role? We can simply say that charisma, that 'personal, extraordinary gift of an individual', as Max Weber has defined it, if it cannot be transmitted, can – according to the famous German sociologist – give birth to a new tradition, it can become institutionalized in structures and practices which, without its initial impulse, would not have seen the light of day.   Charisma is not necessarily sterile and one cannot count on its brevity nor can one be sure it will leave no mark.

Notes to Chapter 2

1. 'Démission des Français ou rénovation de la France?,' *Preuves* 96, February 1959.
2. *L'Express* 897, September 16–22, 1968.
3. Max Weber, *Le savant et le politique* (The Scientist and Politics), Plon, Paris, 1963, collection 10/18, pp. 159–60.
4. Cf. the well known work of M. Ostrogorsky, *La démocratie et l'organisation des partis politiques*, Calmann-Lévy, Paris, 1903 (2 volumes).
5. '. . . In June 1940,' he said in 1947, 'in the general state of collapse, when the people could not make themselves heard, it is true that I assumed power and kept it until I was able to transfer it to the National Assembly. . . .', Press Conference, April 24, 1947. In May 1958 he proclaimed: 'Do people think that at sixty-seven I am going to start a career as a dictator?', Press Conference, May 19, 1958.
6. Speech addressed to the National Assembly, June 1, 1958.
7. Radio-Television broadcast, January 29, 1960.
8. Radio-Television interview, December 15, 1965.
9. I.F.O.P. poll taken from a representative sample of the French adult population: answers to the question: 'If a government were to be formed, who would you like to see as President of the Council from among the following politicians?', *Sondages* 1958, 3, p. 66.
10. This is the only occasion on which the number of 'dissatisfied' equalled the number of those 'satisfied'. The dissatisfied were fewer, even in April 1969, the morning after the negative result was given to the referendum.
11. Perhaps Antoine Pinay, too, in 1952. There are no opinion polls enabling us to verify this.
12. From the findings of Gallup Poll (London), *Gallup Election Handbook*, 1966. The question asked was the same as in France: 'Are you satisfied or dissatisfied with X . . . as Prime Minister?'
13. This point had already been noted by François Bourricaud in 'L'arbitre, le public et les oppositions', *Revue de l'Action populaire*, 193, December 1965.
14. The intensity of pro-gaullism and anti-gaullism increases, partly due to the campaign, in the election years: this is especially true for 1962 (a realigning election), then 1965 and 1968, less so in 1967 (a maintaining election). Anti-gaullism was fairly intense too in 1963, because of the miners' strike.
15. Cf. *Sondages* 1958, 3, p. 8.
16. Philip Converse and Georges Dupeux, 'Eisenhower et de Gaulle. Les généraux devant l'opinion', *Revue française de science politique*, XII, I, March 1962, especially pp. 58–64.
17. *Sondages* 1958, 3, p. 8.
18. The figures and facts for this table (No. 6) have been taken from two I.F.O.P. surveys, one on January 7–16, 1967, the other on February 2–10, 1967; cf. *Sondages* 1967, 3, pp. 23–4.

19. I.F.O.P. survey, January 7–16, 1967. *Sondages* 1967, 3, diagrams p. 24.
20. François Goguel, 'L'électorat gaulliste', *Nouvelle frontière*, January 5, 1964, p. 31. The referendum of October 28, 1962 was on the election of the President of the Republic by direct universal suffrage (61.7 per cent voted YES); the second question of the referendum of October 21, 1945 (when 66.3 per cent voted YES) concerned the limiting of the powers of the Constituent Assembly elected the same day, in favour of the Provisional Government.
21. 'Twenty Years of Opinion Polls', 66-page report given by these I.F.O.P. specialists at the first reunion of the *Société française de sociologie*, in October 1965. Our quotation is an extract from the Introduction, p. 11. (2)
22. These figures are the percentage, for each political current, of those 'satisfied' (80 per cent of the U.N.R. voters, for example) and of those 'dissatisfied' (1 per cent of the U.N.R.), the remainder (19 per cent) representing those who did not show a political preference.
23. I.F.O.P. surveys, *Sondages* 1966, 1, p. 40, and 1967, 4, p. 58.
24. The two polls upon which our analysis is based are not wholly comparable: in 1962 those questioned were asked to consider their standard of living in relation to the five preceding years, in 1967 in relation to the preceding year.

CHAPTER III

A Voter-Directed Party
A Dominant Party

DEFINITION

In his classic work on political parties,[1] Maurice Duverger makes a fundamental distinction between 'cadre' parties, like the French Radical Party, flexible, loosely organized and with no party whip, more concerned with the quality than the number of their members, and on the other hand 'mass parties', such as the French Socialist or Communist Party, which are tightly structured, have a strong party whip and endeavour to recruit and train the greatest possible number of activists. The former type of party is a legacy of the broadening democracy of the nineteenth century, the latter the consequence of the rise of socialism at the beginning of the twentieth century. When applied to the situation in France, this typology fits fairly well up to the transformation of the U.N.R. party in 1962. If we look at gaullism, it is clear enough that the R.P.F., founded in 1947 by General de Gaulle, is a 'mass party': it recruits its members in hundreds of thousands, places them in a framework of hierarchical and disciplined organization, moulds them in its officer-training schools and party assemblies, organizes – rather like the Communist Party – huge meetings and enormous popular gatherings, fund-raising campaigns and the door-to-door sale of its newspapers, while at the same time increasing its parallel organizations in the hope of influencing many different milieux. Conversely, there is no doubt that the *Centre national des Républicains sociaux*, which was to gather together the old R.P.F. gaullists minus de Gaulle after the General himself had forced the R.P.F. into a state of suspended activity, is a 'cadre party', non-militant, loosely disciplined and dominated to a great extent by its parliamentarians and what remained of those councillors elected in 1947. But what is the *Union des démocrates pour la République*? A mass party? It certainly has more members than the socialist S.F.I.O. party, but they do not play the vital role normally given to activists in mass parties. A cadre party? It has undoubtedly aimed at this, but the notabilities have hardly been won over by gaullism up to now; moreover all the efforts of the U.N.R. and later of the U.D.R. to take root by winning seats in the departmental and town councils have met with poor results. In fact the U.D.R. looked neither to its militants nor to the notabilities but to the voters. The U.D.R. is a 'voter party', so another type of party, omitted from Maurice Duverger's analysis, namely the 'voter-directed party', must be added to the parties of notabilities, such as the *Fédération nationale des Républicains indépendants*, and the parties of activists, such as the *Front du progrès*. This new addition is a typical feature of contemporary political life in western industrial democracies.[2]

The voter-directed party objects to ideological dogmatism, contrary to the 'militant' or mass-directed party which tends to make a god of it or at least to express a certain reverence towards it. For the voter party a minimum of shared values is enough and this enables it to appeal to a very wide clientèle. In this respect, the ideas of the nation on the right and of social equality on the left are the strongest foundations of such parties, as the basic values of the Conservative and Labour parties in Great Britain illustrate. In France, gaullism was in a better position than any other political movement to adopt this model. All gaullists hold with General de Gaulle 'a precise image of France', from the voters to the activists and dignitaries of the movement, from the veteran gaullists to its more recent supporters, from left-wing gaullists to the more conservative. In 1940, as in 1962, despite the defeat inflicted by Germany and the loss of an empire, gaullism was able to rekindle a feeling of pride in the French nation and a taste for French grandeur. It was André Malraux who better than anyone else put into words the essence of gaullism, when, quoting Pasquini, he exclaimed at the U.N.R.-U.D.T. party conference at Nice, 'Whereas others have behind them the history of their party, we have behind us the history of our whole country'.[3] And Malraux goes on to contrast gaullism which unites, with the old parties which divide, and General de Gaulle 'a man of history who has taken upon himself the guardianship of France, and for whom France will not readily find a replacement' with 'the politicians who will always be waiting around the corner'.[4] The only article of the gaullist faith consists in the belief that ideologies pass away, but that nations remain and constitute the driving force behind all history.[5] In all other aspects gaullism is at the same time, and by its very nature, an empiricism; those ideologists in the party who would like to force gaullism into an iron cage of doctrine – whether it be a doctrine of the State, as with Michel Debré, a doctrine of social democracy as with the late René Capitant, or one of the 'common good' with former M.R.P. members – have little hope of accomplishing this because their success would ruin any hope that gaullism has of uniting the nation around itself.[6] The gaullists' national ideal thus coincides with their electoral interests: it is to their advantage to become a non-doctrinaire, non-sectarian party. The power lies rather with the pragmatists, notably Georges Pompidou, Jacques Chaban-Delmas and Roger Frey. The latter, quoting Raymond Aron, stated: '. . . In the affluent society towards which Western Europe is gradually moving, no political party has a doctrine as such. . . . Our society is not without its problems . . . but it does not have one big problem. . . . As from now on, an intelligent, pragmatic party, with the aid of the simple majority voting system and an expanding economy, is able to remain in power even when the particular events instrumental to its obtaining that power have faded into the past.' [7] Is this electioneering, political opportunism? Not necessarily. Wherever political aims are involved – in this case the independence and grandeur of France – or the means of attaining them – a strong state – the gaullists know how to take electoral risks, as in 1962 at the time of the referendum on the election of the President of the Republic by universal suffrage, in 1965 when they provoked a crisis in the Common Market on the eve of the presidential election, or in 1969 when, during the election campaign, Georges Pompidou refused to make any concessions – reveal the name of his Prime Minister for instance – despite the difficulties he was up against.

Unlike the notability or cadre parties, the voter party fully acknowledges mass democracy and group solidarity, and challenges the liberal philosophy of individualism in the name of which the French right and centre have always refused to submit to discipline. The voter party does not consider the national battle won once it has won over the notabilities. Even if, as all groups do, it shelters a more or less open oligarchy, neither by conception nor in essence is it elitist. It is popular. That is why it does not abhor mass demonstrations and all those manifestations of political activity to which the parties of notabilities do not give a thought, and which seem to be the monopoly of the activist parties. But the voter party differs from the latter in that it does not call into question either in principle or in practice the social and political system of which it is a part; for this reason it can rely on the elections, with their integrating function, and on the electors who participate in the democratic system, rather than on the notabilities, re-creating their lost paradise of a restricted franchise, or on the activists dreaming of their Utopias. In this respect it could be said that the R.P.F. had already fulfilled the necessary requirements for the creation of a voter party, but it could not see its way to accepting the rules of the game nor find a means of changing them. Therefore the R.P.F. could only be a party of activists. Once in power, the U.D.R. became, through the normal course of events, a voter party, for it had shaped the political system to its own liking.

In a way, all parties are at the same time parties of activists, parties of notabilities and voter parties. But the important point lies in knowing upon what the parties themselves put the emphasis, and for what reason. The U.D.R., an essentially nationalist party, guardian of the new institutions, has to rely on the electors alone for its survival, for the preservation of its institutional accomplishments and its pursuit of French grandeur. Its very nature and structure derive directly from this situation. But this party, of a type new to France, is like a foreign body within the French party system, which the latter finds difficult to assimilate.

A DOMINANT PARTY

The French political system, until 1962, was in fact characterized by a system of many parties which expressed essentially either an ideology or sectarian interests. Maurice Duverger has written that 'the representation of interests is firmly assured. The citizens entrust their deputies with the defence of local and private interests. They do not look to the deputies for the expression of the public interest nor for the actual government and administration of the country. Total representation therefore does not exist.' [8]

Since it is weak both socially and politically, the French political party resembles a pressure group or a sect and therefore cannot fulfil its proper political function of arbitrating between interests and ideals. The everyday decisions are taken by short-lived and shifting coalitions of party leaders. Parties of notabilities and activists – who are fighting for ideals as diametrically opposed as Christian democracy, socialism and communism – coexist without too much difficulty, since no one party is in a dominant position, and since elections periodically give each the possibility of asserting its originality and the hope of obtaining a little more power though never enough to govern alone. Such a system cannot subsist if a voter party is really successful and outgrows the divisions of particular interests and ideologies, for it is then capable of becoming a majority party, a dominant party. This is precisely what has happened in France since 1962, though not without doubts, fears and bitterness. Normally – when there is no revolution in the air – parties of notabilities and activists can live peacefully together. The appearance on the political scene of a voter-oriented party in a multiparty system can only lead either to the elimination of the voter party or, alternatively, to the transformation of the system itself into a dominant party system or a two-party system.

THE SOCIOLOGY OF THE GAULLIST ELECTORATE

Apart from the actual number of voters, the best of electorates can only be defined in ideological terms. Hence the left's criticism of gaullism with its electorate comprised mostly of women, old people and a large proportion of the non-working population, is explicitly or implicitly related to a certain ideal of society where politics would be essentially the activity of men, young people and the productive members of the community. If the analysis takes for its model French society as it is now, and for the ideal electorate that which comes nearest to the actual electorate, then the gaullist electorate is increasingly the most representative and the best one can envisage if one is a democrat or a nationalist. The U.D.R. general secretary, Robert Poujade, thus praised the diversity of gaullism as a reflection of French diversity in the words: 'Gaullism is not an interest group. It is not specifically a working-class party, of which I could name one, nor is it an association of civil servants, of which I could name another, nor is it anti-clerical in outlook, as another party has been, nor does it represent the upper class. Gaullism is a mystical doctrine of national unity.' [9]

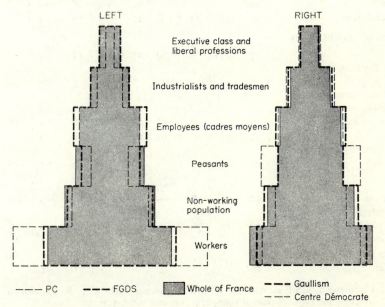

Fig. 7. *Comparison of the socio-professional composition of the different electorates with that of the adult population in metropolitan France, according to the occupation of the head of the family.* (I.F.O.P. February 1967)

The gaullist electorate is the only one in which women are in a majority, as they are also in the French adult population. It is true that it includes proportionately too many women to reflect exactly the total population, but the Federation of the Left has too many men and the Communist Party as the Centre Démocrate has far too many. As to age,

TABLE 12: *The sociological composition of the gaullist electorate*
(*Source:* I.F.O.P.)

% Categories	(1) France (adults) %	(2) U.N.R. 1958 %	diff. col. 1	(3) U.N.R. 1962 %	diff. col. 1	(4) Fifth Rep. 1967 %	diff. col. 1	(5) U.D.R.–R.I 1968 %	diff. col. 1
Sex									
male	48	44	(−4)	43	−5	42	−6	46	−2
female	52	56	(+4)	57	+5	58	+6	54	+2
Age									
20/21–34 years	30 ⎫			29	−1	29	−1		
35–49 years	26 ⎬ (80)	77	(−3)	24	−2	26	—	55	−1
50–64 years	26 ⎭			30	+4	26	—		
65 years and over	18 (20)	23	(+3)	17	−1	19	+1	45	+1
Occupation of head of family									
peasants	17 (23)	7	(−16)	21	+4	16	−1	18	+1
liberal professions, executive class	5 ⎫ (14)	27	(+13)	7	+2	5	—	6	+1
industrial & commercial employers	10 ⎭			10	—	11	+1	14	+4
employees (cadres moyens)	15 (13)	19	(+6)	16	+1	16	+1	18	+3
workers	31 (35)	26	(−9)	28	−3	28	−3	25	−6
retired & non-working population	22 (15)	21	(+6)	18	−4	24	+2	19	−3
Residence									
rural districts	37 (38)	38	—	—	—	34	−3	40	+3
urban districts:									
less than 20,000 inhabitants	13 (29)	30	(+1)	—	—	16	+3	16	+3
20 to 100,000 inhabitants	13 (16)	11	(−5)	—	—	14	+1	11	−2
more than 100,000 inhabitants	19 ⎫ (17)	21	(+4)	—	—	19	—	19	—
Paris region	18 ⎭			—	—	17	−1	14	−4

1. From the I.N.S.E.E. and the I.F.O.P. *Sondages* 1960, 4, p. 8. Figures in brackets for 1958. *Sondages* 1966, 2, p. 12, and 1967, 3, p. 52.
2. *Sondages* 1960, 4, p. 19.
3. I.F.O.P. survey, November 1962.
4. *Sondages* 1967, 3, p. 52.
5. *Sondages* 1968, 2, p. 101.

N.B. The vertical arrow indicates that the percentages have been calculated vertically in relation to the whole column, in each category (sex, age, etc.).

again it is the gaullist electorate which most nearly approximates to the age pyramid in France: here the communist and centre electorates are 'too young'. From a socio-professional point of view, the communists are under-represented among the peasants, and very much over-represented among the workers; the centrists have 'too many' peasants. All things considered, it is the gaullists and the Federation of the Left who come nearest to the normal distribution of the French electorate (see *Figure 7* and *Table 12*). Finally, if one considers only the sociological composition of the French electorate and that of the party electorates, it is the gaullist electorate which since February 1967 has shown itself to be the most representative with an average deviation from the norm of only 1½ points, followed by the Federation of the Left with 2 points, the Centre Démocrate with over 3 points, and lastly the Communist Party with over 5 points (*Figure 8*). The peculiarity of the communists in French political society can be gauged by looking first and foremost at the distortion in its electorate. The gaullists and the Federation of the Left are more or less on the same level, in that their electorates make up

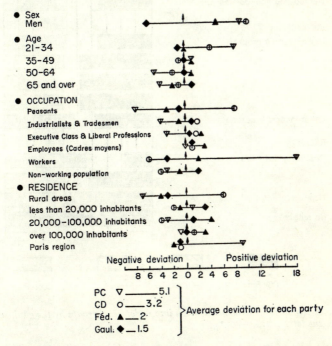

Fig. 8. *Differences in percentage between the socio-professional composition of the different electorates and that of the adult population in metropolitan France.* (I.F.O.P. February 1967)

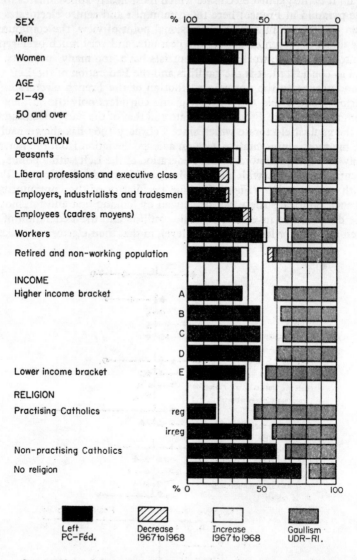

SEX
Men
Women

AGE
21–49
50 and over

OCCUPATION
Peasants
Liberal professions and executive class
Employers, industrialists and tradesmen
Employees (cadres moyens)
Workers
Retired and non-working population

INCOME
Higher income bracket   A
B
C
D
Lower income bracket   E

RELIGION
Practising Catholics   reg
irreg
Non-practising Catholics
No religion

% 100   50   0

% 0   50   100

Left
PC–Féd.

Decrease
1967 to 1968

Increase
1967 to 1968

Gaullism
UDR–RI.

Fig. 9. A comparison of the penetration into sociological groups by the gaullists and the left.

a fairly representative sample of the French adult population. This means, no doubt, that the Federation or its future equivalent is probably in a more favourable position than any other group on the left as far as the creation of a voter-directed party capable of opposing gaullism is concerned. But there is still no question of this, and the similarity in composition of the gaullist and Federation electorates must not let one forget the differences in their respective strength. Thus, in order to appreciate the extent to which gaullism has been successful in penetrating the various socio-professional classes in France, a comparison has to be made with the entire left, the Federation and the Communist Party grouped together (*Figure 9* and *Table 13*). What emerges as most striking from this comparison is the extraordinary way in which gaullism and the left have complemented one another within the French electorate. This is clearly shown in the table – only here and there do the centrists play a part, and then only a very slight one, among the liberal professions, the upper grades of executives, the highest income brackets and the practising Catholics. Moreover, its presence was felt less between 1967 and 1968, since the dramatic events of May 1968 undoubtedly reinforced the political tendency in France towards a sort of two party system. Another point to be noted is that the best criterion for distinguishing gaullism from the left is not one of income: the gaullist electorate has more of both the richest and the poorest sectors of society than the left. Nor is it one of occupation: the gaullists receive the support of 30 per cent of the French workers, and the same number of employees and managers as the left. What distinguishes the two is a cultural criterion, namely religion: the great majority of the 'non-religious' vote for the left, while most of the practising Catholics vote gaullist, or at any rate do not vote for the left.

Leaving aside this typically French characteristic, the analysis of the penetration by the gaullists and the left into the various strata of society can still be said to show two different, complementary electorates, the stuff from which two voter-directed parties could be made. This view of things leads one to the rather surprising conclusion that gaullism is to the left in France what the Conservative Party is to the Labour Party in Great Britain, despite the social and cultural differences between the two countries (*Table 14*): that is to say, a large female vote versus a large male vote, old versus young, less working class versus working class, etc.

We have here a whole series of observations which give support to the theses of such political writers and theorists as Maurice Duverger, for example, who has seen an evolution in France during the last few years towards a two-party system. The idea is all the more credible since the presidential election of December 1965 showed that this evolution was not bound to the person of de Gaulle: in this election, if the gaullist

TABLE 13: *A comparison between the sociological penetration of the gaullists and the left*

(*Source*: I.F.O.P.)

Categories	Gaullists		Left (Comm. Party + Fed. Left)	
	(1)	(2)	(1)	(2)
% ⟶	Jan. 1967	June 1968	Jan. 1967	June 1968
Sex				
male	34	35	43	43
female	41	46	33	34
Age				
21–49 years	37	38	39	40
50 years and over	40	43	34	37
Occupation				
peasants	45	48	27	32
liberal professions, executive class	44	48	24	19
industrial & commercial employers		53		23
employees, cadres moyens	35	40	40	36
workers	30	31	49	51
retired and non-working population	43	42	34	40
Monthly Income				
higher income bracket A	41	—	35	—
B	38	—	47	—
C	36	—	49	—
D	40	—	48	—
lower income bracket E	49	—	39	—
Residence				
rural districts	—	47	—	34
less than 20,000 inhabitants	—	45	—	34
20 to 100,000 inhabitants (urban districts)	—	35	—	50
more than 100,000 inhabitants	—	40	—	39
Paris region	—	30	—	42
Religion				
regular practising catholics	55	—	17	—
occasional practising catholics	42	—	41	—
non-practising catholics	33	—	60	—
agnostic	18	—	77	—
Television				
possess it	40	—	43	—
do not possess it	40	—	45	—

1. I.F.O.P. survey, January 20–30, 1967. Cf. *Sondages* 1967, 3, pp. 55 and 57.
2. All of 4,565 interviews given in two I.F.O.P. opinion polls before the first ballot of the general elections; cf. *Sondages* 1968, 2, p. 102.

N.B. The horizontal arrow indicates that the percentages have been calculated, for each survey, in relation to the whole line in each category (male, female, etc.). Example: of 100 men declaring their intention to vote in June 1968, 35 are gaullists; 43 vote for the left, 12 for the P.D.M. (Centre) and 10 others (including P.S.U.).

TABLE 14: *Gaullism v. the left in France,*
Conservative v. Labour in Great Britain

	France			Great Britain		
	Gaullism	Communist Party + Fed. Left	difference Gaullism/ Left	Conservative Party	Labour Party	difference Con./Lab.
Sex % →	I.F.O.P. January 1967 (1)			Gallup Poll October 1964 (2)		
male	34	43	−9	40	49	−9
female	41	33	+8	45	39	+6
Age % →	I.F.O.P. December 1966 (3)					
50–64 years	39	45	−6	44	40	−4
65 years and over	43	40	+3	46	44	+2
Social Classes % →	I.F.O.P. January 1967 (1)					
workers	30	49	−19	33	53	−20

1. I.F.O.P. survey, January 20–30, 1967. Cf. *Sondages* 1967, 3, pp. 55 and 57.

2. Henry Durant, Director, Gallup Poll: 'Voting Behaviour in Britain, 1945–64' *in*: Richard Rose, *Studies in British Politics*, A Reader in Political Sociology, Macmillan, London, 1966, pp. 122–8.

3. M. and R. Fichelet, G. Michelat and Michel Simon, 'The French, Politics, and the Communist Party', *Cahiers du Communisme*, December 12, 1967, pp. 14–15 (percentages recalculated after elimination of the 'don't knows').

N.B. The horizontal arrow indicates that the percentages have been calculated, for each survey, horizontally, in relation to the whole line in each category.

electorate increased numerically it also showed more particularism and more similarity with the electorate of the left than did the gaullist electorate in the 1967 general elections, for example (*Table 15*). In composition it was clearly older, less agricultural, more working class, and one might say more unproductive.

On the contrary, the electorate that voted for Georges Pompidou as President in June 1969 was closer sociologically to the gaullist 'general election' electorate than to the 'presidential' electorate of General de Gaulle. Georges Pompidou won the votes of exactly the same percentage of men (35 per cent) and women (46 per cent) as the U.D.R. candidates in June 1968, whereas Charles de Gaulle in 1965 had attracted an extra 5 per cent of the male vote. General de Gaulle's popularity was also stronger than that of the U.D.R. or Pompidou amongst the older age group. Compared with the gaullist candidates at the 1967 and 1968 legislative elections, de Gaulle was less successful

TABLE 15: *Comparison between the electorates of de Gaulle and the gaullists*
(*Source*: I.F.O.P.)

Categories	% ↓ (1) whole of France	Sociological composition (2) General de Gaulle 1965	% diff. col. 1	(3) Fifth Republic 1967	% diff. col. 1	% Sociological penetration → (4) General de Gaulle 1965	(5) Fifth Republic 1967	(6) Georges Pompidou 1969
Sex								
male	48	43	−5	42	−6	40	34	35
female	52	57	+5	58	+6	46	41	46
Age								
21–34 years	30	25	−5	29	−1	36	} 37	38
35–49 years	26	23	−3	26	—	36		38
50–64 years	26	29	+3	26	—	48	} 40	41
65 years and over	18	23	+5	19	+1	61		54
Occupation of head of family								
peasants	17	13	−4	16	−1	37	45	47
liberal prof. and executive class	5	4	−1	5	—	34	} 44	44
indust. and commercial employers	10	11	+1	11	+1	45		43
employees (cadres moyens)	15	16	+1	16	+1	39	35	35
workers	31	28	−3	28	−3	42	30	32
retired and non-working population	22	28	+6	24	+2	57	43	51

1. From the I.N.S.E.E. and I.F.O.P. *Sondages* 1967, 3, p. 52.
2. Before the first ballot of the presidential election.
3. I.F.O.P. survey of February 17–23, 1967. *Sondages* 1967, 3, p. 52.
4. Before the first ballot of the presidential election – percentages calculated from the 100 people who gave an opinion. The sample taken as a whole: 43 per cent of the votes for de Gaulle.
5. I.F.O.P. survey of January 20–30, 1967. Cf. *Sondages* 1967, 3, pp. 55 and 57.
6. I.F.O.P. survey of May 23–4, 1969. *Le Monde*, June 1–2, 1969.

among the peasants, the executives and the liberal professions, while Pompidou's popularity was on the same level as that of the party. On the other hand, de Gaulle was more successful among the workers than were the U.D.R. and Républicains indépendants, whereas Georges Pompidou did not fare much better than they did (*Tables 13* and *15*).

It would appear that, quite independently of the person of General de Gaulle, the gaullist electorate had found in March 1967 and June 1968, under the direction of Georges Pompidou, the specific socio-professional basis it needed if it were to become a large modern conservative party.

It is this, no doubt, that explains the final NO to the referendum of April 27, 1969 and the election of Georges Pompidou as President of the Republic on June 15, 1969.

GEOGRAPHICAL AND POLITICAL DISTRIBUTION OF THE GAULLIST ELECTORATE

In order to draw a map of the political distribution of gaullism, of its strongholds and its weak position, its progress and its gains, we have based our survey only on the general elections: November 1958, November 1962, March 1967 and June 1968.[10]

The dynamics of gaullism are fairly visible if one looks at the list of constituencies won either in a straight fight or by electoral pacts in 1962 and 1967 and retained thereafter (*Table 16*). Of these 116 metropolitan seats, 78 (67 per cent) were wrested from the opposition, for the most part as early as November 1962; the remainder – 38 seats (33 per cent) – fell to the majority as a result of electoral alliances with outgoing deputies, slightly more in 1967 than in 1962.

The moderate right is obviously the chief victim of the gaullist electoral expansion: the parliamentary group of Independents and Peasants in 1959 counted 108 members plus 10 allies, but in 1962 the group could not be reconstituted because the 30 deputies required by the parliamentary rules could not be found. In the only constituencies which are examined here, namely those which remained in gaullist hands after they had been won in 1962 or 1967, in November 1962 the moderates lost about 40 seats plus 10 of their re-elected deputies, to gaullism. The outright losses were fewer but the defections of those elected were still more numerous – about 15 – in March 1967. Taking together 1962 and 1967, the moderates conceded 66 constituencies to the gaullists, that is 55 per cent of those they had held in 1959. The Christian democrats of the M.R.P., for their part, conceded 29 constituencies, only one fifth of them through alliances, the rest through defeat or forfeiture. Their loss is clearly smaller than that of the moderates but then the M.R.P. also had less to lose: in 1959 the group

TABLE 16: *The dynamics of the majority* (seats won outright or by the conversion of an outgoing deputy, and held thereafter)

Seats won or brought in by 'converts' at the expense of . . .	I November 1962		II March 1967		Total
	Wins	*Converts*	*Wins*	*Converts*	
1. Moderates	39	10	2	15	66
2. M.R.P.	15	3	8	3	29
3. Various right-wing	—	1	—	—	1
4. Radicals	4	3	3	3	13
5. Socialists	2	—	3	—	5
6. Communists	—	—	2	—	2
Total	60	17	18	21	116

TABLE 17: *Ups and downs of electoral successes: June 1968 and March 1967 (Metropolitan France)*

1967: losses to the advantage of . . . *or:* 1968: gains at the expense of . . .	I March 1967	II June 1968
	seats lost (to the advantage of . . .)	*seats re-taken and seats won* = Total (at the expense of . . .)*
1. Centrists: Moderates	6 ⎫	4+ 3 = 7 ⎫
2. Centrists: M.R.P.	1 ⎬ 8	3+ 5 = 8 ⎬ 17
3. Centrists: Radicals	1 ⎭	0+ 2 = 2 ⎭
4. F.G.D.S.: Radicals	3 ⎫	4+ 6 = 10 ⎫
5. F.G.D.S.: Convention	11 ⎬ 37	11+ 0 = 11 ⎬ 55
6. F.G.D.S.: Socialists	23 ⎭	27+ 7 = 34 ⎭
7. P.S.U.	3	3+ 1 = 4
8. Communists	25	28+10 = 38
Total	73	80+34 = 114

* for the first time during the Fifth Republic.

of the Républicains populaires and of the Democratic Centre in the National Assembly had only 50 members, plus 6 allies. Proportionally, therefore, the M.R.P. losses are almost equivalent to those of the moderates: 51 per cent as against 55 per cent. The left, on the other hand, with the exception of the radicals who surrendered 13 seats, does not seem to run the risk of being weakened by gaullism. The socialists and communists were the only parliamentary opposition groups which lost none of their elected deputies to gaullism either in 1962 or in 1967.[11] The seats they lost 'permanently' to gaullism numbered only 2 in 1962, and 5 in 1967. Only the right and centre, therefore, have suffered greatly from the gaullist implantation even if, as will be shown below, in some elections a certain number of marginal left-wing seats have changed hands.

If we no longer consider the gaullist electoral phenomenon in terms of its dynamics but in terms of its more or less favourable political context – the elections of March 1967 and June 1968 will serve as examples (*Table 17*) – then the contest is again between the left and the gaullists.

In March 1967, a difficult electoral year for the gaullists, of the 73 metropolitan constituencies they lost, 40 went to the non-communist left and 25 to the communists, making a total of 65 to the left (89 per cent), as against 8 to the right and centre. From a legislative point of view, 1968 was a good year for the gaullists as they won back 73 seats from the left, and 7 seats from the right and centre. They also won 34 constituencies they had never before held: 10 from the right and centre, the other 24 from the left. Of the total gaullist gains, 85 per cent can be accounted for by the losses of the non-communist left – 59 seats – and of the Communist Party – 38 seats. The electoral pendulum swings from gaullism to the left, just as it swings from Tory to Labour in Great Britain.

We have tried to assess the electoral strength and weakness of gaullism after the general election of June 1968. It is however difficult to establish a classification of constituencies based on the lead of the majority party. The existence of a second ballot in France, with all the possibilities of electoral pacts and vote transfers it involves, does in fact cloud the issue. We have therefore preferred to classify the constituencies according to the number of times the gaullists have won the seat in general elections since 1958, modified on the assumption that, from the gaullist point of view, the more recent a defeat, the more dangerous it is for them. In 1958, gaullism had not yet established its real political and electoral foundations, so an isolated success or defeat at that time is only of marginal significance for the present survey. The same cannot be said for 1962, and even less so for 1967 or 1968. With these considerations in mind, one can classify the 470 constituencies of metropolitan France as follows: 210 *safe seats* (44.7 per cent) held by the gaullists or their 'converts' since 1962 at least, and for 7 out of 10 since 1958; 88 *marginal seats* (18.7 per cent) which the opposition took from the majority in one of the two key elections of 1962 and 1967, or even in 1958. Thus two different kinds of constituency can be distinguished, the one comprising 62 constituencies held by the gaullists in 1962 and 1968

TABLE 18. *Classification of the constituencies in metropolitan France, from the point of view of gaullism in 1968.*

Types of constituency (number/percentage)	November 1958	November 1962	March 1967	June 1968
1. 'Safe' seats (210/44.7%)		110 + 38 R+		
			60 + 2 R	
2. 'Marginal' seats (88/18.7%)			7 + 1 R	
				18
		33 + 6 R		
		22 + 1 R		
3. 'Very marginal' seats (52/11.1%)				17 + 1 R
				34
4. 'Opposition' seats (120/25.5%)		1		
		5 + 1 R		
		5		
	26			
		82		

+R = 'rallié' or convert. Unbroken line = gaullist win ; Dotted line = opposition win in the relative general election

but lost in 1967, and the other comprising 26 constituencies held as from 1967, but which the opposition still successfully retained or had sometimes won back in 1962; 52 *very marginal seats* (11.1 per cent), of primary importance in an election, either because they had never been part of gaullist territory before 1968, or – for a third of them – because, won by the gaullists in 1958, they had been lost both in 1962 and 1967 and were only recovered in 1968; finally, the 120 *opposition* constituencies (only 25.5 per cent in 1968) of which two-thirds have never been won by the majority (*Table 18*). The above classification is obviously imperfect. For example, a constituency in the 'very marginal' seat group, because it was taken from the opposition as late as 1968, might well prove in practice to be much safer than a theoretically 'safe' seat, especially if it had been won as a result of the departure of an important right-wing notability who had held it securely for many years. It is essential therefore to draw some finer distinctions.

As may be expected, the 'converts' to gaullism have in four cases out of five been firmly established deputies or notabilities who have really strengthened the bases of the majority by bringing their voters with them. Without denying the political reasons behind these partnerships, one can say that they offered the notabilities a double tactical advantage: firstly, they were saved from having to deal with a gaullist opponent [12] and secondly, they earned the gratitude of the central government. The gaullists also gained from the partnerships by extending their influence into areas which would otherwise have been forbidden territory. Of the 50 constituencies thus secured by the majority, 38 have been consistently held since 1958 by the 'converts', 29 of these 38 being personal strongholds: the electors have consistently returned the same man to the Palais-Bourbon since the beginning of the Fifth Republic; such is the case with Clermont-Montagne (Puy-de-Dôme – second constituency) where Valéry Giscard d'Estaing [13] has been elected on the first ballot in every election since 1958, like 6 of his Républicains indépendants colleagues.[14] The U.D.R., for its part, counts about 73 personal strongholds, of which only 2 have regularly elected their representatives on the first ballot since 1958: the constituency of Bayeux (Calvados – fourth constituency) faithful to Raymond Triboulet, and that of Saumur (Maine-et-Loire – third constituency) to Philippe Rivain.

These 102 'permanent' representatives in the various Assemblies of the Fifth Republic – 73 gaullists and 29 converts – clearly guarantee an element of continuity to the majority and provide it with the bulk of its ministerial, parliamentary and party officials. This is the case with Jacques Chaban-Delmas, Robert Boulin, Achille Péretti, Jean Taittinger, René Tomasini amongst the gaullists, with Valéry Giscard d'Estaing, Raymond Marcellin, Jean Chamant, Raymond Mondon, Jean de Broglie and Roland Boscary-Monsservin among the Républicains indépendants, and with Maurice Schumann of the Républicains populaires allies of the U.D.R.

The geographical distribution of the gaullist expansion (see *Map*) clearly reveals its areas of strength and weakness in the country. The blackest patches represent the 148 constituencies held since 1958, and they are reinforced by the 62 constituencies won in 1962 and subsequently retained. The real strongholds of gaullism can clearly be distinguished: eastern France and Savoie, where the support of the converts proved important; western France, Paris and the major part of the Paris area, with the exception of the communist suburbs; the southern parts of the Massif Central and Corsica. These areas coincide, on the whole, with the catholic strongholds, although also with the French non-

Map.

Penetration of the gaullist majority in 1968.

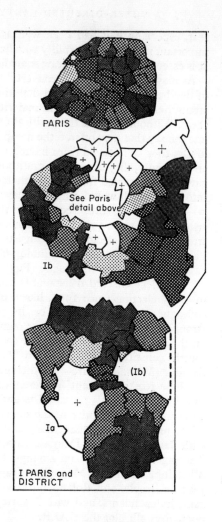

PARIS

See Paris detail above

Ib

(Ib)

Ia

I PARIS and DISTRICT

Catholic right. François Goguel pointed out in 1967 the importance of the votes cast for the 'Fifth Republic' candidates in northern France, in the central regions and the south-west, where the right had obtained poor results at the end of the Third Republic and throughout the Fourth.[15] The successes and failures of the gaullists over a fairly long series of general elections indicate that the most discerning map is the one showing the deputies elected rather than the votes gained, since it reveals the gaullist weakness in the regions which are traditionally not part of the strongholds of the right. The gaullist constituencies in the north and the Pas-de-Calais, excluding the towns of Lille and Calais,

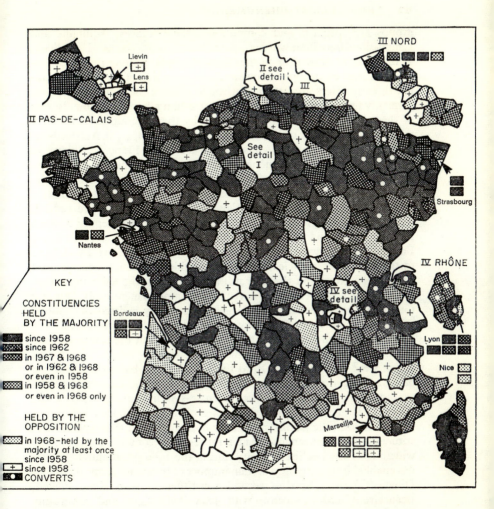

are far from being 'safe seats', whilst the opposition strongholds remain relatively numerous. The gaullist gains and losses are there of an essentially provisional nature. The same is true of the centre of France, with the exception of a few converted constituencies, and of the south-east, where the gaullists' success in the Gironde for example has dwindled sadly after their outstanding victories in 1958.

The regions most resistant to gaullism are precisely the strongholds of the left, the communist suburbs of Paris, and especially the Seine-Saint-Denis; the socialist-communist mining areas in the north and in the Pas-de-Calais, the Rhône delta and Marseilles, where the opposing groups are socialists and communists; the Pyrénées, Aquitaine and Languedoc-Roussillon where the socialists have succeeded the radicals, as in the areas bordering on the Massif Central. Among the 82 constituencies held by the opposition since the beginning of the Fifth Republic, three-quarters are bastions of the left where the gaullist candidate generally finds himself playing what is for him a hopeless game. Eleven of these constituencies have been held by the communists since 1958 without a break, that of Waldeck Rochet, for example, at Aubervilliers (Seine St Denis – third constituency), and of François Billoux at Marseilles (Bouches-du-Rhône – fourth); 21 have constantly remained faithful to the Socialists, as for example, Arras to Guy Mollet (Pas-de-Calais – first constituency), Abbeville to Max Lejeune (Somme – fourth), Narbonne to Francis Vals (Aude – second); 6 are radical, Tarbes (Hautes-Pyrénées – first), for instance, whose deputy is René Billières, or Cahors (Lot – first) which still regularly supports Maurice Faure despite his waverings between the centre and the left. In addition to these 38 constituencies, there are 10 which, although contested by the various groups on the left, still remain within the left-wing camp; plus 12 which the centre has never held on a permanent basis. Out of a total of 82 constituencies which have successfully resisted the gaullist expansion since 1958, 60 belong to the left. Of the remainder, a very few have been the subject of bitter clashes between the centre and the left – this was the case in Vendôme (Loir-et-Cher – third constituency) which went from the M.R.P. to the S.F.I.O. and back again, but the others are bastions of the moderate right or of the centre. Here the candidates of the majority fared even less well than they did in the strongholds of the left, and more often than not withdrew before the second ballot. The gaullists can only hope to win in this type of constituency if the entrenched leader retires or becomes a convert. The widening of the gaullist majority during the 1969 presidential election has enabled it to integrate a certain number of resistance areas, including Dinan (Côtes-du-Nord – second constituency) with René Pleven, Beaucaire (Gard – second) with Jean Poudevigne and Albertville (Savoie – second) with Joseph Fontanet.[16] Here again the right and the centre have shown themselves less capable of holding out against gaullism than the left. One might almost say that the gaullists have captured or converted the different right-wing electorates but they have had to fight, with varying results, only against the left.

CONCLUSION: A DOMINANT PARTY OF THE RIGHT

François Goguel, in one of his articles,[17] estimated that there were between 2,700,000 and 3,000,000 voters who had voted for the left, including communists, socialists and mendesist radicals, on January 2,

1956, who cast their votes for General de Gaulle and not for François Mitterrand at the presidential election on December 5, 1965. This figure – three million out of some ten million gaullist voters – was a substantial contribution of the left to gaullism and encouraged the left-wing gaullists' hopes of playing a more important role in the majority.

But the political and electoral evolution has not led towards a strengthening of the left wing within the gaullist ranks. The influence of ideology and of General de Gaulle's personal electorate in the gaullist phenomenon has doubtless been exaggerated.[18] However that may be, it has become clear since 1968–9 that gaullism has managed to amalgamate the various right-wing groups, and is faced by a totally disunited left.

A study of the opinion polls and of the gaullist successes in the general elections of 1958, 1962, 1967 and 1968 confirms the opposition between gaullism and the left and the common interests that bring together the gaullists, the centre and the moderates. For some who dreamed of bringing together workers and executives, left and right alike, it will be a disappointment that gaullism has in the end only managed to unite the right. But this in itself is no mean achievement and had never before been realized in France.

The creation of a large party of the right, with no great weakness in any particular region or any one social category, capable of assuming power alone, was not easy nor was it of little import. In any case it is probably preferable to leave to the left the opportunity and the responsibility for defending its own ideals.

Notes to Chapter 3

1. Maurice Duverger, *Les Partis Politiques,* 3rd edition revised and published, A. Colin, Paris, 1958, Chapter XII, p. 476.
2. The concept of a 'voter party' has much in common with the idea of a 'catch-all party' outlined by Otto Kirchheimer in: Joseph La Palombara and Myron Weiner ed., *Political Parties and Political Development,* Princeton, 1966, pp. 177–200. John S. Ambler rightly applies this concept to the U.D.R. party in his article 'The Democratic Union for the Republic: to survive de Gaulle', *Rice University Studies* 54, 3, summer 1968, pp. 1–51. Peter D. Trooboff had applied it previously to the unsuccessful federation of Gaston Defferre: Peter D. Trooboff, *Le catch-allisme et Gaston Defferre,* Professor Otto Kirchheimer's seminar in Comparative Politics, May 18, 1964. Columbia College, p. 30.
3. Party Conference at Nice, November 1963.
4. Speech of October 30, 1962 and of December 15, 1965, at the Palais des Sports, Paris – on the day after the referendum on the direct election of the President of the Republic by universal suffrage in 1962,

and on the eve of the second ballot of the presidential election in 1965.

5. Cf. Michel Debré, *Au service de la Nation*, Stock, Paris, 1963, in particular pp. 273–9.
6. On the ideology of the U.N.R. cf. Jean Charlot, *L'U.N.R.*, A. Colin, Paris, Chapter XI.
7. Raymond Aron in *Le Figaro*, quoted by Roger Frey, speech made at third Party Conference of the U.N.R.–U.D.T. at Nice, November 23, 1963.
8. Maurice Duverger, 'La démocratie du XXe siècle', *La Nef* 6, April–June 1961, p. 43.
9. *La Nation*, January 29, 1969.
10. In the 470 metropolitan constituencies defined by the electoral boundary law in 1958 and modified in 1967. In order to reflect this slight change the gaullist votes in 1958 and 1962 have been reconsidered within the new structure of the constituencies in the Paris region.
11. The socialists were to witness in June 1968 the conversion to gaullism of their former deputy Arthur Conte, defeated in 1967 by a communist, at Perpignan, in the second constituency of the Pyrénées Orientales.
12. Of the thirty-eight notabilities who joined the majority and brought with them their constituencies, held continuously either by the same deputy or by one of their group until 1958 inclusive, fourteen had no gaullist opponent in the general elections previous to their joining the gaullist majority. But it is probable that they would have encountered gaullist opposition had they not joined the gaullist ranks in 1962 or in 1967. This was the case more often in 1962 (eight out of seventeen converts) than in 1967 (six out of nineteen).
13. His replacement by his acting substitute when he assumes a government post has not been taken into account.
14. The other six R.I. deputies being: R. Boscary-Monsservin (Aveyron – 1st), Y. du Halgouët (Morbihan – 4th), G. Pianta (Haute-Savoie – 2nd), C. Bonnet (Morbihan – 2nd), I. Renouard (Ille-&-Vilaine – 4th), and A. Beauguitte (Meuse – 2nd).
15. Cf. in particular his article on the general election of March 1967 in the *Revue française de science politique*, June 1967, p. 447.
16. The post-1968 conversions have not been taken into account in *Figure 1* and *Table 18*.
17. François Goguel, 'Combien y a-t-il en d'électeurs de gauche parmi ceux qui ont voté le 5 décembre 1965 pour le général de Gaulle?' *Revue française de science politique*, XVII, February 1, 1967, pp. 65–9.
18. With reference to this subject, see the article by René Remond showing that gaullism does not coincide exactly with the right: 'Le gaullisme à la lumière du printemps 68', *France-Forum*, Nos. 90–1, October–November 1968, pp. 25–8.

PART TWO

THE GAULLISM OF THE GAULLIST GROUPS

CHAPTER IV

The Gaullists

THE THREE AGES OF GAULLISM

1940

Who are the gaullists? A few weeks after General de Gaulle's broadcast from London on June 18, 1940, they were only a meagre band of the first Free Frenchmen. 'You represent half of France,' the three hundred active male inhabitants of the island of Sein, who had all left for England, were told when they landed in Portsmouth at the end of June. 'At the end of July,' General de Gaulle records in his War Memoirs,[1] 'the total number barely reached seven thousand.' Of these many were unknown individuals of low rank, and few were notabilities or army officers: 'Hourly the passage via Lisbon or the landing in Liverpool of such and such a well-known politician or famous general was announced,' de Gaulle remembers, 'but the news was soon denied. . . .'[2]

In the chapter of his memoirs entitled 'Free France' he gives examples of numerous changes of mind, from that of General Weygand, whom he begged – on June 20th – to put himself at the head of the Resistance, assured of his complete obedience, to that of Noguès, the Commander-in-Chief in North Africa and the Resident General in Morocco, who had gone so far as to protest against the armistice and declare that he could only put it into effect with 'shame on his head'[3].

Of France's proconsuls in the Empire only General Catroux, governor-general of Indo-China, and General Legentilhomme, commander of the troops in the Somali Coast, refused the armistice; they were immediately deprived of their offices. In July the Governor Félix Eboué, 'this ardently French black man', brought over the Chad to the Free French cause. Most of the first Free French were thus virtually unknown people: Magrin-Verneret (called Monclar), Koenig, Dewavrin (called Passy), de Hauteclocque (called Leclerc), d'Argenlieu, Cabanier and a few other soldiers; the only exception as far as notoriety was concerned was Vice-Admiral Muselier.[4] With the help of d'Argenlieu he organized the first naval units; Magrin-Verneret (Monclar) and

Koenig organized the first land units, while Pigeaud and Rancourt set up the first air force units. Tissier, Dewavrin (Passy), Hettier de Boislambert formed the first état-major of the General. Geoffroy de Courcel served him as personal secretary, aide-de-camp and interpreter 'and, often, as a good adviser'.[5] Professor René Cassin, Antoine, Pierre-Olivier Lapie, Escarra, Hackin, René Pleven, Denis, Maurice Schumann, Jean Massip and Bingen made up the non-military entourage.[6] They were the first 'Companions',* those of St Stephens House and of Carlton Gardens, on British territory because, as Sir Winston Churchill and General de Gaulle agreed, 'England is an island, France the headland of a continent, America another world.'[7]

In France a handful of men refused from the first to give way. Most of them had not heard the appeal of June 18th but their resistance gave proof of a similar spirit. Air Marshal Cochet urged his men to pursue the fight underground; the prefect of Chartres, Jean Moulin, refused to sign the 'agreement' foisting the executions and rapes in Saint-Georges-sur-Eure on the Senegalese infantry – he tried to commit suicide so as not to give way under torture.[8] Among the very first, Etienne Achavanne, on June 20th, sabotaged the telephone cable between the Boos airfield and the Feldkommandatur of Rouen; he was captured, condemned to death and executed on July 6, 1940.[9] A few communists with Marcel Paul, a few Catholics with Edmond Michelet, a few non-Catholics with Daniel Mayer, a few Jews with 'the writer X', a few soldiers like Colonel Rivet, Colonel Mollard and Captain Henri Frenay, formed the first pockets of resistance. One of the first *Réseaux* was created at the Musée de l'Homme, by Boris Vildé, Anatole Lewitzky and Germaine Tillion. Jean Texcier in mid-July wrote his 'advice to the occupied', a real 'little handbook on dignity'.[10]

Already Passy, Rémy, Jack (Jacques Mansion), Weil-Curiel and a few others were trying to forge links between the Resistance in France and Free France. But 'virtually all the French population, stupefied by the military disaster, numbed by the exodus, "conditioned" by a well-orchestrated propaganda, welcomed Pétain as a saviour, the armistice as a deliverance and, furthermore, with the help of Marshal Pétain's first message, they soon saw the defeat as a deserved punishment. To want to go on fighting . . . was to fight against the current, to give way to impulse, to show a lack of reason, to cut oneself off from the bruised national community. It could only be the feat of a very small number. . . .'[11]

* Translator's note: title given to those who were awarded the highest resistance decoration 'Compagnon de la Libération' and by extension to gaullist activists.

1947

The gaullists were much more numerous when the R.P.F. (*Rassemblement du peuple français*) was officially created by General de Gaulle in Strasbourg on April 7, 1947. People rushed to join, and on the evening of April 15th the general secretary of the R.P.F., Jacques Soustelle, declared that there were 12,700 new members each day in the Seine alone. On May 10th, Jacques Baumel announced that there were 810,000 members, of whom 103,000 came from the Paris district; their number was to reach a million before the movement was 'demobilized' by General de Gaulle in 1952. The gaullists of the war, of the first age, had not been forgotten and from among them were drawn the major part of the officers of the new movement. The secretaries were recruited by a triumvirate composed of Jacques Soustelle, one of the leaders of the B.C.R.A. (the Central Bureau of Information and Action) at the end of the war; Jacques Baumel, who had been made responsible for political agitation in the southern zone in the R.O.P. (Recruiting, Organization, Propaganda) before serving as a liaison between the two zones to establish the M.U.R. (The United Movements of the Resistance), which was to establish the new authorities after the Liberation; and lastly Colonel Rémy, the Secret Agent No. 1 of Free France, who knew better than anyone else the members of the *Réseaux*. Roughly a fortnight before the official creation of the *Rassemblement*, a circular letter bearing the number (1), dated March 22, 1947, coming from the 'provisional secretariat' of one knows not what organization, invited the local secretaries recruited by Soustelle, Baumel and Rémy to seek 'irreproachable activists' in the Resistance movements and the clubs of former Free Frenchmen. They were told to be careful to guard against all risk of 'infiltration' (communists), of 'people clearing themselves' (vichyites) and 'reactionary deviation' (nationalist extreme right?). The headquarters staff of the R.P.F. in any case came straight from the Resistance. Of the 43 people whom General de Gaulle asked between 1947 and 1953 to become members of the supreme committee of the Rassemblement (which was first its Executive Committee then its Conseil de Direction) 15 came from the Resistance, 13 from the Free French, 6 had served in both; altogether 34 had taken some part in the Resistance. Only 4 had no military decoration; 8 were Companions of the Liberation: Baumel, de Bénouville, Billotte, Chaban-Delmas, Koenig, Malraux, Morandat and Rémy. The scanty bands of the army of shadows formed and trained the army of those who upheld General de Gaulle's policy.

1958

Some ten telephone calls sufficed in June 1958 for the teams to re-form and *réseaux* to spring back to life. But gaullism entered on a new phase –

that of the exercise of power; this enabled it to confront with reality the ideas and objective it had nurtured throughout the Fourth Republic, in the fields of the institutions, the economy, social and foreign policy. 'Between 1947 and 1949,' Georges Pompidou remembered some twenty years later, 'when General de Gaulle was no longer in power, he charged me with a "work group", which was in no way public, to study the general problems of the country. There were with me, grouped around Gaston Palewski, Michel Debré, Albin Chalandon, Raymond Aron, Louis Vallon, etc. We had ideas on many things. No doubt we were not right about everything. But we tried to think things out seriously and much has remained which has been useful during these ten years of government.' [12]

Having tasted power without compromise, the purest, most intransigent gaullists, like Michel Debré, discovered how difficult it was to live without it: 'I have already had to relinquish power,' confided the former Prime Minister of the General, 'and one must always be ready to do so. The feelings one experiences when this occurs . . . vary according to the circumstances of the departure. When one has tasted action, it is difficult to retire into the ivory tower of thought . . . when one has taken part in public affairs, it is difficult to return to private affairs . . . when one wants to bring action to bear on the needs of the future, it is not easy to take refuge in the contemplation of the present. . . . But life is made up of vanquished difficulties. . . .' [13]

Great courage was needed to become a gaullist in 1940, a certain amount of merit to become, and, above all, to remain one during the Fourth Republic; after 1958, one might find personal advantage in becoming a gaullist. For the *Union pour la nouvelle République* was a fortunate party which found power in its cradle and won an election before it had time to organize itself. A party with an unusual destiny in so far as it was 'first a ministerial team, then a central committee to select candidates for a general election, then the strongest parliamentary group in the National Assembly, and finally – at last – a party . . .'.[14]

Gaullism had to guard against the number, not of the electors, but of the candidates-for-responsibility; it had feared deviations. Applications for membership were carefully examined and membership was limited to the modest number – contrasted with the R.P.F. – of 24,000 in 1959, 50,000 in 1962 at the end of the Algerian war, between 100,000 and 150,000 today in so far as it can be evaluated.[15] In the selection of U.N.R. candidates for the general election, in November 1958, friendships made at 5, rue de Solférino, during the R.P.F. period were decisive: the applications were scrutinized by men who had been members of the party machine of the *Rassemblement* – Roger Frey, Jacques Baumel, Jacques Marette, together with Olivier Guichard,

Jacques Foccart, Jacques Richard, Pierre Lefranc, René Rivière, not to mention the leaders of the movement, Debré, Chaban-Delmas, Malraux, Michelet, Soustelle.[16] The gaullist past of those chosen in 1958 guaranteed their loyalty when faced with the trial of power. If they succumbed they were excluded, rejected, abandoned to anti-gaullism without power.

THE GENERATIONS OF GAULLISTS

Gaullism is therefore first a story – the story of thirty years of history; 'a film in episodes' Georges Pompidou said one day,[17] from the heroic gaullism of 1940 to the activist gaullism of 1947, to gaullism in power in 1958. Forged in the war, gaullism did not become a mere club of ex-service men, for it turned to politics with the R.P.F., but the gaullism of 1940 has long kept, and still keeps though less clearly, its value as an example, a symbol, an emotional force within political gaullism.

The individual itineraries of the gaullists are obviously multiple and complex. Of those who went through the Resistance, for example, some – like Leclerc – remained in the army, others went back to their villages, returned to their jobs without becoming interested in politics. Others, such as Mendès-France, have never been attracted by gaullism in politics. Some have broken off their links, like Billotte in 1952, though he was to return ten years later, or like Soustelle in 1960. On the other hand, there have been some 'conversions' which political considerations alone cannot completely explain – like that of the progressist Emmanuel d'Astier de la Vigerie in 1965; symbolically he passed away when the man whom he respectfully called 'the man of high stature' had retired to Ireland, to meditate alone whilst his successor was being elected. Some, like Maurice Schumann, returned to the gaullist fold, others – like René Pleven – found it difficult to make up their minds. . . . The necessities of the day pushed this man forward, forced that man back. Who could have predicted in 1958 that the three Prime Ministers of General de Gaulle under the Fifth Republic would be Michel Debré, Georges Pompidou and Maurice Couve de Murville? Jacques Soustelle was expected but he disappeared; Jacques Chaban-Delmas had to be patient.

But over and above individual fates, the situation of the gaullists within gaullism can only be understood if one takes into account the different political generations: the different periods of gaullism have each engendered their generation of gaullists who are far from having the same personality and carrying the same weight within the movement. A generation, in political terms, is one that has shared the same experiences, the same memories and the same emotions; it does not always speak the same language as the generation that precedes or follows it.

THE GAULLISTS OF THE FIRST GENERATION

The gaullists of the first generation, the 'historic gaullists' as they are sometimes called within the movement, have in common the shame of May 1940, the pride in August 1944, in Paris liberated. They have a special, personal link with the leader of June 18th; they are the real 'Companions', the Companions of the Liberation. They have the feeling, justified but heady, of being the happy few who were right, who were strong while the majority remained weak and hesitant. They are people who made history, and their hearts thumped when they heard André Malraux – quoting Pasquini – say to the delegates at the U.N.R. congress in Nice: 'While all the others have behind them the history of their parties, we have behind us the history of our country.'[18] For a long time the symbols of gaullism – the flag with its 'Cross of Lorraine', June 18th, the four beats of 'London calling', the companionship – are the signs of their own struggle in the F.F.L. or the F.F.I. In November 1963, for example, the third Party Conference of the U.N.R. was opened by the raising of the colours: the flag with the Cross of Lorraine was hoisted by Pierre Clostermann, surrounded by some thirty Companions of the Liberation, to the sound of the bugle and the four beats of 'London calling'. For them gaullism is their youth, their pride, the forming of their friendships, the friendship of men very different one from another but, as Jacques Chaban-Delmas told us, since de Gaulle gave them the opportunity to live 'the most honourable years of their lives' in 1940–5, these men transfer to one another the gratitude and admiration they have for General de Gaulle.[19] They are more sensitive than others to the appeals made in the name of solidarity, in the name of the past. 'We did not join the General two years ago,' Roger Frey recalled in 1960, 'but for most of us virtually twenty years ago.' [20] When Léon Delbecque resigned from the U.N.R. parliamentary party on October 14, 1959, because he was not allowed to plead for 'the most French solution' in Algeria, Marie-Madeleine Fourcade, the heroine of the Resistance, wrote to him to tell him that his resignation seemed to her 'incomprehensible', his arguments non-valid: 'the interdiction to speak freely, in this case, came from the General and not from the party'.[21] 'Many of our friends,' wrote Raymond Schmittlein, the president of the U.N.R. parliamentary party to Raymond Dronne, on March 2, 1961, 'are upset at the thought that you do not feel yourself bound by the links of friendship that we all feel towards you and they have already noticed for some time that you are drawing away from us. . . . If you would be so good as to give your old friends the pleasure of showing yourself more restrained in your use of language, the matter would go no further.' 'I am a gaullist of 1940,' the deputy of the Sarthe replied, 'and I am too old to change. But my loyalty towards General de

Gaulle does not prevent me from preserving my freedom of expression.'
'It is for me heartrending,' Raymond Schmittlein confessed when he
finally wrote to notify Dronne of his exclusion from the group, 'to see a
Companion of the first hour leave us. . . .' [22]

Some left the gaullist world at the Liberation to return under the
Fifth Republic, as in the case of Pierre Messmer and Maurice Couve de
Murville whom General de Gaulle put in the key positions of defence
and diplomacy. The 'entourage' could not, it is true, be made up of men
belonging to parties, not even of men belonging to the gaullist party, for
the General was above the parties. Malraux had only belonged to the
R.P.F., which was placed under the direct authority of the General.
Jacques Foccart and Pierre Lefranc were in the same position. But most
of the historic gaullists have taken part in all the phases of gaullism:
from the Resistance to the R.P.F., then to the Républicains sociaux, the
U.N.R. and the Fifth Republic – Michel Debré, Jacques Chaban-
Delmas, Edmond Michelet, Roger Frey. . . . In opposition, as in power,
they meet regularly, informally, usually at dinners organized by one or
other of them. It is there that the most important decisions are made, outside any official structure, in the magic circle into which Georges Pompidou is no doubt the only post-1940 gaullist who has managed to enter.

The team of the gaullist leaders was formed during the war by
General de Gaulle.[23] The political gaullism of the Fourth and Fifth
Republics has not made it, but has simply strengthened it by the testing
after the General's resignation in January 1946, the temptations offered
by Antoine Pinay in March 1952, the Algerian problem in 1959–60.

The historic gaullists who remained loyal throughout these periods
have in the movement, and today in the government, an importance out
of all comparison to their small number.

NEW BLOOD

New blood, however, has been brought into gaullism in increasing
quantities during the last few years. In 1964, we noted that since the
creation of the U.N.R. six years earlier the proportion of 'historic'
gaullists was becoming smaller. Until 1962 they had controlled the
executive of the U.N.R., in 1962–4 they became a minority on the
central committee and among the leaders of the gaullist parliamentary
party.[24] But the turning point was the fourth party Conference of the
U.N.R. in Lille, in November 1967.[25] For the first time in the history of
gaullism, the image of the young gaullist is exalted at the expense of that
of the old companion. The political necessity of renewal is ardently
defended by Georges Pompidou: 'For all those who are under thirty,
June 18th, Free France and the Liberation are no more living realities
than the 1914–18 war. For those who are twenty the Fourth Republic,

with its trials and on occasion its shame, is no more than an abstract notion. . . . It is our task to bring in new blood. It is our task to seek out all those who are interested in public affairs, all those who reflect on the problems put before the world of today by an unprecedented scientific and technical evolution, and to convince them that they will find in our midst the means to act and to realize their ambitions, that they will find among us progressive men and ideas for the future. Thus, and only thus, shall we be able to ensure the continuity of the regime and of the ideas which have saved our people from decadence. Thus, but only thus, will gaullism be able to continue its work.' [26] The 'modernists', led by Georges Pompidou, who only joined the gaullists in 1944 through the small door of the General's cabinet, and by the pragmatists among the historic gaullists – in particular Jacques Chaban-Delmas and Roger Frey – prudently tried to prepare gaullism for the period after de Gaulle, tried to transform the movement so that it would remain in harmony with the changing country. They have come up against some left-wing gaullists, such as René Capitant and Louis Vallon, and against those who feel nostalgia for the past, like Raymond Réthoré 'tired of hearing that we have come to the end of gaullism', or like Raymond Triboulet, the first Prefect of liberated France, for whom gaullism remains 'first and foremost the flame of the Resistance' which will never go out, or like that obscure activist Connas who was worried about the authentic nature of the gaullism of so many gaullists. But the renewal had already occurred among the rank and file, and when, playing on both sides at the same time, Jacques Chaban-Delmas and Roger Frey tried to get the activists to agree to the new statutes drawn up by Michel Habib-Deloncle by appealing to the loyalty born of the common struggles in the past, they were not listened to and had to find a compromise.[27] The negligible effect of this sentimental appeal to the past symbolizes the end of an epoch, in which the former leaders of the Resistance still dominated the gaullist Party Conference.

All the general secretaries of the U.N.R. since it first came into being in October 1958 – Roger Frey, Albin Chalandon, Jacques Richard, Roger Dusseaulx, Louis Terrenoire, Jacques Baumel – were gaullists of the Resistance and of the R.P.F. The General Secretary chosen by the new gaullist party, *Union des démocrates pour la Ve République* (U.D.Ve) after the Party Conference at Lille, Robert Poujade, was twelve in 1940 and nineteen in 1947 when he began to take an active part in politics in the R.P.F.[28] He came to gaullism by way of politics – deeply hostile to the 'Republic of the Parties' – and not through the Resistance. In Dijon, in the general election of March 1967, he defeated the local hero, Canon Kir, who had ruled over the town since the end of the war. Younger and more dynamic, Poujade had given proof of his competence in economic and urban affairs when he sat on the Committee for the

Expansion of Dijon, the Committee for the Regional Development of Burgundy and the Economic and Social Council. The executive bureau of the *Union des démocrates pour la Ve République*, which replaced in 1967 the former political committee of the U.N.R., marked the elimination of some fifty gaullists born between 1897 and 1925, 1913 on average, some forty of whom were gaullists of the first generation. On the other hand, it opened its doors to some ten gaullists born around 1922, who were therefore under twenty in 1940, so that the number of gaullists too young to have taken part in the Resistance was practically equal to that of the 'historic' gaullists. This is the controlled renewal of the first generation by the intermediary generation of the R.P.F. gaullists symbolized by Robert Poujade.

The study of the governmental circle of the Fifth Republic, from the Cabinet presided over by General de Gaulle in 1958 to that of Jacques Chaban-Delmas some eleven years later, confirms this movement for renewal (see *Table 19*). Under General de Gaulle, the gaullism of the war predominated: 62 per cent of the Ministers were either Companions of the Liberation or had Resistance medals; to which party they belonged was a detail: André Boulloche, the socialist, was the equal of André Malraux, the gaullist, for they were both Companions of the Liberation – Eugène Thomas, the socialist, Louis Jacquinot, the moderate, Jacques Soustelle, Michel Debré and Edmond Michelet, the gaullists, all had a Resistance medal with a 'rosette'; * the orthodox gaullists in fact made up only five twenty-fourths of the members of the Government, scarcely more than a fifth. From 1968 onwards, the situation was reversed: from then on it was more important to have the U.D.R. label – 87 per cent of the Ministers of Couve de Murville's Cabinet, or even that of a neighbouring party and ally such as the Républicains indépendants (R.I.), rather than to have Resistance decorations. Roughly half the ministers had none, 15 per cent were too young to have won any, for they were fifteen or under in 1940: these include Valéry Giscard d'Estaing, Philippe Mallaud, Jacques Limouzy, Bernard Pons, André Fanton, Jacques Chirac. The 'young wolves' were no longer heroes; they were intellectuals with a diploma from the Paris School of Political Science, the Polytechnic or the National School of Administration. In ten years, gaullism had become 'normalized'; instead of the royal way opened by the war, the road followed was now the classical road – from party to parliament, from parliament to government. The renewal of the government circle depended less on wartime friendships than on political necessities: in April 1969 Jacques Chaban-Delmas took over half his ministers from outside the former government, thus widening the party, as Georges Pompidou had promised during the presidential campaign (see *Table 20*).

* Translator's note: = a bar.

TABLE 19: *Resistance activities, partisanship and ministerial responsibilities*

	Government				
	de Gaulle	Debré	Pompidou	Couve de Murville	Chaban-Delmas
Ministers	24 members (July '58)	27 members (Jan. '59)	29 members (April '62)	31 members (July '68)	39 members (June '69)
Compagnons de la Libération (Companions of the Liberation)	3	3	6	4	5
Rosette de la Résistance (Resistance Bar)	5	5	1	3	6
Médaille de la Résistance (Resistance Medal)	7	7	13	8	9
Total	15 (62%)	15 (55%)	20 (69%)	15 (48%)	20 (51%)
15 years old or less in 1940	—	1 (4%)	2 (7%)	5 (16%)	6 (15%)
Partisanship (1)	5 (21%)	8 (30%)	16 (55%)	27 (87%)	29 (74%)

1. Members of the *Républicains sociaux*, of the U.N.R.–U.D.T. or of the U.D.R. depending on the period, or a very close allegiance to them (e.g. André Malraux); the percentages are calculated in relation to the total number of ministers in each government.

TABLE 20: *Changes in the composition of the government*

New members of the government	Debré (January '59)	Pompidou (April '62)	Couve de Murville (July '68)	Chaban-Delmas (June '69)
Number (percentage)	9 (33%)	10 (34%)	8 (26%)	20 (51%)

LOYALTY IN A CHANGING MOVEMENT

'The world needs a renaissance,' Georges Pompidou declared on June 25, 1969 in his first official message, thus placing his seven-year Presidency under the sign of the renaissance to come.[29] 'Is it the end of a renaissance?' Pierre Lefranc, the president of the National Association in favour of the Action of General de Gaulle, had questioned a little while before. For him the renaissance had begun on June 18, 1940 after 'the loss of all illusion'; 'if de Gaulle goes,' he went on, 'what will happen to this country for which we have acquired so much taste, what will happen to the renaissance of France?'[30] 'The end of a gaullism, or the end of gaullism?'

Since 1965 the gaullists had been preparing the 'after-de Gaulle' period. With anguish, with a feeling of guilt or a sense of reality, as the case may be; the end came more quickly, more dramatically than had been expected. However, as might have been expected, a few gaullists discreetly followed de Gaulle. Once he had gone, the political adventure had lost its epic quality and they had lost interest. André Malraux left the Government to which since 1958 he had given his witticisms. In June 1969, for the first time, his voice was not heard during a major national election. His political speeches needed giants, uncommon destinies, the great wind of history. . . . For Malraux, as for de Gaulle, France held more interest than the French and one can well imagine his feelings on the evening of April 27, 1969 when the people said NO to de Gaulle, by reading his speech delivered during the 1965 election: 'France, Bernanos wrote, created Joan of Arc, Saint-Just, Clemenceau. . . . She has not finished creating the great. That is her task! Ours is to see they are not burnt.' [31] Maurice Couve de Murville, after ten years at the Foreign Office implementing the General's foreign policy, and a single year at Matignon as Prime Minister, also left the Government, and Michel Debré declared: '. . . Now with the installation of a new President of the Republic, a major period of our lives comes to an end and our emotion is all the greater as we see you leave, because you have been the last of General de Gaulle's Prime Ministers. . . .' [32] René Capitant dreamed of converting the left to gaullism, of changing the condition of the workers by the association of employers and workers, which de Gaulle alone, with the approbation of the people obtained by a referendum, could impose on the right, on his own parliamentary majority. His faith has not been weakened by the reply to the referendum in April 1969, the departure of General de Gaulle and the election of Georges Pompidou: '. . . If the nation has sent General de Gaulle away, the people may also one day send Pompidou away before his seven years are up'; and he added, 'de Gaulle is not dead. . . . Do you think he will bow before those who want to bury his projects? Perhaps those who have caused de Gaulle to go will find him tomorrow even more dangerous for them than he was yesterday. . . . The only unity we accept is unity around de Gaulle and his programme and not around Giscard and Duhamel.' [33] But René Capitant was soon to die, as was General de Gaulle himself – without having had the time to finish his memoirs.

Even if the noisy controversies of the gaullist left were expected and were of little consequence, they were not the only expressions of a fear of 'revisionism' within a gaullism suddenly conscious that it had an ideology. At the beginning of May 1969 Michel Debré, Louis Joxe and Pierre Messmer founded an association entitled *Amicale présence et action du gaullisme* to defend the spirit of 'a precise image of France developed by General de Gaulle . . . a policy of national independence, of modernization of the administration, of economic and social reform within the framework of the Fifth Republic.'[34] Towards the beginning of July, on the initiative of General de Gaulle's son-in-law Jacques Vendroux, a parliamentary group, Actuality and Influence of Gaullism, was formed to 'act within the majority'.[35] On Saturday, July 5th, at the central committee meeting of the U.D.R., Jacques Chaban-Delmas showed some concern about the interpretations the creation of this group might give rise to, and declared: 'We are the true heirs of gaullism.' For his part, Robert Poujade, the general secretary of the U.D.R., remarked with humour to the journalists, 'Our conclusion was that all the members of the parliamentary party could belong to this group for they are all irrefutable gaullists. I have not been asked to be its president. But although I do not usually join parliamentary groups, I might make an exception for this one. . . .'[36]

In a majority party there are necessarily different ideological currents, representing internal pressure groups. The gaullism of Valéry Giscard d'Estaing and Jacques Duhamel is in its essence institutional and does not go beyond the recognition of the need for a majority capable of ensuring France's political stability. The gaullism of Michel Debré comprises an ardent defence of the authority of the state and of the international independence of France. The gaullism of René Capitant and Louis Vallon is above all concerned with the progress of society. Inevitably the President of the Republic, Georges Pompidou, and Jacques Chaban-Delmas, the Prime Minister, have to maintain a certain equilibrium, while defending a 'certain view of France'. The only problem is to know to what extent the various groups will continue to believe in the need for concerted and common decisions. A voter-oriented party – contrary to an activist-oriented party – has far less to fear from a certain ideological adaptability than it has from a unique and total political doctrine imposed on all members, for this would lead to schism.

Robert Poujade saw the problem clearly when he said to the central committee of the U.D.R., 'there is no question of our becoming a sect, but we have a message to convey'.[37] Apart from a few gaullist left-wing personalities and fringe groups, the majority of the party seems to have realized this over the last twelve years.

Notes to Chapter 4

1. Volume I, *L'Appel, 1940–2*, p. 100 in the Livre de Poche edition (Plon).
2. Ibid., pp. 105–6.
3. Ibid., p. 91–2. Among these 'evasions' was that of Jean Monnet, who reproached de Gaulle with having set up an organization which might

have appeared in France as having been created under the protection of England, and he felt that the effort to save France could not originate in London (p. 106).

4. Ibid., p. 97.
5. Ibid., pp. 107–8.
6. Ibid., p. 107. A year later, on September 19, 1941, the non-military services of Free France numbered 96 people, of whom 35 were women; the ensemble of the *états-majors* consisted of 280 military men and 70 civilians, including 65 women (Paul-Marie de la Gorce, *De Gaulle entre deux mondes*, A. Fayard, Paris, 1964, p. 218).
7. Volume I, *L'Appel, 1940–2*, p. 112.
8. Henri Noguères, ed., *Histoire de la Résistance en France*, Volume I, June 1940–June 1941, R. Laffont, Paris, 1967, pp. 23–5.
9. Ibid., pp. 30 and 32.
10. Ibid., pp. 76–7
11. Ibid., pp. 33–4.
12. Interview in *L'Express* 846, September 4–10, 1967, p. 19.
13. Interview in *Réalités*, 'Dix ans de pouvoir', March 1968, p. 48.
14. Jean Charlot, *L'U.N.R., étude du pouvoir au sein d'un parti politique*, A. Colin, Paris, 1967, p. 23.
15. Cf. Ibid., Diagram No. 2, p. 116 and following chapter.
16. Cf. Ibid., pp. 41–2.
17. Speech at the U.N.R.-U.D.T. parliamentary study days, Dinard, September 24, 1964.
18. Speech, November 24, 1963.
19. Interview, June 23, 1965.
20. Speech, the U.N.R.-U.D.T. National Council, St-Mandé, October 22–3, 1960.
21. Unedited correspondence, October 23, 1959.
22. Unedited correspondence, letter from R. Schmittlein to R. Dronne, March 2, 1961; reply of R. Dronne, March 3rd; notification of expulsion on November 21, 1961.
23. Cf. Jean Charlot, op. cit., pp. 296–304.
24. Ibid., pp. 250–4.
25. Cf. Jean Charlot, 'L'Après-gaullisme', *Revue française de science politique*, XVIII, February 1, 1968, pp. 68–76.
26. Speech given by Georges Pompidou, Prime Minister, at the Party Conference at Lille, November 26, 1967.
27. Cf. following chapter.
28. He joined in his year of 'khâgne' at Montpellier. In 1948, he went to the Ecole Normale Supérieure and was active on a national level: he was national secretary of the R.P.F. students. He organized the review of the intellectuals of the movement, *Liberté de L'Esprit*. He was then secretary of the Federation of the Social Republicans of the Côte d'Or, in 1955, then of the U.N.R. as from 1958. In March 1967, he defeated Canon Kir at Dijon, and became a deputy. He was re-elected in June 1968.
29. 'Message au Parlement', *Le Monde*, June 27, 1969.

30. 'Libres Opinions', *Le Monde*, May 17, 1969.
31. Speech, December 15, 1965, at the Palais des Sports, Paris.
32. Intervention at the last Cabinet Council meeting of the Couve de Murville administration, June 19, 1969. Cf. *Le Monde*, June 21, 1969.
33. June 18, 1969, before the members of the 'Popular Gaullist Union'. Cf. *Le Monde*, June 20, 1969.
34. The General Secretary of the association is Roger Stéphane; its headquarters are at 12, rue Ernest-Psichari, Paris 7ᵉ. Cf. *La Nation*, May 7, 1969.
35. Presided over by Hubert Germain, Companion of the Liberation, deputy for Paris, the bureau of this Friendly Society also includes three vice-presidents, MM. Plantier, Clostermann, Béraud, and a general secretary, Michel de Grailly. The first list of names of the deputies who were members of the Society included, apart from Jacques Vendroux and the five former members, MM. Michel Le Tac, Pasqua, Poujade, Le Bault de la Morinière, Neuwirth, Jacquet, Lacombe, Mercier, Poncelet, Marcenet, Tricout, Vallon, Sanguinetti, Herzog, Jacques-Philippe Vendroux, Abdoulker Moussa Ali, Tomasini and Carter – the founders wanted to limit the Society to a total membership of about forty. Cf. *La Nation*, July 3rd and *Le Monde*, July 4, 1969.

    On September 9, 1969, on the eve of the parliamentary days at Amboise, only about twenty of the deputies who were members of the Friendly Society met together at Noisy-Le-Roi to determine their doctrine. Neither a splinter group nor an integrationist, they aim, according to one of them, to be the 'knot in the handkerchief' which will constantly remind the U.D.R. and the majority of the gaullist doctrine. Cf. *Le Monde*, September 11, 1969. The most gaullian of the gaullists feel the more or less veiled criticisms made by the widened majority to the team that was in power 1968-9, including General de Gaulle. Cf. the article of Jacques Vendroux in *Le Figaro*, September 16th and the reply of *La Nation*, September 18, 1969. The speech of Michel Debré, at Amboise, tried to stress quite clearly, nevertheless, the unity and cohesion of the U.D.R. parliamentary party. The Friendly Society counted very much on the strengthening that would be brought by Maurice Couve de Murville, to whom Pierre Clostermann sacrificed his parliamentary seat, in the Yvelines. But the former Prime Minister was beaten by Michel Rocard, leader of the P.S.U.
36. *Le Monde*, July 5, 1969.
37. Ibid.

CHAPTER V

The Gaullist Organizations

THE NATURE OF THE ORGANIZATIONS

The gaullist organizations are certainly numerous. We have listed some
thirty different ones and this may not be all.[1] The situation becomes
clearer, however, if we take into account the size and above all the roles
of each of them, for it is these two factors which finally decide, according
to the problems and the moment, whether or not they will be active.
Some of them are permanently mobilized: first of all the gaullist
'parties', the *Union des démocrates pour la République*, the *Fédération
nationale des Républicains indépendants*, to which can be added the
Centre démocratie et progrès and the *Union de la gauche Vᵉ République*;
next come the 'specialized' movements which take charge of the non-
party supporters and the less 'politicized' gaullists, from every milieu
and at every level. There are other organizations which are only inter-
mittently active: the associations giving strong support to General de
Gaulle, such as the *Association nationale pour le soutien de l'action du
Général de Gaulle* (the National Association for the support of General
de Gaulle's action) which, while de Gaulle was in power, only came to
life when there was a referendum or a presidential election but which,
on these occasions, played a major role; there are also special associations, like the *Service d'action civique* (S.A.C.) and the *Comités de
défense de la République* (C.D.R.) whose aims are respectively order and
free speech at gaullist meetings and the preservation of law and order
throughout the country.[2] The rational division of these organizations
into categories, according to the work they do, does not satisfactorily
explain all the gaullist associations; personal struggles and, even more,
conflict of opinion cause rivalry between organizations which could
otherwise combine since they fulfil the same role. In this respect, the
classification that corresponds most closely to the political reality of gaullism is that which distinguishes three main components: firstly, the gaullist
left wing, individualist and divided; secondly, the moderate right,
ambitious and organized but still a minority; finally, the mass of gaullists,
forming the biggest section of the majority, who represent gaullism
proper, who control the most important posts and intend to keep them.

I. THE GAULLIST LEFT WING

DIVERSE CURRENTS OF OPINION

The tragedy of the gaullist left is that it always feels a desperate need to justify itself: to the left, that it is genuinely left wing; to the gaullists, that it is more gaullist than all of them put together, apart from General de Gaulle himself of course, and he claims that he is not a gaullist. In short, it is always and on all sides suspected of disloyalty.

The majority of left-wing gaullists are gaullist in outlook in that they favour the foreign policy of General de Gaulle; they accept the institutions of the Fifth Republic but are somewhat embarrassed by gaullist economic and social policy. The *Groupe des vingt-neuf* (Group of twenty-nine) is the most representative in this respect. Its founder members come unquestionably, and came quite recently, from the left: they include the late Emmanuel d'Astier de la Vigerie, who died in 1969 and had been head of the progressive daily newspaper *Libération*; Pierre Le Brun, the former National Secretary of the C.G.T., who died in 1970; the late André Philip, a former socialist S.F.I.O. minister, afterwards a member of the P.S.U.; David Rousset, co-founder in 1948, with Sartre, Camus and Breton, of the *Rassemblement démocratique révolutionnaire*; Philippe Dechartre, a former mendesist candidate at the general election of January 1956; Jean-Marie Domenach, director of *Esprit* and a left-wing Catholic; former journalists, such as Roger Stéphane of *L'Observateur*, or Robert Barrat of *Témoignage Chrétien*, and so on. 'We are democrats,' they declared jointly in their appeal in May 1966, 'and some of us are socialists. We consider the dispute over institutions as a thing of the past. . . . The most important thing in our eyes is foreign policy. Together with a great number of left-wing voters and with most of the progressive forces throughout the world, we give our support to an international policy of peace founded on the refusal to become part of either one of the dominant blocks, on an enlarged and reconciled Europe and on co-operation with the developing countries and with the neutral nations.' They remarked that this 'policy [is] at the present time being pursued in the name of France'.[3] 'We wish to show that the left can, in good faith, be gaullist. But that it can also give gaullism the conscience of a left-wing party,' one of the 'twenty-nine' was later to state.[4]

The *Front du progrès* which, in April 1964, succeeded the *Mouvement pour la Communauté*, also places the emphasis on foreign policy, as is shown by the order of its fundamental aims: 'world solidarity – the freedom of peoples – the building of an independent Europe – the coming of a civilization in which the human individual would be the overriding consideration'.[5] The leader of the *Front du progrès*, Jacques Dauer, is one of the 'twenty-nine'; he is anything but an orthodox gaullist: at the general election of November, 1958, for example, he was responsible for encouraging the presentation of independent candidates for *Renouveau et Fidélité* against the U.N.R. He dreamed of a party of activists, pure and uncompromising. 'Activists,' he proclaimed in *Le Télégramme de Paris*, 'your candidates are men who have wielded the brushes and the glue-pot, who have not drawn their punches. They compromised themselves when the politicians thought only of lining their pockets, at a time when it was dangerous, praiseworthy and ridiculously heroic. They are activists. They had suffered.' [6] Jacques Dauer is the type of gaullist more fitted to stay in the wilderness than to pace the corridors of power. He dreads the integration and the drowning of the *Front du progrès*, of the whole gaullist left, in the majority.[7]

The *Union démocratique du travail (U.D.T.)*, which joined the U.N.R. of its own accord, after their joint success in the general election of November 1962, reconstituted itself as a group, but only a shadow of its former self, in 1969 after the General's departure. It is principally preoccupied with home affairs although still remaining a strong supporter of General de Gaulle's foreign policy. The late René Capitant, one of its leading men, defended with passion and with great political integrity a certain notion of democracy; he venerated those whom Michel Debré would willingly destroy – Jean-Jacques Rousseau, Bergson, even Alain – since he was suspicious of the 'Leviathan State'. For René Capitant 'it is in relation to democracy that we must judge nationalism', and not vice-versa.[8] His gaullism derived essentially from the fact that General de Gaulle, when he established a system of direct democracy through the election of the President of the Republic by direct universal suffrage, through the use of the referendum and the right of dissolution of the Assembly, restored to the people their sovereignty, which had till then been seized by the parties in parliament. But René Capitant pushed his logic to the point of condemning, on the grounds of deviation, the existence of a true gaullist party in the Fifth Republic: the aim of gaullism, he considered, is not to found a party but a regime, by converting the opposition parties to gaullism, that is to say, to the new institutions.[9] This represents an idealistic and individualistic view of political life which ignores the role of parties and groups in the political behaviour of men; in the eyes of other left-wing gaullists like Philippe Dechartre and of gaullists in general, the views of Capitant were also masochistic, causing one to lament the gaullist victories on account of their conservatism and to dream 'rather surprisingly' of a replacement of the majority.[10] For the gaullists of the U.D.T., René Capitant and Louis Vallon for example, moved to gaullism because of their disappointment with the left; they stayed only because they had faith in the revolutionary spirit of General de Gaulle, despite the fundamental conservatism, in their opinion, of the majority of gaullists. They awaited the grand 'social reform' that the General was expected to impose upon the majority in the same way that he had earlier imposed Algerian independence upon them – by drawing his support from the people, if necessary, through a referendum. 'Gaullism,' René Capitant wrote, 'is pregnant with something else, something which was indicated in its early years but which has not even begun to see the light of day, which is still awaited by the three million voters of the left who, even in the communist party ranks, still vote despite everything for the hero of June 18th, something which he promised to do and which he cannot go back on without comprising all he has done before and his very legend.' [11] In 1965–6 the gaullists of the U.D.T. thought they had finally found in the 'pan-capitalist' idea of Marcel Loichot the way to non-violent social revolution: all workers would be given access to the ownership of the means of production by sharing between the capitalist-owners and the workers the increase of wealth due to self-financing. At the present rate of growth in production, more than a quarter of the present assets could thus be transferred to the workers within twenty years. This is the aim of the famous 'Vallon amendment' to article 33 of the bill made law on July 12, 1965 on the participation of the workers in the profits resulting from auto-financing. For René Capitant, who was won over by the idea, pan-capitalism 'is not *a* solution but *the* solution'.

General de Gaulle himself referred to this in his press conference of October 28, 1966: 'It is not negligible to have provided in a recent law that the workers, under certain conditions, will have a right to share in the increase in value of capital.' This form of participation was not, however, acceptable to the trade unions, and met with resistance from the employers' organizations and with apathy from the government and from the greater part of the parliamentary majority.[12] It is understandable that the gaullists of the U.D.T. asked themselves, even before the departure of General de Gaulle, what exactly was the significance of their inclusion in the majority. 'Was the U.D.T. right to combine forces with the U.N.R. in 1962?' René Capitant asked – four years later. 'Has not the moment come for the movement to loosen the ties? After all, the other gaullist parties – the M.R.P. gaullists and independent gaullists from all parties – had guaranteed their independence before joining the ranks. I do not wish for a split, but I am not afraid of one either!' [13] Their links with the majority of gaullists became clearly more strained after the departure of the General, their only hope, on April 27, 1969. Relations were strained to breaking point, and were finally broken off for Louis Vallon by his exclusion from the U.D.R.

ACTION FROM WITHOUT OR FROM WITHIN?

The eternal tactical problem of active minorities is to know whether to act from without or from within the majority organization. Between the presidential election of 1965 and the general election of 1967, the different political trends of the gaullist left thought they had found the solution to the problem in the formula that Edgar Faure had applied to the problem of decolonization: 'independence within interdependence'; the left-wing gaullists clearly placed their political action within their contract with the majority, with all the obligations that followed: unity of candidature, the exercise of a party whip, etc. On the other hand, in order to safeguard their individuality and have more influence, they organized themselves so as to form alongside the U.N.R. and the Républicains indépendants the third wing of the gaullist triptych. With this in mind, the *Convention de la Gauche Ve République* was founded in Paris on October 8, 1966. Under Philippe Dechartre, its general secretary, it united five left-wing gaullist organizations, of unequal weight: the *Front du progrès*, the *Centre de la Réforme républicaine*, the *Cercle Jules Vallès*, the *Association nouveau régime* and the *Clubs Ve République*. Three groups remained outside this federation: the members of the U.D.T., still integrated in the U.N.R. and whose departure the Convention could not provoke without breaking with the major part of the majority; the *Front travailliste* of Yvon Morandat, Lucien Junillon and Bernard Farbmann, composed chiefly of former S.F.I.O. members, with whom the Convention worked while awaiting the coalition it desired and finally achieved in March 1969; lastly, the *Groupe des vingt-neuf*, which intends to remain more of a philosophical than a politically militant club but which allows its members to belong to the Convention as well. To describe the latter, Philippe Dechartre could use the same words as Valéry Giscard d'Estaing did when speaking of the Républicains indépendants: 'A young and modern party whose task is to function as a laboratory for political research and study', a movement of 'internal controversy waged within the limits of discipline implied by its agreement to form part of the majority . . . pressure from without . . . remaining the specific means of action of the opposition'.[14] The following message was cabled to the organizers of the constitutive committee of the Convention by the polemist Philippe de Saint-Robert: 'Send you support for building structures capable of restoring balance to majority and bringing it out of unfortunate position of immobility and feeble neo-radicalism'.[15]

In the *Comité d'Action pour la Ve République* which, under the presidency of Prime Minister Georges Pompidou, listed in 1966–7 prospective candidates drawn from all the different trends in the majority, the gaullist left can count on nine individuals: three from the U.D.T. group,

Pierre Billotte, René Capitant, Léo Hamon, and six others, Louis Joxe, Edgard Pisani, Edgar Faure, Maurice Schumann, David Rousset and André Malraux. This includes too many leaders for an organization that is still weak and incomplete. Moreover the gaullist left presented few serious candidates for nomination, which is why it obtained so few, in particular, from the movements that had most recently joined the majority: the *Front du progrès*, for example, which had hoped for a dozen nominations, obtained only four [16] and did not have a single deputy elected. The *Convention de la Gauche Ve République* had only twelve candidates, and when it reported back to the groups composing it on December 17, 1966, one of its five supporting organizations, the *Clubs Ve République*, withdrew. 'To go where?' Philippe Dechartre asked. In fact, loyalty to the majority prevailed: 'The triumph of our ideas depends partly on the triumph of the majority,' Edgard Pisani was to declare. Louis Vallon showed more optimism: 'The number of back-seats offered to the left-wing gaullists is small,' he said, 'but with the support of General de Gaulle we shall find a way of extending our influence.[17]

Moreover, the gaullist left found satisfaction in the move towards unity that was ratified by the presence at their conference of men such as Louis Joxe, Edgard Pisani, Louis Vallon, Bernard Farbmann, François Sarda, who broadened the appeal of the *Convention de la Gauche Ve République* until it regrouped almost the entire gaullist left. The Convention concluded officially from this that it 'is henceforth recognized as being the third wing in the triptych of the majority'.[18]

During the afternoon of January 13, 1967, on the initiative of Louis Joxe, about sixty 'Fifth Republic' candidates – former M.R.P. members including Maurice Schumann, members of the *Convention de la Gauche Ve République* with Philippe Dechartre, or of the *Front travailliste* with Louis Junillon, finally Edgard Pisani's circle – met for a working party, followed by a reception attended by Georges Pompidou and Olivier Guichard.[19] They arranged another meeting to be held after the general election. But at this second meeting on March 21, 1967, only twenty-two deputies took part, not enough to form a parliamentary group independent of the U.D.V^e group, as the Républicains indépendants had been able to do. It was then unanimously decided that they would ally themselves to the U.D.V^e group. In fact, the gaullists of the left did not manage to maintain this position: under pressure from the Prime Minister and from the principal gaullist leaders, those who might have led the 'gaullist left' finally joined the U.D.V^e group, Louis Joxe, Edgard Pisani, Edgar Faure for example. This meant that it was of little importance that Maurice Schumann and René Capitant did not join the group but were simply allies: the third wing of the triptych did not exist in parliament and lost any serious hope of organizing itself outside parliament.[20] In October 1967, the *Front du progrès* in its turn withdrew from the *Convention de la Gauche Ve République*, which it accused of allowing itself to be absorbed by the gaullist majority because it had participated in the attempt of the U.N.R.-U.D.T. at Lille to expand the party.[21] On October 22, 1967 Jacques Dauer, general secretary of the *Front du progrès*, was excluded from the *Convention de la Gauche Ve République* on account of his 'false and untimely statements'; in fact his real offence was that he wanted to remain on the borderline between the majority and the opposition, to recognize the Elysée while at the same time criticizing and condemning Matignon.[22] On November 10, 1967, René Capitant and Louis Vallon challenged the plans of the U.N.R.-U.D.T. for expansion, by their refusal to go to the Party Conference at Lille. They contrasted Georges Pompidou with General de Gaulle, the U.N.R. party with gaullism, the parliamentary majority with the popular, presidential majority.[23] Léo Hamon, also a left-wing gaullist of the U.D.T., recalled in vain that 'political influence can neither be obtained nor exerted by splinter groups, even if they are outstanding', nor is it derived from 'writing an article in a newspaper, however well written it may be', and that the left-wing gaullists ought to 'combine their action', or divisions would continue to plague the gaullist left as they do the whole of the French left.[24]

General de Gaulle's defeat over the referendum and his replacement at the Elysée by Georges Pompidou, in April–May–June 1969, have obviously accentuated the divisions between part of the gaullist left and the U.D.R. The *Front du progrès* took refuge in 'vigilance and organization' (National Council of June 21, 1969). René Capitant founded a *Union gaulliste populaire* (Popular gaullist union) which, on June 18, 1969, published a virulent manifesto against neo-gaullism: 'On April 27,' it read, 'Charles de Gaulle was overthrown by the action of right-wing forces. If this was so, it was because these forces banked on the new President rejecting the reforms which they did not want and with which they reproached his predecessor for having wished to carry out.' The manifesto called on the heroes of the Resistance, on the young and on the 'mass of workers' to demonstrate their loyalty and confidence in General de Gaulle and to join together in the U.G.P. Jacques Debû-Bridel created a parallel organization, the *Union populaire progressiste* (Popular progressive union), and some dissidents from the *Union des jeunes pour le Progrès* launched a *Front des Jeunes progressistes*.[25] On September 19, 1969, the former *Union démocratique du travail* (U.D.T.), which had been dissolved when it joined the U.N.R. towards the end of 1962, was reconstituted by René Capitant, Louis Vallon, Jacques Debû-Bridel and Michel Cazenave, who at the same time revived the publication of the weekly *Notre République*, which had been suspended after the retirement of General de Gaulle. The U.G.P. and the U.P.P.

immediately joined the reconstituted U.D.T. group. This did not yet represent a total break with the mass of the gaullist forces, but was still open defiance, epitomized in the words of Louis Vallon when, abstaining with David Rousset and three other U.D.R. deputies from giving a vote of confidence in the Chaban-Delmas government, on September 17, 1969, he explained, 'I do not have confidence. . . .'

THE CONTRADICTIONS IN THE GAULLIST LEFT

The gaullist left has not, in fact, managed to rise above its contradictions. It has no real social basis, it is not an electoral force. In March 1967, out of 83 candidates claiming to be part of the gaullist left, taking into account all its shades of political opinion – from the *Front du progrès* through the M.R.P.-Ve République to the U.D.T. – there was one worker and one employee as against 7 employers; all nine, moreover, were overwhelmed by 60 executives and members of the professions: the left-wing gaullist is more often than not an intellectual or a 'technocrat' who has gone through E.N.A. (the National School of Administration) and worked in a Minister's entourage. The supporters of the various left-wing gaullist movements, several thousands at the most, are decidedly fewer in number than the U.D.R. supporters. When it combined with the U.N.R. at the end of 1962, for example, the U.D.T. had at the most generous estimation 5,000 followers, two-fifths of them coming from the Paris region. As for the gaullist voters of the left, if we calculate the figures as two or even three million, their geographical distribution is such that, on its own strength alone, the gaullist left would probably elect only a handful of deputies: some of the former M.R.P. party such as Maurice Schumann and Marie-Madeleine Dienesch, or of the radical party, like Edgar Faure, but hardly anybody more committed to the left than these. An experiment was made in November 1958 with the forefather of the U.D.T., the *Centre de la Réforme républicaine* (C.R.R.): of thirty-five candidates presented, not one was elected – at a time when the newly-formed U.N.R. was barely organized and much less sure of itself than the U.D.R. of today. Therefore, in so far as it wants to play a part in elections and fight for representation within the structures of the majority, the gaullist left, in order to obtain its share of the power, has had to rely on the 'conservative' majority that it challenges, and up until 1968 on Georges Pompidou whom it loathed. It could only hope for – though it could not count on – the backing of General de Gaulle while he remained President of the Republic. For an organization of the left to place in one man all its hopes of transforming a society in which it had no roots, put it in a strange position. The not insignificant success of the weekly *Notre République*, a forum for the gaullist left inspired by the leaders of the

U.D.T., whose circulation in April 1969 was around 8,900; the reper-
cussions of the *appel des vingt-neuf* (the only left-wing gaullists who, as a
group, did not yield to the temptation of fighting elections); the poor
results obtained by left-wing gaullism throughout the country, in
parliament and in the government – all these factors seem to show that
left-wing gaullism would do well to become a philosophical society, a
political club, with no *collective* ambition in the electoral or governmental field. The number of its candidates for the leadership, the
multiplicity and diversity of its groups, the intellectual status of most of
its members would, in this perspective, become a positive advantage
instead of constituting a drawback, as they do at present. The gaullist
'left' cannot win if its aim is to fight against the gaullist 'right' in the
domain of organization, elections and social penetration.

II. 'THE MINORITY IN THE MAJORITY': LA FÉDÉRATION NATIONALE DES RÉPUBLICAINS INDÉPENDANTS (F.N.R.I.)

THE ORIGINS OF THE RÉPUBLICAINS INDÉPENDANTS

History can be ironic: it now seems a well-established fact that Georges
Pompidou himself was responsible for giving Valéry Giscard d'Estaing
the backing of a parliamentary group and of a party by committing two
successive errors of judgment. The first was after the gaullist victory at
the general election of November 1962: the Républicains indépendants
had just broken with the *Centre national des indépendants*, whom they
considered too anti-gaullist, and it was not certain that they would find
the thirty deputies necessary to constitute a parliamentary group in the
Assembly. Some personalities of the U.N.R. party, Albin Chalandon
and friends of Michel Debré in particular, asked Georges Pompidou to
use his influence in order to bring about the formation of a single
majority group, the prefiguration – perhaps – of a large, majority party.
But the Prime Minister was reluctant to do so, probably because he
recalled the old adage: 'Divide and rule'. Five years later, Georges
Pompidou, who was feeling more confident because of his good relationship with parliament and less harried by matters of immediate
concern, sought in vain for the integration he had declined in 1962. For
in January 1966 he had made a second mistake: he had dropped Valéry
Giscard d'Estaing from the government. The Prime Minister did not
appreciate the initiative of his young Finance Minister and his habit of
playing off the Elysée against him. He appointed Michel Debré Minister
of Finance and offered Valéry Giscard d'Estaing the Ministry of Equip-
ment, a demotion that the latter could not accept. He was thus free to

devote both his time and his intelligence to the task of transforming the Républicains indépendants into a real party – especially as, according to the new 'incompatibility rule' in the 1958 Constitution, he was no longer a deputy, having given up this post to become a Minister.

In 1962–3, those 'indépendants' who upheld the Fifth Republic simply founded a 'Centre of research and liaison for the co-ordination of the activity of deputies'.

'A party cannot be created with only thirty-six deputies,' Valéry Giscard d'Estaing said. 'Moreover, public opinion would not understand us if we were to form a new party, to introduce yet another political denomination.'[26] In reality, the moderates were still very divided as far as gaullism was concerned. Some, including Antoine Pinay, hoped to win over their support to form a centre force in conjunction with the Christian democrats and the radicals.[27]

Valéry Giscard d'Estaing, however, had plainly sided with the gaullists by defending the idea of a 'contract within the majority' among the Républicains indépendants. The traditional freedom of vote of the moderates, he explained, was difficult to justify at a time when the voters no longer accepted it; the Finance Minister thus concluded that 'the assistance we give to the government will be probed by our votes in parliament'. He faced strong resistance, notably from Marcel Anthonioz and Roland Boscary Monsservin.[28] For many months contact between the *Centre national des indépendants* and the *Centre d'études et de liaison* of the Républicains indépendants was fairly fluid. Circulars reach all organizations whatever their origin: in political life separation is rarely brutal, especially when it occurs on the right.

By 1965, when the presidential election was imminent, the final break had come. Michel Poniatowski, the closest colleague of Valéry Giscard d'Estaing, produced the idea of the *Clubs Perspectives et Réalités*, which were to be 'laboratories for the elaboration of doctrine' but also political 'breeding-grounds' for the Républicains indépendants. A team comprising Xavier de la Fournière, Jacques Dominati, Jean-François Lemaire and Charles-Noël Hardy was given the task of launching these clubs. The first was founded in Paris in May 1965.[29]

The presidential election marked the real beginning of the organization of the Républicains indépendants: they broke ties with Jean Lecanuet who, at the second ballot, advised his electors to vote for Mitterrand rather than for de Gaulle; as for Valéry Giscard d'Estaing, we have seen that his time was his own. The *Fédération nationale des Républicains indépendants* was registered on June 3, 1966; two days previously the premises of its national Centre at 195 boulevard St Germain had been opened in the presence of three hundred guests including the Prime Minister, Georges Pompidou, who greeted Valéry Giscard d'Estaing with a very biblical piece of advice: 'Increase and multiply.'[30]

THE YES AND THE BUT

The Républicains indépendants wished to be part of the majority, but at the same time different from the majority of this majority, a position epitomized in the words pronounced on January 10, 1967 by Valéry Giscard d'Estaing: 'YES, BUT. . . .' The future lies with them: as the 'younger generation' of the majority, they do not question the fact that one day they will become the most influential element in the majority.

In 1967, people tended to stress the BUT more than the YES of the Républicains indépendants, but this is hindsight. Until April 1969, the Républicains indépendants, and Valéry Giscard d'Estaing in particular, recalled constantly that they were nevertheless a component of the majority and as such accepted all the consequences involved, especially the refusal to precipitate a crisis. 'The group of Républicains indé-pendants . . . acts within the framework of the institutions of the Fifth Republic. It has chosen to act within the majority . . . traditionally respectful of the freedom of vote of each deputy, it is convinced of the need to reach a conclusion concerning the major problems so that after objective discussion unity of view may be reached': this is the charter of the group, defined after the election of March 1967 and re-adopted after that of June 1968. The Républicains indépendants have always sup-ported the majority in moments of difficulty. In October 1967, during a debate of censure, Valéry Giscard d'Estaing replied to those who reproached the Républicains indépendants for saying 'Yes . . . but' to governmental policy but 'no' to governmental crisis: 'we refuse to consider crisis as a means of government, and a member of the majority can only censure the government in the case of a grave national crisis.' [31] A 'national crisis for France' did arise in May 1968; Valéry Giscard d'Estaing recognized the fact. But his colleagues did not censure the government because they did not wish to 'add the terrors of the unknown to the disorder already existing'; the former minister, on May 30th, called for the departure of Georges Pompidou and the expansion of the government but he remained firm in his support of the presi-dential institution and of General de Gaulle: 'If this function did not exist,' he declared on May 22nd, 'and if it had not been assumed by the present holder, everything would have been swept away.' [32] 'To be quite honest,' he told French television viewers on June 28th, 'only the four minutes of General de Gaulle's intervention, on the afternoon of May 30th, were tuned in to the wavelength of what was happening.' [33]

The electoral discipline of the Républicains indépendants is the most clear indication of their adhesion to the majority. In December 1965, they supported without hesitation the candidacy of General de Gaulle to the Presidency, despite the fact that Jean Lecanuet was also a candi-date. In March 1967, they agreed even at the first ballot that there should be only one 'Fifth Republic' candidate in each constituency, as General de Gaulle, Georges Pompidou and the U.N.R. wished.[34] But in June 1968, at the first ballot, they broke this rule in forty-six constituencies, all – except for one – held by the opposition; at the second ballot, however, they maintained total electoral discipline by withdrawing in favour of the best placed majority candidate. At the referendum of April 27, 1969, on regionalism and the reform of the Senate, four-fifths of the Républicains indépendants deputies campaigned for the YES, despite the abstention of Valéry Giscard d'Estaing who, in the end, supported Georges Pompidou after the NO at the referendum had caused the departure of General de Gaulle. Thus the YES prevailed over the BUT.

The latter, however, is not a mere superficiality: it is expressed not only in political choice but even in the kind of men and type of organization which the *Fédération nationale des Républicains indépendants* represents. The Républicains indépendants see themselves as 'liberals, in the centre politically and pro-European'. While advocating the restoration of Executive authority in the Fifth Republic, they are at the same time more 'orleanist' and more 'parliamentary' than their gaullist partners. Their catchword is 'discussion'. On August 17, 1967, after the government's demand for special powers, following General de Gaulle's stand on the Middle East conflict and more particularly on Quebec, Valéry Giscard d'Estaing called a meeting of the executive committee of the F.N.R.I. and afterwards broadcast a thundering statement on the 'single-handed exercise of power'; 'discussion,' he stated, 'does not weaken authority. It can show authority the way and ensure real national cohesion.' [35] During the debate of censure on May 22, 1968, Valéry Giscard d'Estaing again called upon the government to reorganize itself and invited it to broaden its political basis by drawing upon the support of the centre, the centre left and perhaps even the left. On June 14th, he proclaimed on television the threefold electoral slogan of the Républicains indépendants: 'A choice in favour of order, discussion and the reuniting of all Frenchmen.' While remaining on the majority side, the Républicains indépendants drew closer to the centre ranks in their common fear of authority and power that is not shared, and their apprehension of two large, rival blocks which would tear the nation apart.[36] The Républicains indépendants do not share with the centrists their faith in a supra-national Europe but share, nonetheless, their impatience with a European policy that marks time. Their economic liberalism is, ultimately, in the purest tradition of the classical right: the reduction of national expenditure, the fight against the deterioration of currency because of a respect for economic and, above all, financial forces, the belief in individual initiative and in a market economy, the limitation to a strict minimum of state intervention.[37]

The party programme of the Républicains indépendants is lacking in precision and it is difficult to forecast the policy they would endorse if they managed to become, as they hope to, the 'majority of the majority'. The fact is that – until July 1969 at least – the Républicains indépendants did not really consider themselves as being in power, despite the personal participation in the government of a few of them and the total backing that they gave to the majority: the initiative and direction of political matters are normally the prerogative of the most important of the gaullist forces; the Républicains indépendants therefore saw themselves as the future 'reserve' of the majority. Thus they did not have to elaborate any of the details of a programme which would be out

TABLE 21: *The sixty-two Independent Republican deputies elected in June 1968 (socio-professional characteristics)*

(Statistics taken from *Réponses* 2, October 22, 1968)

Categories	Number	Percentage
Age		
under 30 years	2	3.2
30 to 39 years	4	6.4
40 to 49 years	27	43.6
50 to 64 years	24	38.7
over 65 years	5	8.1
Family		
single	2	3.2
married, no children	8	12.9
married, 1 to 3 children	34	54.8
married, more than 3 children	18	29.1
Occupation		
liberal professions:		
doctors	11 ⎫	17.9 ⎫
chemists	3 ⎬ 25	4.8 ⎬ 40.4
lawyers	9 ⎪	14.5 ⎪
journalists	2 ⎭	3.2 ⎭
peasants, industrialists, tradesmen:		
peasants	11 ⎫	17.8 ⎫
industrialists	8 ⎬ 22	12.9 ⎬ 35.5
tradesmen	3 ⎭	4.8 ⎭
executive class:		
higher civil servants	9 ⎫ 11	14.5 ⎫ 17.7
university teachers	2 ⎭	3.2 ⎭
white-collar workers	4	6.4
Cursus honorum		
deputies-mayors*	54	87

* In France, the two offices of deputy and mayor can be held concurrently.

of date when applied and which would limit their scope for action; [38] it sufficed to define a few guiding principles and, above all, to create a style, to popularize a brand image. From this point of view, the Giscardians are clearly distinguishable from the traditional right: 'future' and 'change', 'youth' and 'drive', 'efficiency' and 'realism', 'authority' and 'stability' are the traits of a modern right, active and attractive – which corresponds well to the youthful, intelligent, sportive personality that the party has chosen for its leader. The typical profile of the Républicain indépendant deputy would be depicted as follows: 'a *young* man, with a *balanced* conception of family life, *responsible* in his approach to political activity at all levels, and in his choice of profession, open-minded, as his interest in the many national problems proves'.[39] A statistical survey reveals that, on some of these points, things are rather different in reality (see *Table 21*).

THE NATURE AND ORGANIZATION OF THE RÉPUBLICAINS INDÉPENDANTS

The difference in nature between the kind of political formation represented by the F.N.R.I. and that of the U.D.R. is striking. The U.D.R. is a party of electors, wide open to many different social strata, drawing its electoral strength on a national level; the F.N.R.I., on the other hand, is a party of notabilities, strongly rooted in local political life, taking its party officials from among the social élite of the nation. This phenomenon is moreover in line with the wishes of the Républicain indé-pendants who, at the time of the opening of their National Centre, specified their intention to choose their candidates for the general elections from amongst those 'personalities already bearing responsibilities in local affairs', and to 'enlist the support of regional notabilities'. They would not make the 'same mistake as the U.N.R.' by 'para-chuting' candidates in order to 'rouse' the constituencies. 'No party enrolment, no membership card, no organized recruitment'[40]: the F.N.R.I. is an example of the classical 'cadre party', as defined by Maurice Duverger. The Républicains indépendants work from the double postulate that France is fundamentally a country of moderates and that the moderates will never be a disciplined group, that they cannot be organized into a strong political formation; at most, they can be influenced in certain directions. This line of reasoning takes into account the intermediaries, the notabilities, rather than the voters. The organization of the Républicains indépendants proceeds from this liberal and élitist vision of French society and of political life in France.

The existence of secondary organizations allows them to make contact with bodies whose sympathy for the Giscardian movement would not go as far as political involvement, for instance the *Clubs*

Perspectives et Réalités, specialized clubs, the Young Républicains indépendants, the Ladies' Committee. Like the communists, the Républicains indépendants attach the greatest importance to these 'intermediary circles' [41] which link them with the outside world; but instead of plunging them into the masses, they ensure contact with the élites.

The *Clubs Perspectives et Réalités*, as we have seen, preceded the organization of the F.N.R.I. On the occasion of their Third National Convention on December 7 and 8, 1968 they officially grouped some 700 delegates representing the 2,700 members of 38 different clubs, spread over the whole of France. The home towns of the spokesmen and chairmen, about 20 in all, give some idea of the most active of the clubs: Paris, Lille, Nantes, Angers, Périgueux, Royan and Toulouse.[42] The most important figure in the *Clubs* is their national General Secretary, Charles-Noël Hardy, who by virtue of this post is also one of the nine members of the executive committee of the Républicains indépendants.[43] In February 1969, the clubs decided to begin publication of a monthly bulletin and a series of booklets; to launch a collection of works of which the first two would be on economic progress and business respectively; to organize committees of municipal and regional administration, for the purpose of training and informing local officials.[44] The new clubs are almost always opened by Valéry Giscard d'Estaing. The president of the Républicains indépendants and Michel Poniatowski never fail to give encouragement to the clubs at their general assemblies or national conventions.

Beside these local clubs, the Républicains indépendants want to organize specialized clubs on a national level. Today there are two: the *Club Tiers Monde*, presided over by M. Lizop, and the *Club Sigma*, for scientific matters, under the guidance of M. Rocard, the father of the P.S.U. general secretary. The creation of an agricultural club and of a club specializing in trade union problems are also envisaged.

The *Jeunes Républicains indépendants* (J.R.I.) were founded in October 1966 by about thirty young supporters gathered at Dixmont. Their first national committee comprised some young ex-C.N.I., some ex-U.N.R. and some former *Action française*.[45] The results obtained did not meet their expectations and in November 1968 the young deputy for the Hautes-Alpes, Paul Dijoud, was given the job of relaunching the movement. He secured its representation on the executive committee of the Républicains indépendants. At the end of 1967, the J.R.I. claimed 300 members; now the movement numbers more than 3,000 – which seems a lot, even taking into account the events of May 1968 which speeded up the recruitment of young people by all the specialized groups.

The influence of the women, who are grouped in a *Commission féminine* (Ladies' Committee) within the movement, seems even more limited. After the failure of an autonomous organization, created for women who were Républicains indépendant partisans, the Ladies' Committee became simply a liaison body, at national and regional level. The president of its national committee is Mme Boyé-Carré, mother of four and lawyer at the Court of Appeal, but its spokesman at the top level of the F.N.R.I. organization is a man, Claude Guichard, deputy for the Dordogne. Neither the executive committee of the F.N.R.I. nor the parliamentary group of the Républicains indépendants has any women members.[46] It would seem, in fact, that of all the 'secondary organizations' only the *Clubs Perspectives et Réalités* have, up to now, a real existence and some importance within the R.I. movement.

The way in which Michel Poniatowski has organized the Républicains indépendants is a clear indication of the twofold purpose of the Giscardians. They want to create a modern party and to draw support for it from the notabilities. The F.N.R.I. has a permanent staff of about fifteen, whose work programme is reviewed and specified every three months. Three of these specialize in political canvassing and are sent out as scouts for about six weeks into a region that is still without an R.I. organization. Their role is to do fieldwork, to make a thorough study of the political 'market', and to locate, in particular, all those who have some influence in the region. Their reports are studied by Valéry Giscard d'Estaing and Michel Poniatowski who then discuss with them in Paris. A second team, more politically orientated, is then sent out to contact those persons capable of forming the initial core of the F.N.R.I. in the region. The people concerned are then received individually in Paris by the president of the R.I. and the secretary general, who will decide in the last resort. The process ends with the solemn inauguration of the new federation for which one of the five permanent federation 'envoys' at national level assumes responsibility.

By July 1, 1967, officially six out of twenty-one regions in the programme had already established regional R.I. federations: the Paris region, Basse-Normandie, Champagne, Bourgogne, Auvergne and Aquitania; two others were in the process of being formed: Rhône-Alpes and Provence-Côte d'Azur-Corse.[47] By February 1969, only five regions were without R.I. federations.

A DUAL POWER

The power in the *Fédération nationale des Républicains indépendants* theoretically derives from the national congress, or the 'Conseil fédéral' (federal council) which annually groups the deputies and their 'suppléants', and senators; representatives – a maximum of 30 – of the managing committee of the regional federations (departmental in the case of the Paris region); members of the economic council; 3 representatives for each of the *Clubs Perspectives et Réalités*; 3 for each of the J.R.I. (Young R.I.) clubs; finally 5 representatives of the Ladies' Committee. It is the federal council which elects for a one-year term the president of the Federation, its general secretary and its executive committee.

The legislative body of the F.N.R.I. is the 'Comité directeur' (managing committee), more limited in size since its basic composition is the executive committee of the party, the committees of the parliamentary groups and the presidents of the regional federations (departmental for the Paris region), plus one representative for each 'secondary organization' (Clubs, J.R.I., Ladies' Committee), two representatives from the economic council and, if desired, two persons co-opted by the managing committee. It meets as a rule every two months. Nominations of prospective candidates are made under its authority.[48]

In actual fact, the power belongs to the executive committee of the party, that is to say the staff of the president Valéry Giscard d'Estaing: Michel Poniatowski, secretary general; Michel d'Ornano, treasurer; and six other close colleagues of Valéry Giscard d'Estaing, each in charge of one particular sector: Jean de Broglie (doctrine), Jean-Pierre Soisson (expansion of the movement), Paul Dijoud (youth), Claude Guichard (women), Charles-Noël Hardy, the only non-parliamentarian in the team (*Clubs Perspectives et Réalités*), and finally Alain Griotteray (press). Nine men in all, of whom four are ex-students of the National School of Administration and most of them are very young, as is their leader. The latter has at his disposal a real brains-trust, placed directly under his authority, together with the *section économique d'information et d'études*, where higher civil servants from all the ministries, but above all from the Ministry of Finance, briefed and advised him before he returned to his post as Finance Minister in 1969, and with the even more discreet *section d'information politique*, which attempts to anticipate the political trends of the government and of the other parties. Organized in this way, the party machine is a reliable and efficient instrument in the hands of Valéry Giscard d'Estaing.

The latter, however, can only use the services of the party machine within certain political limits. He comes up against another power not under his control, that of the parliamentary party of the Républicains indépendants. An analysis of the election addresses of the R.I. candidates at the general election of March 1967 reveals that only a third of the outgoing deputies re-adopted either wholly or partially the 'YES, BUT . . .' tactic of Valéry Giscard d'Estaing; the percentage of the YES BUTs is not much higher among the new candidates; 56 per cent of the R.I. candidates referred to de Gaulle himself as against only 18 per cent to Valéry Giscard d'Estaing. The 'Giscardians' are in a minority in the parliamentary party of the Républicain indépendants in the National Assembly: it is much more 'gaullist' in inclination and certainly more cautious than the leaders of the F.N.R.I.[49] Some of the group's leaders are of gaullist origin, for example, the late Raymond Mondon, its president until 1969, who was a former R.P.F. deputy, and two of its vice-presidents, Raymond Boisdé – also a former R.P.F. deputy – and Jean de Broglie, a former Conseiller national (national councillor) of the R.P.F. Even more numerous are those who were of gaullist sympathy during the Resistance. The greater part of the parliamentary party's committee is composed of experienced parliamentarians, who have sat in the National Assembly for a considerable time, and who are not prepared to jeopardize their positions.[50] Finally, the R.I. ministers, especially Raymond Marcellin, are not lacking in influence although they sit neither on the committee of the parliamentary party (the same is true for the U.D.R.) nor on the executive committee of the F.N.R.I. (on the contrary, U.D.R. ministers do sit on the executive committee of their party) – in theory this ensures the separation of powers, in fact the rule is applied lest the ministers exercise too great a hold over their friends.

So it is that, from time to time, the sudden outbursts of Valéry Giscard d'Estaing are censured by his political friends. The statement of August 17, 1967 on the 'single-handed exercise of power' provoked among the Républicains indépendants a series of ministerial counter-statements, strongly encouraged, it is true, by the Elysée. 'Mr Giscard d'Estaing,' Raymond Marcellin wrote, 'asks General de Gaulle to give up being General de Gaulle and suggests to him that he should force himself to govern as Mr Giscard d'Estaing would, if the electors were to select him for the supreme office. . . . It seems clear that, if the French people do not succeed in electing a President of the Republic who has the courage to exercise the rights that the Constitution bestows upon him, the regime will gradually move back to that of government by assembly, which we have already experienced.' [51] More recently, the only R.I. deputy for Paris, Jacques Dominati, president of the Parisian federation of the movement, declared in his turn: 'The image given of the Républicains indépendants is false when it is shown as criticizing systematically and without restraint the government's action; this Michel Poniatowski, the general secretary of our Federation, does whenever he has an opportunity, as he did recently in the review L'Economie.' [52]

But the most serious crisis the Républicains indépendants have undergone was linked with the referendum of April 27, 1969. Whilst the parliamentary party of the R.I. in the National Assembly had, on March 27th, with a very large majority opted for the YES, Valéry Giscard d'Estaing on April 14th, criticizing the timing of the referendum and the complexity of the text to be voted, concluded: 'For my part, it is with regret but with conviction that I decline to give my assent to this referendum.' [53] Four-fifths of the deputies refused to follow their talented leader, but the F.N.R.I. and all its subsidiary organizations remained faithful to him. 'A rebel with a future' was *The Times* headline. The victory of the NO at the referendum justified him politically, and his conversion to the candidacy of Georges Pompidou, after a fruitless attempt to persuade Antoine Pinay to stand, reconciled him with his political friends and enabled him to recover the post of Finance Minister which he had lost in January 1966.

The figures are, on the whole, impressive: 33 deputies in 1962, 42 in 1967, 62 in 1968; the success undeniable, a party created from nothing; a more liberal and European policy imposed on the majority, while the future has not been mortgaged, and the party's long term aims are clear. 'In normal political circumstances, that is to say in 1972,' Valéry Giscard d'Estaing announced, 'I would have run for the Presidency. . . .' Two years earlier he had confided to *L'Express*: 'It will take us five years to come out of the wilderness. We will make the most of this period by organizing a two-fold structure, political and professional; twenty men for each region, politically committed and professionally competent, clubs capable of maintaining talks and contacts with the new notables. We should have a hundred deputies by 1972.' [54] However much more open and united the majority of the majority may be, it still remains a rival, the more so as the Républicains indépendants will, from now on, have to reckon with the centrists who were converted in 1969, in particular Jacques Duhamel, René Pleven, Joseph Fontanet, Jean Poudevigne, and their *Centre démocratie et progrès* which also claims that 'by joining the widened majority . . . it has become the stimulus and the instigator of it'.

III. 'THE MAJORITY OF THE MAJORITY': L'UNION DES DÉMOCRATES POUR LA RÉPUBLIQUE (U.D.R.)

The 'Union for the New Republic' (U.N.R.), we wrote in 1964–5, 'is first of all a ministerial team, then a central committee for the selection of candidates for the general election, then the largest parliamentary party in the National Assembly and finally – at last – a party.' [55] A young party blessed by the gods of power, the U.N.R. began to grow exceedingly fast; all it needed now was to gain strength. On the electoral and parliamentary level, its foundations had already been laid in 1962; each general election brought with it some minor changes and a new title: U.N.R.-U.D.T. in 1962, U.D.Vᵉ in 1967, and U.D.R. in 1968.[56] Its party organization, on the other hand, long remained weak, as if cut off from the government-parliamentary group circuit. But since 1967 and the Lille Party Conference, an effort has been made to strengthen the party and reintegrate it into the power system of the majority of the gaullists.

THE PARLIAMENTARY PARTY

After the elections of November 1962, which are a proof, even in France, of the advantages to be gained from a disciplined vote and the close associations it encourages in public opinion between the government and majority parties, the gaullist deputies accepted the British model of an Executive which governs, of a majority which gives its support while exerting to a maximum its power of influence over the government, of an opposition which criticizes, and of a nation which has the final word in each general election. The U.D.R. deputies, therefore, do not seek to undermine the policy of the government nor do they dissociate themselves from its actions, however unpopular they may be. This does not mean, however, that they simply allow themselves to be manipulated by those in power.[57]

The organization and functioning of the U.D.R. party in the National Assembly illustrate the double desire to make the deputies of the majority partners of the government in the formulation of policy and at the same time to safeguard the power of decision-making and the authority of the government.

PRESSURE ON POLICY

The participation of the parliamentary party is facilitated primarily by its sub-division into regional groups and study groups. It is interesting to note here that the 'jacobins' of gaullism, Michel Debré in particular, for whom all institutionalization of local or particular interests runs counter to the national and general interest, have been obliged to accept this, first at the level of group organization, then at party level and recently with regard to the organization of the public powers.

In 1959, the U.N.R. deputies were seated within that part of the National Assembly reserved for them by drawing lots. They were similarly divided into sub-groups at random. By trying to avoid any risk of splinter activity or of 'parish pump' politics, they had created artificial sub-groups which had no real reason for existence and were consequently never able to function. In 1960 the idea of having sub-groups with compatible interests was adopted; but by December 1962 the regional sub-groups had asserted themselves and all the U.N.R.-U.D.T. deputies from a particular region could be found sitting side by side in the National Assembly. It became general for these regional sub-groups to have as fair a representation as possible at the highest level, that is on the executive committee. In 1965, this practice became a statutory rule: 21 of the 27 elected members of the executive committee are elected within the framework of the region from which they come. These 21 regions are the same as the 21 programme regions, but they have been regrouped into bigger units so as to give two seats to the regions with more than 30 constituencies, and one seat only to the others.[58]

Parallel to these regional sub-groups, permanent specialized study groups were constituted, especially after 1962. They are organized at the discretion of the executive committee which determines their number, the scope of their activity and their powers. They are the party equivalent of the parliamentary committees in the Assembly. Each permanent study group normally includes all the U.D.R. deputies belonging to the corresponding committee in the Assembly. Every U.D.R. deputy, according to the new statutes of the parliamentary party adopted in July 1968, belongs to at least one permanent study group.[59]

These specialized study groups (*groupes d'études spécialisés,* or G.E.S.) are, in principle, the privileged meeting point of the government and the majority of its majority. In April 1963, for example, a report emphasizes the favourable results obtained at this level: '. . . The ministers presented to the G.E.S. the broad lines of the legislative programme . . . the groups were informed by M. Dumas [60] of various rough drafts of bills sufficiently in advance to allow them to study the drafts thoroughly and to put forward their suggestions *before* the bill was presented. . . . The function of the specialized U.N.R.-U.D.T. study groups as go-between has provided a new basis, formerly unknown, for work in parliament.' [61] The willingness to collaborate varies in reality according to the ministers and the projects involved, and the participation of the U.D.R. deputies in the study groups remains relatively poor, despite all the statutory obligations. An internal circular of the U.D.R. group, issued on September 26, 1968, fixes the number of permanent study groups at six: agriculture, social affairs, economic and financial affairs, national education and youth, town and country planning, foreign affairs.[62] Since 1968 the party rules have also provided for the creation of *ad hoc* groups, called *comités d'action parlementaire* (Parliamentary Party Study Groups), 'for each branch of parliamentary activity which requires the elaboration and execution of fundamental reforms.' [63] The circular of September 26, 1968 mentioned the creation of six of these groups: for university reform, information and social and cultural affairs, the problem of prices, employment, reform of the regulations governing the civil service and industrial democracy. Moreover, these study groups were used as a framework within which the U.D.R. parliamentary party could work on the study days at La Baule, on September 10, 11 and 12, 1968. A good example of this is the group specializing in 'university reform', headed by Michel Habib-Deloncle with, as its Chairman, the 'Vice-Chancellor' Capelle, before whom the Minister of Education, Edgar Faure, had come to defend his general reform for higher education. These groups do not, however, seem to have played any active role at the Palais-Bourbon during the parliamentary sessions.[64]

The conclusions we reached in 1964–5 still seem valid: some groups, including that concerned with agriculture, because they have a dynamic leader and regular contacts with professional organizations in their own branch, have a real influence on governmental activity; there are few deputies in the groups but their members form a dynamic, competent and loyal nucleus. Nevertheless, in most cases, the specialized study groups are not the active and influential intermediaries between the principal group of the majority and the government that they are thought to be; the government has no desire to prolong further the time needed for a bill to become law, and thus it is not in favour of allowing the U.D.R. study group to benefit automatically from a preliminary control.[65] As for the U.D.R. deputies themselves, cramped by an overloaded timetable as are all deputies, they rarely see the necessity for adding to their committee work in the Assembly by further discussion in group committees. In fact, the compromise between government projects and the wishes of the U.D.R. deputies is essentially worked out by the party leaders' intermediary in the executive committee and in the committees of the Assembly, as well as in the full meeting of the party members when the problem is particularly thorny.[66]

Thus the most effective way of allowing the parliamentary party a positive influence probably consists in increasing the number of those in the party who are in a position to participate in discussions with the government as representatives of the whole group. By multiplying the number of front benchers, the influence of the party is increased because it becomes more difficult for the government to choose and control its parliamentary spokesmen; on the other hand, the government gains in voluntary support because the participation of interested parties in the making of decisions integrates them into the political process.

During the first legislature (1958–62), the front benchers of the U.N.R. party represented 17.5 per cent of the total number of its members and allies; in the second legislature (1962–7), their proportion rose to 30.4 per cent despite the overall increase in the party's numbers. In the present legislature, with a record party of 291 members and allies, the proportion of front benchers is 33.7 per cent. This increase can be explained by the coinciding of two phenomena: owing to the increase in the total number of gaullist deputies, it became necessary to strengthen their officer ranks and to delegate responsibilities in order to give coherence to a mass which would otherwise be undisciplined; at the same time, precisely because the party was gaining in strength, the gaullist parliamentary party was able to hold many more responsible official positions in the Assembly (see *Table 22*). These are the advantages of the majority and the disadvantages of the opposition in a majority-party system. The best and most ambitious of the gaullist parliamentarians have, since 1962, been entrusted with responsibilities which allow them to play a part and give them a real opportunity to influence governmental action. They use their energies to facilitate the work of the government, as the parliamentarians in Great Britain do instead of using them against the government. The rules of the U.N.R. parliamentary party encourage, moreover, this wide participation in the decision-making process, thereby avoiding the risk of 'pluralism' which would give all the power to a few. At the same time the rules organize at Secretary level in the Assembly committees 'the rotation necessary for the greatest possible number of party members or allies to accede to official posts'.[67]

TABLE 22: *The leaders of the gaullist parliamentary party*

Functions	Dec. 1958 (U.N.R.)		Dec. 1962 (U.N.R.–U.D.T.)		April 1967 (U.D.V^e)		July 1968 (U.D.R.)	
	number	%	number	%	number	%	number	%
1. in the parliamentary party:	12	5.8	29	12.4	29	14.7	42	14.4
executive committee (elected members)	12	5.8	22	9.4	22	11.2	33	11.3
other responsibilities	—	——	7	3.0	7	3.5	9	3.1
2. in the Assembly:	24	11.7	42	18.0	39	19.8	56	19.3
bureau of the Assembly	8	3.9	11	4.7	8	4.1	12	4.1
bureaux of the committees	16	7.8	31	13.3	31	15.7	44*	15.2
Total	36	17.5	71	30.4	68	34.5	98	33.7
number in the party (allies included)	206	100.0	233	100.0	197	100.0	291	100.0

*The increase in the number of U.D.R. posts was partly due to the refusal of the *Républicains indépendants* to accept responsibilities at this level after the failure of Valéry Giscard d'Estaing to be re-elected to the post of president of the Finance Committee, the post being filled by Jean Taittinger, the U.D.R. candidate.

THE STRUCTURE OF THE PARLIAMENTARY PARTY

Apart from a few key-posts, such as president of the parliamentary party or of the permanent committees in the Assembly, which until 1969 were generally filled in compliance with the wishes of the Prime Minister and the President of the Republic, the battle for all the other major posts within the parliamentary party is lively and the result is not known beforehand. For example, the elections for office on the executive committee, contrary to general opinion, are well-contested and in April each year take a good day to complete. The candidates always outnumber the posts available and each time out-going officers are beaten. If the victors in the majority are 'gaullists of the first generation' and long-standing deputies, it is not because of any obligation to elect them but simply because the average U.D.R. deputy chooses them.

Although authority is shared, and this is largely on an elective basis, it still remains under the control of the most important officials of the parliamentary party, in particular of the president assisted by the five vice-presidents and the administrative services of the party. A *deputy president*, freely chosen by the president from among the five vice-presidents elected to the executive committee, supervises the organiza-tion and the administration of the parliamentary party, prepares the executive committee's discussions of government and private bills, oral and written questions from the members of the parliamentary party and of claims registered by socio-professional organizations. The *second vice-president* is responsible for auditing the accounts of the parliamentary party and for facilitating relations with the ministries; when a delegation from the parliamentary party wishes to disclose a general problem of interest to a particular region or department, this vice-president arranges the appointment and attends the meeting.[68] The *third vice-president* is in charge of the committees. In each of the six big committees in the Assembly there is a U.D.R. 'whip' jointly proposed by the executive committee and the U.D.R. committee members of the committee involved and nominated by the president.[69] His role is to inform the vice-president responsible for 'committees' of the views expressed and the work done on these committees by the U.D.R. deputies who, in accordance with the statutes of the group, have to attend meetings regularly and to respect the party line. The vice-president for 'committees' can thus at this level apply the general lines of the policy decided by the executive committee of the parlia-mentary party. The *fourth vice-president* is responsible for the *comités d'action parlementaire* (Parliamentary Party Study Groups) and, above all, for facilitating relations with the party as a whole and with external organizations. His task is essentially to inform the party of the requests and demands of socio-professional groups and to draw up, for the benefit of the president of the parliamentary party, specimen letters which the U.D.R. deputies will be invited to send to these groups. The *fifth vice-president* is in charge of relations with the 'permanent study groups'. He ensures the liaison between them and the executive committee which determines how their decisions will be put into effect. Finally, two 'assistants', nominated by the president and responsible to him, ensure the relations of the parliamentary party with the press, radio and television. They alone have the authority to pass on the information that the party, the executive committee or the president decide to diffuse; the communiqués of the permanent study groups or of any other U.D.R. sub-groups must also be sent out through them.[70]

At the top of this hierarchy is the president of the parliamentary party, a post which Marc Jacquet has held since June 1969. He is responsible for the cohesion and the discipline of the party, which means that he has to avoid crises rather than solve them; he also represents the party in all aspects of parliamentary activity and in all its outside relations, especially at the top level at Matignon and, on occasion, at the Elysée. This is a difficult task: 'One needs the gift of ubiquity to perform the job well,' admitted Louis Terrenoire who himself did not find it easy at a time when there were divisions in the party linked to the Algerian problem. 'One also needs the gift of administration and public speaking, not to mention the typical sort of parliamentary work that is done in the corridors.' [71] It is a thankless task too: the president only makes news when he is being challenged, that is, when he fails in his duty as co-ordinator of the party, or when he himself is the challenger, that is, when he refuses to play the game of the majority government and intends to set himself or the parliamentary party above the government. He is rarely spoken about when he is fulfilling his duty as he should.[72]

The U.D.R. group, like any group of this size and because it is the parliamentary expression of a 'voter-directed party', is divided into clans and groups of differing and changing opinions; it needs a 'peace-maker' at the top. The clans range from supporters of Debré, who are less numerous, to supporters of Pompidou, who are in the lead, and between these two extremes we find the friends of Jacques Chaban-Delmas, of Roger Frey and of Maurice Couve de Murville. But more clear cut and more stable wings of opinion are also discernible: first the gaullist left which has its roots in the U.D.T., and which is gathered together in certain of the specialized study groups, such as the one dealing with 'social affairs' or the parliamentary party specialized study group concerned with 'participation in industry'; then the former Christian democrats who follow closely both social problems and European problems; finally the conservative and authoritarian

right, which groups together individuals of a similar political tempera-
ment rather than actually forming a trend of opinion. This diversity
provokes extremely keen discussion within the group – all the more so
when the majority is comfortable, as it was from June 1968 – yet not
in itself firm enough to cause a split: the parliamentary parties in
Britain, both Conservative and Labour, are no less aggressive, yet
splintering rarely occurs. On the contrary, it would appear that the
gaullist parliamentary party has found a sound balance in controlled
participation, a positive view of the influence of the parliamentarian
and an organization established over a period fraught with deep internal
crises between 1958 and 1962, then 'broken in' during three legislatures,
and tested during the new crises of May 1968 and April–May–June
1969. The creation of a parliamentary association called *Amicale
présence et action du gaullisme*, which has about forty members drawn
from the parliamentary party, the most 'gaullian' gaullists, shows that
there is a certain apprehension among some members although it does
not appear to have changed in any way the life of the parliamentary
party. Michel Debré, the most intransigent defender of continuity
and of fidelity to the doctrines of General de Gaulle, called upon all
the gaullist deputies on September 11, 1969, at the parliamentary
party meeting at Amboise, to remain united around the new Head of
State, Georges Pompidou, 'who, being responsible for the fundamental
running of the State, has our wholehearted support, our confidence,
our hopes. We are solidly behind him when he acts at the national
level' – and of the head of the government, Jacques Chaban-Delmas,
he declared: '. . . he is one of us, or rather at our head, because in his
capacity as Prime Minister he is head of the parliamentary majority,
that is, of our party in parliament above all. Our duty is to give him
our assistance, all the more willingly as the period is fraught with
difficulties'. The men have changed, de Gaulle himself has departed,
but the philosophy concerning the power of the state, of parliament
and of the majority party remains the same as it was in 1962 and earlier
in the new institutional context of the Fifth Republic.

THE PARTY

Unlike the parliamentary party, the party machine underwent transformation more recently, in 1967. Until then, the U.N.R. was virtually
only a group of ministers and a parliamentary party. The gaullist
party machine was isolated from power owing to the fear of extremist
action from the militants during the Algerian period, and the uncertainty
as to how to deal with them. The party was active only at election time,
when it prepared the dossiers of the candidates and organized the
election campaign. While this situation was convenient as a short-term

measure, it became dangerous seen in the perspective of the 'after-de Gaulle' period, when gaullism would need many more local inter-mediaries, that is, party officials, supporters, 'opinion leaders', etc. This supposed that the U.N.R. party machine would succeed in overcoming this 'incapacity to exist' which Robert Poujade drew attention to in a report aiming at its transformation.

In March 1967, Georges Pompidou was ready to give his support to this change; the narrowness of their electoral victory showed that it was necessary and the Prime Minister deliberately asserted his authority as leader of the U.N.R.-U.D.T. The movement underwent a radical change. Its General Secretary, Jacques Baumel, who had held the post since December 22, 1962, was replaced by 5 national secretaries: Jean Charbonnel (relations with external organizations), Robert Poujade (elections), André Fanton (public relations), Jean Taittinger (treasurer) and René Tomasini (party expansion). Each week, the five national secretaries met at Matignon with Georges Pompidou in the chair. The meeting was also attended by Roger Frey (Minister of State responsible for relations with Parliament) and, if necessary, by the presidents of the gaullist parliamentary party: Henri Rey for the Assembly, Jacques Soufflet for the Senate. Every fortnight this meeting was followed, under the same conditions, by a meeting of the new 'executive committee', which had 26 members: the 9 presidents plus Michel Debré and Jacques Chaban-Delmas *ex officio*; 5 deputies elected by the parliamentary party in the National Assembly; 1 senator elected by the parliamentary party in the Senate; 5 members of the former supreme body of the movement, the political committee, chosen by them; finally 4 co-opted members.[73] The aim was clear: to give the movement a direct and regular means of access to the Prime Minister, thus giving the movement, as the parliamentary party, the possibility of influencing governmental action; the aim was also to give the Prime Minister, in exchange, a direct hold on the party through its collegiate management. It was with this perspective that Michel Habib-Deloncle drew up the reform of the U.N.R.-U.D.T. statutes which were to be ratified at the fourth national Party Conference at Lille. But the attack from those who wanted greater democracy within the movement, together with the revolt of the veteran gaullists, the first-generation gaullists, almost upset the well-laid plans at Lille, much to the astonishment of the new leaders and outside observers who imagined the party to be monolithic.

THE PARTY CONFERENCE AT LILLE (NOVEMBER 24–6, 1967)

It included, first of all, a revolt of the 'veteran' gaullists, who were well aware that their fellow gaullists were ready to turn over the page of historic gaullism. Like the old trade unionists of the C.F.T.C. who could not make up their minds to drop, in the name of the revival and broadening of their organization, the 'Christian' reference which had drawn them to it, these former voluntary combatants could not abandon a certain ritual present in gaullism. Their fear of change was expressed notably on the occasion of the discussion in committee of a name for the transformed movement. The chairman proposed the title '*Union des démocrates sociaux pour la V*e *Republique*'. Some of the militants demanded an explicit reference to gaullism in the new title. More numerous were those who pleaded, as did Bertrand Flornoy, for the status quo: 'Why,' he asked, 'should we change the name of a movement which has united us for nine years?'; the changing of the name might have been the price paid for a successful broadening of the movement but 'it has been made a prerequisite'. What was needed was a return 'to the spirit and the methods of the R.P.F.' Those who did not believe in the existence of a party patriotism within the U.N.R.-U.D.T. were surprised by the strength and vigour of these reactions. The innovators, however, knew how to overcome these hesitations by multiplying the references to General de Gaulle and by affirming their loyalty to the spirit of gaullism. Michel Habib-Deloncle was responsible for the text amending the party constitution and his relative youthfulness might have seemed suspect to the veteran gaullists; he took great care to remind them that he too had been in the Resistance. Georges Pompidou cleverly took a mid-way position between the past and the future which, he thought, should be united in one and the same movement: 'Beyond being a call to men from other political families, [he declared] the significance of this Party Conference lies, in my opinion, in opening fully our movement to young people. This does not mean we have to disavow past action, nor exclude those who since 1940 have fought first to liberate France, and then to put it on its feet again. Nothing great has ever been built on a foundation of ingratitude. After all, young people have no more rights than others and political youth often has nothing to do with one's real age! But not to be concerned about the political education of the younger generation and not to concentrate all our efforts on winning them over to our ideas and inviting them to participate in our activity, would be to reason in the same way as our opponents and to admit like them that gaullism has been merely an interlude. . . .'

The current which finally was most difficult to dam concerned the internal democratization of the movement. Mingled rather obscurely with this was a real desire for increased participation among the activists and, for some individuals, a move against Pompidou. The two currents were united in demanding the immediate and direct election by the Party Conference of a single general secretary who could talk as an equal with the Prime Minister. Jacques Chaban-Delmas and Roger Frey tried without success to preserve the clauses they had drawn up – namely a collegiate secretariat to be elected by the central committee – by appealing to common emotions which had their roots in the struggles in which they had fought together for so many years. The faint echo of this appeal to the past symbolized the end of an era in which the gaullist party conference was still dominated by the heroes of the Resistance and of the free French. A compromise was therefore necessary: the platform agreed to accept a single general secretary, while the militants accepted his election by the central committee.[74]

AFTER LILLE

The *Union des démocrates pour la République* as it emerged from the Party Conference at Lille, and from the political evolution that both gaullism and France had undergone since 1967, is a transformation of the former *Union pour la nouvelle République*, both as regards the leaders and the structures and the activities of the movement.

From the point of view of its leaders, as we saw in the previous chapter, what happened was that the generation of old-time gaullists were replaced by the intermediate generation of gaullists of the R.P.F. period, who were too young to have been active in the Resistance but old enough to have been avowed gaullists during the crossing of the political desert. A change was made in the post of general secretary of the movement: Jacques Baumel, Companion of the Liberation and formerly assistant secretary general of the R.P.F. was replaced by Robert Poujade, who in 1940 was only twelve years old and made his début in gaullism by joining the youth movement of the R.P.F. This change was undoubtedly both deliberate and symbolic. At the same time, the gaullist family circle was extended to include the Fourth Republic converts: Marie-Madeleine Dienesch, for the Républicains populaires, Philippe Dechartre for the gaullist left, were their representatives on the executive committee holding the new title of 'associate members'. The right to dual membership was recognized in accordance with the statutes (article 4 of the statutes), subject to the approval of the central committee of the movement; the U.D.R. thus remained within the established tradition of gaullism, that of '*rassemblement*'.

At the same time the party structure was completed. First of all, at the top comes the *Bureau exécutif* with 9 *ex officio* members and 2 associate members out of a total of 28, so that a large majority of elected members (elected by the central committee) replaces the former *Commission politique* (political committee) which, with more than 60 members, three-quarters of whom were *ex officio*, was neither representative nor viable and only had the power to ratify decisions taken elsewhere. The political committee was, in effect, dominated by a group of ministers and former ministers who were automatically members; the executive committee (*Bureau exécutif*), on the contrary, only has 2 acting government members *ex officio* – the Prime Minister and another minister appointed by him, who will normally be the Minister of State responsible for relations with Parliament. The other *ex officio* members of the executive committee are the president of the Assembly, the president of the gaullist parliamentary parties and all former gaullist prime ministers. Instead of being, as it was before, a sort of sub-committee of the Council of Ministers, the decision-making body of the movement is now elected and thus brings together the most prominent members of the movement, whether ministers or not.[75]

The party machine was restructured at the same time: the constituency, closest to the activists, the contact point with the electorate, replaced the traditional departmental federation as the basic unit. Parallel to this, the U.D.R., like the Républicains indépendants, was organized within each of the twenty-one regions; the proposals concerning the new party constitution had made provision for establishing regional councils, but the Party Conference at Lille made them compulsory. Since October 1968, the U.D.R. has made a point of organizing regional study days, which not only publicize regionalization but at the same time stress, at the regional level, the existence and the strength of the gaullist movement.[76] This is a campaign within a larger campaign for 'participation', in which participation in industry, in education and in regional matters is closely linked with participation in the U.D.R., as a folder edited in February 1969 shows. First there were the reforms that the U.D.R. undertook to carry out to 'build the France of tomorrow', followed by the invitation to participate in the efforts and work at the U.D.R. by becoming a member and being as united as on May 30, 1968, which is illustrated by the face of de Gaulle pictured against the background of the gaullist demonstration, from la Concorde to l'Etoile. The U.D.R. has rediscovered the party activist which the U.N.R. had for a long time neglected, first out of fear, then from force of habit. In 1959, the U.N.R. had hardly more than 25,000 members; in 1960 it had 35,000; in 1961, 50,000; in 1963, 86,000 as against some 150,000 according to the party.[77] In April 1968 the U.D.R. started an internal monthly bulletin called *Démocrates*,[78] and announced the launching of a massive nationwide campaign for membership, with a reference to Napoleon who said: 'Victory goes to the large battalions.' 'Membership,' Robert Poujade reminded the U.D.R. leaders, 'is a token and a proof of loyalty.' The campaign as planned was thrown off course by the events of May 1968, but it would appear that these events brought more members to the gaullist movement than all their propaganda efforts combined. Right in the middle of

August 1968, the department dealing with membership announced that 500 applications were coming in daily.[79] This rhythm for applications has not slackened since June 1968. In March 1969, the U.D.R. claimed that some 180,000 cards had been delivered to the federations. Taking into account the cards printed but not used and the exaggerations that are usual in this kind of estimate, one could still say that the U.D.R. managed in 1970 to double the actual number of its 1963 membership, rising from 80,000 to 160,000. This is a high figure for France, but at the same time fairly low for a voter-directed party which, if we compare it to corresponding European parties, should count its members in hundreds of thousands and not in tens of thousands.

As a buttress to the existence of the U.D.R., its General Secretary, Robert Poujade, contrary to the authoritarian administrative traditions of gaullism, has built around him a team whose two key members are Jean Charbonnel, Deputy General Secretary responsible for external relations and for social and economic activity, and Jean Valleix, national organization delegate. He has to deal with membership, with the effectiveness of the local and regional sections of the movement, the training of its officials and the organization of the U.D.R. campaigns. One other national delegate, Michel Herson, deals in particular with electoral problems such as investitures, electoral research and analyses etc. Jean Charbonnel, an ex-student of the Ecole Normale (like Robert Poujade) and a former minister, ensures the liaison of the U.D.R. with outside organizations, especially with the parallel organizations of the movement: *Clubs Ve République 'Nouvelle Frontière'* which organize conferences; *L'Université moderne*, which is led by Léo Hamon, and backs University reform; the *Centre féminin d'études et d'information*, (C.F.E.I.) presided over by Mme Rossolin Grandville, who seeks to promote the activity of women within the gaullist movement; finally the *Union des jeunes pour le Progrès* (U.J.P.), an independent movement of young gaullists with Robert Grossmann as president. This is, in short, the exact equivalent of what is found in the Républicains indépendants and in most modern parties. It is difficult to estimate the validity and importance of these organizations; the U.D.R. clubs seem to be less vital than the *Clubs Perspectives et Réalités* of the Républicains indépendants, though the present effort to reanimate them might be successful; the U.J.P. on the contrary has more members and a wider geographical base than the Young Independent Republicans (J.R.I.).[80] Jean Charbonnel is also responsible for the liaison between the U.D.R. and the professional or trade union organizations of industry, commerce, agriculture and craftsmen.

Thus relieved of the administration of the movement, its general secretary can devote himself entirely to its official representation and its political promotion. The U.D.R. party image corresponds partly to the image that the general secretary personally embodies: intelligence, a positive but controlled enthusiasm, and youthfulness.

A slogan and two posters in April 1968 epitomize this new image that gaullism seeks to give of itself. The slogan, printed on both posters, is: 'To build with us the France of tomorrow – join the Union of Democrats for the Fifth Republic (U.D.V^e)'; the first poster shows an anonymous crowd of men inviting other men to join in and lend a hand in modernizing the country; the second shows a young couple – probably middle class managerial – and their child, a little boy, standing apart from the crowd, calling their fellow-men to build their lives and their family happiness by taking part in the common effort. A call to the young, a call to participation, the modernist ideology of progress and individual happiness: the message it contains resembles more closely that of the British Conservative Party than that of traditional gaullism, in spite of the reference to France and the idea of participation in a national effort. Except for the red, white and blue, all the gaullist symbols have now disappeared: neither the Cross of Lorraine nor de Gaulle himself are shown or referred to on the new posters. But they were brought discreetly into the folder, more political by nature, for the campaign for the referendum of April 1969.

The most 'gaullian' of the gaullists, those most sensitive to the ex-servicemen spirit and to a certain gaullist sentimentality, feel slightly frustrated in this 'modern', 'efficient' party which is being built. Many of them, it seems, well before the departure of the General, had already found themselves more at ease in certain parallel associations, quite independent of the U.D.R. party; in the *Association nationale pour le soutien de l'action du Général de Gaulle* (Association for the support of the action of General de Gaulle), which has its head office in the old R.P.F. building at 5, rue de Solférino; then in the *Association pour la Ve République*, created by Malraux, led by Jean Runel, formerly a pro Free France partisan; finally in the C.D.R. – *Comités de défense de la République* – launched on the initiative of General de Gaulle himself in his key speech of May 30, 1968, and directed by Pierre Lefranc, one of the General's entourage who is also leader of the *Association nationale pour le soutien de l'action du Général de Gaulle* in the rue de Solferino. The C.D.R. groups are often presented as fascist-style groups; the former U.D.R. Minister of Education, Edgar Faure, sanctioned this interpretation in a public controversy with the C.D.R. of Dijon, in connection with the reform on education. The C.D.R. were indignant at these accusations 'especially since they had been created precisely to combat the attempts to seize power of certain extremist minorities whose totalitarian character is unquestionable'; they stated positively their willingness to 'defend the Republic with the same conviction and the same energy if ever a fascist threat were to appear'.[81] Beyond any question of polemic, it seems fairly clear that the C.D.R. represent for certain 'Resistance' gaullists quite simply a means of working together for the same ideal: the defence of freedom. There is no doubt that they would have fought for freedom and would have been only too happy to be of use again, if the need had arisen in 1968 or in 1961. But this is not to say that they would refuse to accept the defeat of gaullism by the normal democratic means of free elections. 'Is gaullism the U.D.R. or the C.D.R.?', Pierre Viansson-Ponté asked in *Le Monde* on January 10, 1969. It seems to us that unless something happens that is unforeseen and really dramatic, gaullism will be increasingly identified with the U.D.R. and decreasingly with the C.D.R., in so far as the gaullist past fades more and more into the past. Evidence of this fact can be seen in the proposed transformation of the very loyal and active *Association nationale pour le soutien de l'action du Général de Gaulle* into the guardian of a centre of documentation and research on General de Gaulle.

Notes to Chapter 5

1. Twelve to the left of the U.D.R.: the *Union de la gauche Vᵉ République* (Philippe Dechartre), the *Front du progrès* (J. Dauer), the *Groupe des vingt-neuf* (F. Sarda), the *Cercle Jules Vallès* (G. Cordouin), the *Clubs Vᵉ République* (J. Peillet), the *Centre de la Réforme républicaine* (G. Beaujolin), *Association nouveau régime* (J-J. Meier), the *Front travailliste* (M. Farbmann), the *Union gaulliste populaire* (René Capitant), the *Union populaire progressiste* (M. Cazenave), the *Front des Jeunes progressistes* ('break-aways' from the U.J.P.), and the *Union démocratique du travail* (U.D.T., Louis Vallon); three to the right, with the 'Giscardians': the *Fédération nationale des Républicains indépendants* (V. Giscard d'Estaing), the *Jeunes Républicains indépendants* (B. Lup), and the *Fédération nationale des Clubs Perspectives et Réalités* (C. Hardy), not taking into account the *Centre démocratie et progrès* (J. Duhamel); finally, fourteen on the 'orthodox' gaullist side: the *Union des démocrates pour la République* (R. Poujade), the *Rassemblement du peuple français* (J. Foccart), which is 'suspended' but has not been dissolved, the *Association nationale pour le soutien de l'action du Général de Gaulle* (P. Lefranc), the *Association pour la Vᵉ République* (A. Malraux), the *Union des Jeunes pour le Progrès* (R. Grossmann), the *Club Jeune France* (J. C. Fortuit), the *Université moderne* (L. Hamon), the *Centre féminin d'études et d'information* (Mme Rosselin-Grandville), the *Centre d'information civique* (J. C. Barbé), the *Clubs Vᵉ République 'Nouvelle Frontière'* (Mme de Laval), the *Comité de liaison, d'études et d'action républicaines* (B. Chenot), the *Service d'action civique* (P. Comiti), the *Comités de défense de la République* (Y. Lancien) and the *Amicale présence et action du gaullisme* (H. Germain).

2. The importance of these tends, generally, to be underestimated. Cf. Part Three.

3. The appeal in favour of the foreign policy of the Fifth Republic was launched in May 1966, on the eve of the constitutive meeting of the liaison committee of the majority, by twenty-nine personalities, generally hailing from the left-wing circles, who had declared themselves in favour of General de Gaulle at the time of the presidential election of December 1965. The text of this appeal and the list of the first twenty-nine to sign it were published in *Le Monde* on May 11, 1966. On May 12th, Jean-Marie Domenach, director of *Esprit*, pointed out that the appeal was not an election manifesto nor was it evidence of a future regrouping; it was simply the act of some people who supported the gaullist foreign policy. The Group of Twenty-Nine, which gathered more than 200 signatures for its appeal, was organized in November 1966 when it set up a permanent committee and a post of secretary general, held by François Sarda. At the beginning of 1967, it elaborated a project of worker association in the profits of industry. Cf. *Le Monde*, November 5, 1966 and February 11, 1967.

4. *Le Monde*, November 5, 1966. Cf. also in *Notre République* 221, May 27, 1966, the statements made by Jean-Marie Domenach, Pierre Hervé, Pierre Le Brun and David Rousset in the 'Tribune de la gauche'.

5. Statement of general policy, Fourth National Convention, October 15–16, 1967, at Arcachon. Outside its national conventions, the *Front du progrès* organizes 'round table talks'. It claims 5,000 members, half of whom come from the R.P.F. or other gaullist movements, one third former mendesists, the rest recruited directly. Its bulletin, *Notes d'information du Front du progrès*, and its newspaper, *le Télégramme de Paris*, which appears at irregular intervals are controlled by Jacques Dauer, who is a printer by trade. *Le Télégramme de Paris* has, since 1955, been the permanent link between those whom Jacques Dauer gathered round him after his years in the Resistance and then as a militant in the R.P.F., in the group called *Jeunes de la région parisienne*. The *Mouvement pour la Communauté* was created on June 7, 1959, the *Front du progrès* in April 1964.

6. *Le Télégramme de Paris* 37, November 1958. In the same issue, J. Drault, former leader of the service d'ordre on a local level (R.P.F.) and candidate for *Renouveau et Fidélité* in the 16th arrondissement of Paris, wrote: 'We are the activists who, from 1947 to the present day, have . . . seen to the distribution of pamphlets, the sale of newspapers, the sticking of posters, the organization of meetings, and have resisted the violent assaults of the communists.' We are the activists who stand at elections for 'the continuation of the struggle in those areas where the deputies, representatives of the nation, most lack the indispensable qualities of faith, good works and loyalty'.

7. Majority which excluded Jacques Dauer in October 1967 by expelling him from the *Union de la Gauche Ve République*, which preferred, together with Philippe Dechartre, the expansion of the U.N.R.-U.D.T. Cf. *Le Monde*, October 24, 1967.
8. René Capitant, 'Nation et Démocratie', *Esprit*, March 1955, pp. 371–5.
9. Cf. in particular his article in *Notre République* 206, February 11, 1966. 'The Republic itself, Léo Hamon (and the former U.D.T. member who supported at Lille the expansion of the U.N.R.-U.D.T.) retorted, the Republic which was triumphant in the nineteenth century, was only victorious because it had its party behind it. . . . In order to found and consolidate a gaullist Republic . . . a gaullist political force must exist in the country. . . .' *Notre République* 223, June 10, 1966.
10. Cf. the speech of Philippe Dechartre, general secretary of the *Union de la Gauche Ve République* at the Party Conference of the U.N.R.-U.D.T. at Lille, November 25–6, 1967, in which René Capitant and Louis Vallon had refused to participate.
11. *Notre République* 202, January 14, 1966. Cf. also the article of Louis Vallon, 'Pour un référendum social', *Notre République* 242, December 3, 1966.
12. The faith of the gaullists in the Loichot plan cannot be over-exaggerated. For example, 'A reform such as this,' René Capitant wrote 'can lead to a real change in the social regime. . . .' After several decades, we would be faced with a society in which, as M. Loichot rightly says, 'the proletarian state will have disappeared and in which men will have rediscovered their original dignity. . . .' For René Capitant, this will represent the end of the class struggle. *Notre République* 203, January 21, 1966. Cf. on this problem: M. Loichot, *La réforme pancapitaliste*, Laffont, Paris, 1966, and especially the study of Jean Claude Casanova 'L'amendement Vallon', *Revue française de science politique*, XVII(1), February 1967, pp. 97–109.
13. René Capitant, 'l'U.N.R. et l'U.D.T.', *Notre République* 205, February 4, 1966.
14. *Le Télégramme de Paris* 13–14, October–November 1966. Cf. also *Le Nation*, II, October 1966.
15. Quoted by Michel Rodet in *Le Télégramme de Paris* 13–14, October–November 1966. In the editorial of the same issue Jacques Dauer, general secretary of the *Front du progrès*, together with the whole team of the *Télégramme*, declares himself a willing participant in the effort, 'an honest undertaking, a loyal effort, a movement emanating from a free assembly of leading activists after a sincere exchange of views'.
16. Charles d'Aragon, Arnaud, Cordouin and Mercier. For fuller details cf. our study on 'les préparatifs de la majorité', *Cahier de la F.N.S.P.* on the *élections législatives de mars 1967*, A. Colin, Paris. If we add all those who, in March 1967, were neither U.N.R. nor Républicain

indépendant, that is the U.D.T., radicals and M.R.P. gaullists, etc., we arrive at the following results: 83 candidates, of whom 29 are outgoing deputies; only 28 deputies elected, 19 of whom were outgoing deputies (8 of them U.D.T.). This definition of the 'gaullist left' is still a very broad one.

17. *Courrier de la Convention*, weekly bulletin of the *Convention de la Gauche Ve République*, No. 5, December 21, 1966; *Le Monde* December 18–19, 1966.

18. *Le Monde*, December 20, 1966.

19. First indication of a breach in the unity of the gaullist left wing: on the same day Edgar Faure organized a luncheon grouping together some thirty candidates of the same political colour to whom he proposed his leadership: 'You wish to have me as your technical adviser. We haven't yet seen my photo on all the walls, but after a few sessions of physical fitness and make-up, you never know.' The spirit of this repartee was understood to have been directed against Valéry Giscard d'Estaing. On these meetings, cf. *Le Monde*, February 2, 1967.

20. Cf. *Le Monde*, March 23, 1967 and our article on 'L'après-gaullisme', *Revue française de science politique*, XVIII (I, February 1968, pp. 68–76. The role of personalities and the absence of political consensus within the gaullist left were clearly visible during the May 1968 crisis. Edgard Pisani supported the vote of no confidence against the government of Pompidou and, breaking with the majority, created a *Mouvement pour la Réforme* which at the June elections obtained very poor results. He himself was defeated. René Capitant, so as not to have to vote resigned as deputy; he accepted a post in the new government, 'swallowing' – in his own words – 'that grass-snake Pompidou'. He was re-elected a U.D.R. deputy for Paris in June. The other left-wing gaullist deputies remained loyal to the government.

21. *Front du progrès*, *IVe Convention nationale – Arcachon, 14–15 October 1967*. Cf. in particular the report of general policy by Michel Rodet and the closing speech of Jacques Dauer.

22. *Le Monde*, October 24, 1967. Since then ties have been virtually broken between the *Front du progrès* and the U.GV^e.

23. 'Nous n'irons pas à Lille', Notre République 283, November 10, 1967. Other U.D.T. leaders do go to Lille: Pierre Billotte for example (cf. *La Nation*, November 20, 1967).

24. *La Nation*, November 23, 1967.

25. *Le Monde*, June 18, 20 and July 5, 1969 especially. Cf. also in *La Nation* of July 2, 1969 the editorial entitled 'nos progressistes'. The U.G.P. had its headquarters at 18, rue St. Ferdinand, Paris 17e; the U.P.P. at 15, rue des Barres, Paris 4e and the F.J.P. at 33, rue Poussin, Paris 16e.

26. *Le Monde*, January 24, 1963.

27. Thus at the end of January 1963 the independent Senators refused to rejoin the *Centre d'études et de liaison des Républicains indépendants*,

as they had been invited to do by Valéry Giscard d'Estaing, Raymond
Mondon and Aimé Paquet in a personal letter (*Le Monde*, January
1963); on the other hand, the parliamentary party of the Républicains indépendants in the National Assembly did not make use of
the contacts organized by Camille Laurens, general secretary of the
C.N.I., under the direction of Antoine Pinay, between the scattered
members of the moderate 'family' (*Le Monde*, February 9, 1963).

28. *Le Monde*, November 30, 1962.
29. *France moderne* 306, April 1967.
30. *France moderne* 296, June 1966.
31. Speech in the National Assembly, May 20, 1967, during the debate
    of no confidence on the special powers of the government.
32. Explanation of vote in the National Assembly, May 22, 1968, during
    the debate of no confidence relating to the events of May. No
    Républicain indépendant voted the motion of censure.
33. Radio-television speech on June 28, 1968, part of the campaign
    for the general election.
34. Cf. our study on the 'les préparatifs de la majorité', in the *Cahier
    de la Fondation nationale des sciences politiques* on the *élections
    législatives de mars 1967* (A. Colin, Paris).
35. The complete text of this statement was published in *France moderne*
    309, September 7, 1967.
36. On May 22, 1968, Valéry Giscard d'Estaing made the following
    statement in the National Assembly: 'The lesson to be learned from
    these events is that the implementation of important and necessary
    plans for change, in political and social stability, cannot be imposed
    on one half of the French people by the other half. A common
    programme and means of co-operation must be found some day.'
37. Cf. the excellent article of Marie-Christine Kessler, 'M. Valéry
    Giscard d'Estaing et les Républicains indépendants: Juillet 1966–
    Novembre 1967', *Revue française de science politique*, XVIII (I),
    February 1968, pp. 77–93.
38. He also revealed on certain points, the differences of opinion with
    'the majority of the majority'.
39. *Réponses* 2, October 22, 1968, p. 3. The words italicized were in
    block letters in the text of the article. We have shown, moreover,
    with regard to the general election of March 1967, that if the R.I.
    deputies were not particularly young – an average age of more than
    fifty-three and a half years in this legislature – the F.N.R.I. unlike
    the U.N.R. had made a great effort to widen the electoral arena to
    younger men; they thus present no new candidate over sixty-five
    years, and half of their candidates are between forty and fifty years
    old. The 'new' candidates do not, of course, have the best con-
    stituencies, but they are given the opportunity to fabricate their
    first political arms (cf. our study on 'les préparatifs de la majorité',
    Cahier de la F.N.S.P. on the *élections législatives de mars 1967*,
    A. Colin, Paris).
40. *France moderne* 296, June 1966.

41. In *Les Communistes français*, Seuil, Paris, 1968.

42. *Réponses* 10, December 17, 1968, pp. 4–5.

43. *Le Monde*, February 5, 1969, on the general assembly of the *Fédération nationale des Clubs Perspectives et Réalités*, February 1, 1969. This general assembly gathered together officially sixty-five leaders representing forty-four clubs, that is six more than in December 1968 at the time of the Third National Convention of the Clubs. In fact it seems that the number of active clubs is nearer thirty than forty.

44. Ibid.

45. Cf. *Combat*, February 15, 1967: president: J. P. Deroche, aged twenty-six, H.E.C., commercial 'official' in an industrial society, former member of the *Club des Prouvaires* then of *Perspectives et Réalités*; vice-president (provisional): C. M. Chambat, Clermont-Ferrand, aged twenty-four, former member of the *Action française*. The national bureau, elected on February 11, 1969 (cf. *Réponses* of February 1969) no longer has a single founder member. Its president is Bernard Lup, from Grenoble; its general secretary is Philippe Bernard, from Amiens, who is assisted by Florence Canivet and J. L. Olivier from Paris. Out of seven members, the bureau has four from Paris.

46. The national bureau of the Ladies' Committee was elected for two years in 1968. It comprises the woman president, Mme Boyé-Carré, two vice-presidents, Mme de Lattre and Mlle Berthon, a general secretary, Mme Hardy–Baillot and a treasurer, Mme Boda.

47. Map published in *France moderne* 307, May 1967. According to this map the Clubs then numbered twelve and the regional correspondents of the Jeunes R.I. numbered seventeen. The first region to be constituted was Auvergne, the region of Valéry Giscard d'Estaing.

48. The original statutes, which have not been applied, made provision for a general assembly of members with the powers of the present federal council which is much smaller, a managing committee which corresponds on the whole with the present federal council, and a federal council which almost corresponds with the present managing committee. The executive committee, which is the key organ in the present organization, did not exist. The new plan for organization was drawn up by a committee comprising Jean de Broglie, Roger Chinaud, Paul Dijoud, Alain Griotteray and Michel Poniatowski, all close colleagues of Valéry Giscard d'Estaing, and accepted on October 2, 1968 by the provisional bureau of the F.N.R.I. – which corresponds to no body provided for in the statutes but comprising the principal leaders of the parliamentary party and of the party. These mechanisms have been set up too recently for us to study how they really work. Cf. *Réponses* 1, October 15, 1968, p. 7.

49. Cf. our analysis in 'La Campagne de la majorité', *Cahier de la F.N.S.P.*, devoted to the general election of March 1967, A. Colin, Paris.

50. In September 1968, the committee of the R.I. parliamentary party

comprised twelve members: Raymond Mondon, president; Raymond Boisdé, Jean de Broglie, Bertrand Denis, Roland Boscary-Monsservin, and Aimé Paquet, vice-presidents; Christian Bonnet, general secretary; Albert Voilquin, treasurer; Jean Brocard, Alain Griotteray, Michel Poniatowski and René Feit, members – plus two *ex officio* members, the president of the F.N.R.I., Valéry Giscard d'Estaing and the vice-president of the National Assembly, Marcel Anthonioz. The delegations of the parliamentary party, to the Prime Minister for example, usually include R. Mondon, M. Anthonioz, A. Paquet, J. de Broglie, and Michel Poniatowski. The parliamentary party is divided into eight work groups: teaching (led by Olivier Giscard d'Estaing), agriculture (R. Boscary–Monsservin), national defence (M. d'Aillères), finance (A. Paquet), commerce (R. Boisdé) scientific problems (Claude Guichard), foreign affairs (J. de Broglie), and 'repatriates' (F. Icart). Since June 1969, the president of the parliamentary party is A. Paquet, who replaced R. Mondon when he became a Minister.

51. *Le Monde*, September 20, 1967.
52. *Le Monde*, January 28, 1969. *L'Economie*, which appears twice monthly, is one of the three publications of the F.N.R.I. The other two are the weekly, *France moderne*, and a monthly internal liaison bulletin, *Note aux cadres*.
53. *Le Monde*, March 29 and April 16, 1969.
54. *L'Express*, January 9–15, 1967 and *France moderne* 345, May 27, 1969. On the *Centre démocratie et progrès*, whose headquarters are at 6, Cité Martignac, Paris 7ᵉ, cf. *Le Monde*, July 5, 1969.
55. Jean Charlot, *L'U.N.R. – étude du pouvoir au sein d'un parti politique*, A. Colin, Paris, 1967, p. 23. The subsequent pages, like those of Chapters IV and VI, bring the U.N.R. up to date on certain points and on others offer a new interpretation of this first study, in the light of later developments. Thus the organization and power within the parliamentary party have not changed in nature despite the fact that there have been two new legislatures, in 1967 and 1968; but on the other hand, the party was radically restructured after the Party Conference at Lille, in November 1967. It did more than simply change its name from *Union pour la nouvelle République* (U.N.R.) to *Union des démocrates pour la Vᵉ République* (U.D.Vᵉ), and then to *Union des démocrates pour la République* (U.D.R.).
56. U.N.R.-U.D.T. resulting from the fusion with the left-wing gaullists of the *Union démocratique du travail* in December 1962; *Union des démocrates pour la Vᵉ République* after the party expanded to include the M.R.P. and Radicals of the Fifth Republic, and various 'left-wing' gaullist associations in 1967; *Union des démocrates pour la République* in 1968, to recall the victorious title in the June election of the *Union pour la défense de la République*.
57. Cf. Jean Charlot, op. cit., Chapters IV and VI.
58. One seat each for: l'Outre-Mer (Overseas); the Centre-East (Bourgogne and Franche-Comté); Normandy (Haute et Basse–

Normandie). Two seats each for: Paris (ville); the Paris region; the Western regions (Loire and Bretagne); the Centre (Centre, Poitou-Charente, Limousin and Auvergne); the South–West (Aquitaine and Midi-Pyrénées); the East (Alsace, Lorraine and Champagne); Rhône-Alpes; the South-East (Languedoc, Provence, Côte d'Azur-Corse). Article 24 of the statutes of July 9, 1968.

59. Article 18 of the statutes. Membership of the permanent study groups or the specialized study groups (G.E.S.), as they were then called, had been purely optional in all the preceding legislatures.

60. Secretary of State charged, at that time, with the relations with Parliament.

61. Synthesis of the work of the specialized study groups, *Informations et Documents* (of the U.N.R.-U.D.T. parliamentary party in the National Assembly), No. 2, April 30, 1963.

62. Divided into twelve sub-groups: wine-growing, animal and vegetable production (agriculture); work and social security, public health (social affairs); fiscal policy, incomes policy, commerce, distribution, manual trades, building, housing (economic and financial affairs); youth (national education and youth); local and regional planning and administration (town and country planning); Europe, national defence (foreign affairs).

63. Article 19 of the statutes of July 9, 1968.

64. According to several reports, only the group dealing with 'employment' met together, twice, in the six months following the study days at Le Baule. On this subject cf. *Démocrates*, a monthly information pamphlet of the U.D.V^e, No. 4, September–October 1968.

65. Cf. Jean Charlot, *op. cit.*, pp. 153–66.

66. In the case of the Higher Education Act, for example, as we shall see in the following chapter.

67. Article 24 of the statutes of the parliamentary party, of July 9, 1968. This clause was not included in the statutes of 1962 but had, in fact, already been applied. The move against 'pluralism' was aimed at the offices of vice-president, quaestor and secretary of the National Assembly and any other office filled by the vote of the parliamentary party or by the executive committee.

68. When it is a question of personal matters, the deputies generally contact the parliamentary attaché of the Minister concerned. These attachés have an office at the Palais-Bourbon, next to the Bureau of the Ministers, and have frequent contacts with the latter.

69. Article 5 of the statutes of July 9, 1968.

70. All this information is drawn from the statutes of the party (July 9, 1968) and from the circular, signed by the president of the parliamentary party, Henri Rey, dated September 26, 1968.

71. Louis Terrenoire, *De Gaulle et l'Algérie*, Témoignage pour l'Histoire, A. Fayard, Paris, 1964, p. 123.

72. Amongst the 'challenged' presidents can be named Louis Terrenoire, who was president when the party was torn apart by the Algerian problem, from April 1959 till February 1960. For a 'challenging'

president, one can quote Raymond Schmittlein, president from March 1960 to October 1962, this being the only case of a president of the party elected against the 'official' candidate, André Valabrègue. The election of Marc Jacquet, in June 1969, was a 'normal' election, there being no 'official' candidate.

73. For the deputies: Messrs. Vivien, Valleix, Hoffer, Danel and Sabatier; for the Senators: Bayrou; for the political committee: Habib-Deloncle, Sanguinetti, Germain, Hamon and Neuwirth; for the co-opted members: Baumel, Dechartre, Comiti and Narquin.

74. The quotations and observations on the Party Conference at Lille have been taken from documents, notes and interviews made there by the author. Cf. also, on this Party Conference, Chapter IV of this book.

75. That is to say by the central committee which is itself elected by several colleges by the national Assizes (Party Conference) – by 40 parliamentarians and 36 non-parliamentarians, plus about 10 ex officio members, 10 associate members, and 12 co-opted members. In April 1968, the central committee had 118 members. The executive committee comprised 29 members in April 1968: 9 ex officio members: Georges Pompidou, Michel Debré, Jacques Chaban-Delmas, Roger Frey, Henri Rey, Jacques Soufflet, Robert Poujade, Jean Taittinger and René Tomasini; 18 members elected by the Central Committee: Albin Chalandon, Jean Charbonnel, Joseph Comiti, André Fanton, Michel Habib-Deloncle, Léo Hamon, Gabriel Lisette, Robert Menu, Jean Narquin, Lucien Neuwirth, Jean de Préaumont, Bernard Pons, Alexandre Sanguinetti, Jean Valleix, Robert-André Vivien, Robert Bailliard, Guy Baudoin, Jacques Baumel; 2 associate members: Marie-Madeleine Dienesch, Philippe Dechartre.

76. The following are examples of these first regional study days: Marseilles, at the end of October 1968; Charleville-Mézières, November 1968; Bordeaux, December 1968; Tours, February 1969 etc.

77. Cf. Jean Charlot, op. cit., p. 116.

78. The U.N.R. no longer had an internal bulletin addressed expressly to the activists, since the creation at the beginning of 1962 of La Nation and the withdrawal of the Courrier de la nouvelle République, which up till then had given the news of the internal activities of the movement.

79. Démocrates 4, September–October 1968.

80. According to Mr Grossmann, the U.J.P., which was created in 1965, counted 10,000 members (Le Monde, March 18, 1969). This figure seems very exaggerated. The movement claimed to have 2,500 in January 1967 (Notre République, January 13, 1967), 4,300 just before May 1968, 7,300 five months later (Le Monde, October 29, 1968). The organization of the young gaullists has always been hampered by rivalries between individuals. This is why there is also the Club Jeune France led by Jean-Claude Fortuit, a former member of the Cabinet of Jacques Chaban-Delmas, then of that of Michel Habib-Deloncle.

81. Le Monde, January 10, 1969.

CHAPTER VI

The Distribution of Power

THE LEADER OF THE MAJORITY

In a political system that has been 'run in' and has worked well for a considerable number of years, the division of power creates no problem – not that it is always written into the law, for if this were so, power in Great Britain would belong not to the Prime Minister and leader of the majority party but to the Queen; but we do not need a sophisticated political science to determine who governs, with whom, under whose control and how. The analysts of power in a system such as this find in practice a great cohesion which goes far beyond party frontiers. The situation is much less clear in a changing system, such as that of France since 1958–62, which, having broken with its former habits of thought and action, has just passed the crucial stage where the founders of the new system have been replaced by men who may continue, transform or abandon it.

Who is the leader of the majority, for example, in the Fifth Republic? In Great Britain it is without question the leader of the party which has won the last general election; in the United States it is the President; in Federal Germany the Chancellor . . . but who is it in France nowadays? Was it until 1969 General de Gaulle, the President of the Republic? He denied it, for he placed himself not only above the parties but even above the majority which had elected him, so that he might speak and act in the name of public interest, in the name of France. Likewise Georges Pompidou, candidate for the succession and his successor, when speaking to a Genevan journalist said, 'I do not believe that I have what people call a political future. I have a political past. I will perhaps, by the grace of God, have a national destiny, but that is something different'.[1]

What of General de Gaulle, who had a national past when he became President? Already Napoleon I had said that 'to govern with a party is, sooner or later, to become dependent on it. I will not fall into this trap. I rely on the whole nation'. This is a popular attitude, even if it is viewed with a certain scepticism: in November 1965, on the eve of the presidential election, 56 per cent of the French wanted the President of the Republic to be 'outside all political groups'; 23 per cent wanted him to be 'the leader of a majority party', but only 31 per cent of the voters, 43 per cent of the gaullist voters, considered that General de Gaulle had shown himself to be above the parties during his first term of office.[2]

Up till November 1962, General de Gaulle maintained consistently the position of arbitrator. 'The mission which this country has entrusted to me,' he declared on the eve of the general election of November 1958, 'does not allow me to participate in party politics. I shall not therefore intervene in anyone's favour, not even in favour of those who have shown me a marked loyalty and devotion at all times. . . . This impartiality,' he added, 'demands essentially that my name, even in adjectival form, should not be used in the name of any group or candidate.'[3] A curious party indeed, this *Union pour la nouvelle République;* its *raison d'être*, General de Gaulle, does not on principle wish to acknowledge it. 'We find ourselves in a situation,' the General Secretary of the party remarked, 'where we must constantly serve him without being directly under his command.'[4] With time, with the transformation of the institutions resulting from the election of the President of the Republic by universal suffrage, and with the change in the party system based on the emergence of a gaullist majority party, the situation has been radically altered and clarified.

As from November 1962, General de Gaulle abandoned his impartiality and recommended to the voters the candidates who were in favour of the 'New Republic'.[5] When the National Assembly met in March 1967, his position became even clearer after he had spoken disparagingly of the opposition parties in the following words: '. . . even though they join forces and pool their negative attitudes and their spite, they will never be capable of uniting in a positive way to deal with any of the major issues. . . .' The Head of State gave precise voting instructions: he stated that in any case it would be 'both just and desirable' for the present majority to be retained; and he added that 'in the present situation it [was] absolutely necessary'.[6] In November 1967, the day after the Party Conference at Lille, which marked the transformation and the broadening of the U.N.R., General de Gaulle went further than ever before in his support of the gaullist party for the Fifth Republic, without however ceasing to differentiate the respective roles; he stated, 'Come what may, it is the duty of the President of the Republic, as Head of State, to uphold the spirit and the terms of the institutions, and to direct the policy of France throughout the whole period during which he is the sole representative invested by the French people. Moreover, I firmly believe that this is what was so enthusiastically and earnestly demonstrated by those who, in Lille at their Party Conference, endeavoured to adapt our ideas and aspirations to the changing conditions.'[7] One year later, three months after the social and political revolt of May–June 1968, General de Gaulle stated: 'Once more we have proved that in these very unsettled times . . . there is no system of thought, will or action capable of providing the necessary inspiration to France so that it may remain France, except that which events have created and stirred to action since June 1940. . . . We can see, therefore,' he concluded, 'how great must be the need in the future for cohesion and resolution on the part of all those who, throughout the years, have joined, join to-day, or will join in the future, in the task of restoring the nation – a task justified, regulated and inspired in the name of France. This undertaking, although it has been called 'gaullism' since 1940, is but the contemporary manifestation of the impetus of our country. . . .'[8] Thus General de Gaulle's position as head of the majority, and even of the majority of the majority, the U.D.R., became more and more clearly defined. This was simply the proof that the majority had succeeded in its job of 'rassemblement', the re-uniting of the people, for which in vain General de Gaulle had founded the *Rassemblement du peuple français* in 1947. The U.D.R., as a gaullist and hence a national party, as a voter-directed party, and as such open to all social and regional categories, as a disciplined majority party, was naturally cleansed in the General's eyes of the original sin of all other political parties, namely that of their partisan and sectarian nature. De Gaulle could thus emerge as the party leader without betraying his mission.

For Georges Pompidou, who has not the same historical reasons for distrusting political parties and parliament, it will be even easier to become the majority party leader.

This does not, of course, imply that the other major tenet concerning the institutions – that of the separation of powers – will be abandoned.

THE SEPARATION OF POWERS

The excellent work of Ronald Butt on the 'decline' of parliament in Great Britain[9] is well known. The main idea embodied in this book is that we cannot speak of a decline since the House of Commons has never had power, nor has it claimed to have the power, to make and unmake governments, or to lay down the law to the Executive. The golden age of the English parliament is a myth. The Prime Minister and his Cabinet have inherited from the Crown the authority and power to govern, an authority which is quite separate, the author stresses, from that which the government is afforded by the support of parliament, even if the latter is necessary for the government to stay in power. The Cabinet is not the executive committee of the

House but that of the nation; the executive branch neither originates from nor depends on the legislative branch, for it is essentially monarchical. Great Britain is thus a constitutional monarchy in which the real monarch is the Prime Minister, or an 'elected' monarch, in the words of another British political theorist.[10]

As for the House of Commons, it is simply the place where the sovereign explains his or her intentions and actions before the people, thereby submitting to the pressures of the representatives. It is not the place where the subjects discuss amongst themselves the best policy to be followed but where they can thrash out policy with those who govern them. In the last analysis, the sole power of parliament is the essential power of speech: by its mere existence it obliges the government to speak, to state its intentions publicly, to bargain constantly with the majority, and to lay itself open to the criticism of the opposition before the eyes of the whole country which will, in the last resort, be the judge. But, as Charles I had already said, 'a king and a subject are not the same thing' – there is a difference between being one who governs and one who is a member of parliament.

From the time of his Bayeux speech, General de Gaulle was intent on imposing this institutional philosophy, so alien to the French parliamentary tradition. But, in so far as the separation of powers has meant for France a break with the past and consequently an encounter with many strong and active centres of resistance, the gaullists have tended to take from the British model those aspects which encourage the independence of the Executive and to reduce as much as possible the parliamentary right to be completely and continually informed and above all to be the first to hear the explanations of the government on all matters. The definition of the domain of law, the limitation of parliamentary sessions, the overriding influence of the government on the parliamentary timetable, the duality – especially of the Executive – all demonstrate precautions against parliament which can only be explained or justified in terms of a fear of a return to a system of government by assembly.

THE PRESIDENT AND THE PRIME MINISTER

Our 'elected' monarch, the President of the Republic, explains his policy and actions before the National Assembly only through his intermediary, the Prime Minister. Directly elected by the people, he is only responsible to them through the process of a referendum and general or presidential elections; he converses directly with the people when he makes official visits or during his radio and television broadcasts.

In Great Britain the power-confidence circle is single and unbroken –

from the people to the Prime Minister through the largest parliamentary group in the House of Commons, the Prime Minister being the elected leader of this group. In France, under the Fifth Republic, there is a double circle: the one linking the people and the President, the other linking the people and Parliament – between the two circles we find the Prime Minister, nominated by the President and responsible to Parliament. The system is rather complex, but it works well as long as the presidential and parliamentary majorities coincide.

There are many in the opposition ranks who would like to make the Prime Minister the keystone of the system. General de Gaulle was against this and in order to prevent its happening, he was not afraid to change his Prime Minister twice, although not without causing a stir even amongst the majority.[11] The fact is that for General de Gaulle the highest responsibilities cannot be shared and there can be no ambiguity as to who shoulders them; only the President, elected by the whole people, can legitimately assume these responsibilities. If the Prime Minister, because of events and his reactions to them, is forced to come to the front of the political scene and therefore seems indispensable, as was the case with Georges Pompidou in May 1968, he will then have to retire into the background. When Georges Pompidou, who had in 1968 become a simple deputy for the Cantal, confided that he would probably be a candidate at the next presidential election, the General cut short all speculations about this statement by declaring in the Council of Ministers: 'To continue the national task which I have undertaken, I was re-elected by the French people on December 19, 1965 as President of the Republic for a further seven years of office. I have both the duty and the intention to remain in office until the end of my mandate.'[12]

The head of the majority is thus clearly the President of the Republic, as Georges Pompidou himself pointed out before his accession to that office: 'I have always believed,' he said, 'that the leader of the majority in our system is the President of the Republic himself, for he has been elected by the people.' But he was also quite willing to concede to those who put him forward: 'I certainly do not deny that I have a role to play and a certain weight in the present majority.'[13]

The remaining ambiguity over the respective powers of the Prime Minister and the President of the Republic arises from the double meaning that the word 'majority' can have. If it is a question of deciding who holds the power, then of the two the President of the Republic is undeniably the leading man; but if the question is rather one of the parliamentary majority, then it is no longer the President but the Prime Minister, for he is responsible to the Assembly and the President delegates all political action to him whilst reserving the most important policy decisions for himself. 'In our Republic,' General de

Gaulle stated on September 9, 1968, 'it is the Head of State who is always responsible for the highest interests of France, for the stability of her institutions, and for the assurance of continuity in public affairs. His duties and his activity are thus of far-reaching consequence and surpass mere contingencies. . . . But the Prime Minister, chosen and nominated by the Head of State, is directly at grips with circumstances. He has constantly to direct, co-ordinate and follow the activities of the other ministers and administrative departments, to carry statutory law into effect, to direct government participation in legislative matters and in the control of parliament, to keep in contact with facts, opinions and interests; the Prime Minister lives a rough life, without respite, in what is commonly called politics, that is to say in the immediate present, in order to put rapidly into practice the general instructions given to him by the President. Necessity – and principle – set bounds to his action. He must therefore be relieved of his office when the moment calls for it. Yet this replacement in no way implies a transformation in the plans of the state nor does it imply a retreat, since it is the President who determines the aims, the direction and the rhythm.' [14]

Since 1958 the facts have corresponded with this view of the balance of power between the President and the Prime Minister. With this in mind, it was therefore a mistake to think that the candidate who would succeed to the Presidency was automatically the Prime Minister, as people had thought for a long time. This was to consider the Prime Minister as the Vice-President whereas the President of the Republic had always shown a marked opposition to the creation of a Vice-Presidency. If, in the President's opinion, the Prime Minister could be and on occasion had to be relieved of his post, his status obviously could not make him the implicitly chosen successor. Georges Pompidou understood this, he who had received an almost personal nomination for the Presidency when he ceased to be Prime Minister, a point that he did not fail to recall when the occasion arose: 'I do not think,' he stated in Rome, 'that General de Gaulle was discouraging me when, as you remember, he wrote to me and alluded to a national mandate that France might one day give me. He could have been thinking of nothing else but the Presidency, though he himself is no more in control of the voters, the future or my destiny than I am.' [15] All that one can say is that under the Fourth Republic the normal candidate to the Presidency was a president or former president of the Senate, whereas under the Fifth Republic he is a Prime Minister or former Prime Minister.

The President and the Prime Minister, when all is said and done, form an inseparable pair at the head of the state and can only act in mutual confidence. But they are at the same time an unequal pair, for the President always prevails. General de Gaulle, with Michel Debré, Georges Pompidou and Maurice Couve de Murville yesterday, Georges Pompidou and Jacques Chaban-Delmas today, all accept the division of powers between these two offices. The inequality of their respective power, however, should not lead one to underestimate the political role of the Prime Minister in the Fifth Republic, with the implicit reference to the lost paradise of the Fourth – in which the president of the Council was the prisoner of an essentially unstable coalition majority – or to the still-born paradise of the Fifth – whose Constitution had in fact provided under Article 20 that the government should fix and conduct the policy of the nation.[16] The Prime Minister is kept closely informed about everything, even about foreign affairs since he receives the diplomatic dispatches and the ambassadors. He is at the centre of the administrative machinery of government which studies the various solutions and prepares decisions, whilst the Elysée has at its disposal an administration far inferior to that available to the Ministries. The Prime Minister has, finally, a unique power of influence over the President and certain facts show that this power, coupled on occasion with a threat to abandon the office the President has given him, is far from negligible. Thus Georges Pompidou obtained a pardon for General Jouhaud, condemned to death after the putsch of the Generals at Algiers in April 1961; he also managed to persuade General de Gaulle to dissolve the National Assembly on May 30, 1968. The Prime Minister is a member of all the inter-ministerial councils which prepare the most important decisions. In the Algerian affair, for example, all decisions were taken by the President after close and continuous consultation with the minister concerned, Louis Joxe, and with Michel Debré; if the latter finally endorsed a policy of Algerian independence, contrary to what he had hoped for, it was not out of ignorance or blind discipline but in the name of a positive conception of national duty and of the state. The balance is an unequal dualism in which the inequality safeguards the unity of decision while dualism implies a situation of total confidence and collaboration. General de Gaulle himself would have disapproved of the Prime Minister not fully assuming his responsibilities, especially the direction and co-ordination of government and parliamentary business.

The actual mechanism of the preparation and making of decisions at Executive level, after the inevitable hesitations at the start, explains this philosophy and the distribution of power. The Cabinet Councils, which under the Fourth Republic met at Matignon and were not attended by the President of the Republic, have been practically abolished. Michel Debré nevertheless organized at Matignon inter-ministerial councils for the purpose of preparing the smaller meetings at the Elysée; apart from those working in the strictly presidential sector of defence and foreign affairs, the technical advisers from the Elysée were not invited. Georges Pompidou seemed to have broken with this practice when he was Prime Minister: from then on, the technical advisers of the Head of State were present at all the important meetings convened by the Prime Minister. Most of the time, the decisions are made in the restricted council at the Elysée: as in Great Britain, these interministerial committees, limited in each case to a few of the highest officials, tend to strip the government of its theoretical power of collective decision, even of preliminary discussion.[17] Georges Pompidou, when he became President, even went so far as to impose a sort of British Cabinet system, by excluding the Secretaries of State from the meetings of the Council of Ministers.

A meeting point for the coalition parties under the Fourth Republic, the Council of Ministers was certainly more lively and more important. It was here that the Government negotiated its policy. Now, under the system of majority government which has prevailed since 1962, policy is decided at the highest level of responsibility. The Council of Ministers now seems to have the power of approval rather than of actual decision. The famous practice of the 'confessional' is the extreme illustration of this new state of affairs: each time a decision of capital importance is made – for example, in September 1959 on the autodetermination of Algeria, in 1962 on the election of the President by direct universal suffrage and the referendum relating to this, in 1968 on the refusal to devalue the franc – General de Gaulle, in the Council of Ministers, asked each minister in turn to express not his advice, for the decision had already been taken, but his approval or disapproval. With Georges Pompidou the style has changed but the substance has not.

THE EXECUTIVE AND LEGISLATIVE BRANCHES

The Prime Minister is responsible for the good relations of the Executive with parliament and with its supporters in parliament. It is in this respect that he may be seen as the 'leader of the majority'. When Georges Pompidou managed to group together at Matignon in 1966-7, in the *Comité d'action pour la Ve République*, the representatives of all the different groups composing the majority and to lead them united into the first round of the general election, he obviously appeared as leader of a majority, which seemed far from lacking in cohesiveness despite its diversity. At this point the possibility of a permanent delegation of the majority attached to the government was evoked. But immediately after the general election of March 1967 this delegation could not be constituted. Towards the end of September, before Parliament reassembled, the Prime Minister held talks with the presidents of the parliamentary groups, the *Union des démocrates pour* *la Vᵉ République* and the *Fédération nationale des Républicains indépendants*, Henri Rey and Raymond Mondon, and announced that he would receive the committees of the two groups, first separately, then together. Following this, the Républicains indépendants stressed that the separate reception of each of the two groups taking place before the full meeting of the two groups' committees underlined their desire to preserve their own autonomy and their refusal to accept a permanent delegation attached to the majority.[18] The relations between the Prime Minister and the Républicains indépendants had deteriorated from the very beginning of this third legislature, because the executive had used orders in council to take decisions of an economic and social nature without previous consultation. Above all, the U.D.Vᵉ had proposed to the Républicains indépendants the constitution of a permanent delegation in which they would have been represented in proportion to their numbers in parliament but whose decisions would have been binding. They did not intend to lose their right to vote as they wished, nor to disappear in the 'majority of the majority': they were in favour of free joint consultations but refused to commit themselves further. *La Nation* nevertheless congratulated itself on the final agreement on the procedure for consultations, namely twice-monthly meetings of groups first individually, then together, between the groups' committees and the Prime Minister. Thanks to this process which 'avoids the possibility of their outbidding one another', so the gaullist daily paper claimed, 'the groups in the majority will become used to living together and this symbiosis, which corresponds to the majority trend we have recently seen in the country, will perhaps open the way to a wider regrouping in line with the nature of things'.[19] After the elections of June 1968 and until the departure of Maurice Couve de Murville one year later, the procedure of periodic reunions held by the Prime Minister with the committees of the groups was once again adopted by all concerned.[20] Since the presidential election and the widening of the majority to include the *Centre démocratie et progrès* of Jacques Duhamel, in June 1969, the question of the organization of the parliamentary groups within the majority has been resolved, though their regrouping into one single political formation is still awaited.[21] Moreover, the problem has become less acute because the leaders of the different political trends within the majority, notably Valéry Giscard d'Estaing and Jacques Duhamel, are now in the government. The direct relations between the three parliamentary groups involved can thus remain very limited without either interfering with government action or jeopardizing the cohesion of the majority in Parliament.

The essential contacts between the Executive and the Legislative are made finally through the most important group in the majority.

In the course of time a whole web of relations has been woven between the gaullist group and the government, a network of men on Christian-name terms with friendships dating back over twenty-five years; a functional network too, brought into action by successive Prime Ministers.[22] Some men, carefully chosen, play a vital role in these relationships. First of all, the minister charged with managing the government's relations with Parliament, who attends the meetings of the executive committee and the meetings of the parliamentary group; he is a sort of French version of the British Chief Whip and has the same duties; his task is to avoid disputes, to anticipate and smooth out difficulties, to encourage compromises, to ensure discipline; he can ask for the presence of any minister, even the Prime Minister if necessary, before the group or its executive committee; he can press the government for the modification of texts initially proposed, if this is necessary. He works in close collaboration with the Prime Minister whom he sees every morning. It is indicative of a certain political style that for a long while this post was filled by a Secretary of State, Pierre Dumas; not until after the general election of March 1967 was it entrusted to a Minister of State, who knew the gaullists especially well since he was general secretary of the Républicains sociaux – namely Roger Frey. As far as the gaullist deputies are concerned, the person directly in charge of relations with the government is obviously the president of the gaullist group. The least disciplined of all, Raymond Schmittlein, who had to do business with the most dogmatic of the Prime Ministers, Michel Debré, had to recognize that the latter had given him easy access to the head of his cabinet and he was thus kept well informed. The basic mechanism between the government and the majority of its majority is clearly the executive committee of the group, a body fairly limited in size so that frank discussions and secret bargaining can take place amongst them, but a body sufficiently representative for the whole group normally to ratify its actions. But no minister, deputy or group is exempt or excluded from participating in talks between the Executive and the Legislative. Since October 1959, on the initiative of Michel Debré, the Prime Minister has made a habit of attending several times in each session the full meeting of the group. Georges Pompidou multiplied these personal contacts with the gaullist deputies, whom he invited regularly to cocktails at Matignon or, in regional sub-groups, to dinners there. He has made a definite innovation at the Elysée by continuing this practice since his accession to the Presidency. The Prime Minister, whoever he may be, is always present at the yearly parliamentary 'study days' of the group, and ends the discussion by a closing speech. As for the ministers themselves, since 1962 they have ceased to give their explanations to the Assembly committees alone: they have now made a practice of widening their audiences to include the specialized study groups or the full meeting of the gaullist group. 'It is evident that a system of discussion has been really firmly established between the government and the entire parliament', confirmed the president of the Assembly – then Jacques Chaban-Delmas who had criticized Michel Debré's attitude – back in January 1963.[23]

The relationships between the government and the majority have contributed greatly to this. Not that the government has granted all the demands of its majority as to the ways and means of installing consultation. During the parliamentary study days at Pornichet in September, 1961, René Tomasini suggested the setting up of parliamentary secretaries to the government similar to those in Great Britain, who, while adapting themselves to governmental tasks, participate in each ministry in the preparation of bills and ensure a better liaison between the government and the majority. But this met with a veto from General de Gaulle who was opposed to the overlapping of responsibilities and powers. A proposal was made by the U.D.R. group in July 1968 and taken up by Georges Pompidou in the parliamentary study days at La Baule that September, to designate within the group teams of specialists, each charged with maintaining a permanent contact with a member of the government. This proposal was similarly rejected by the Prime Minister, Maurice Couve de Murville, who was not anxious to hinder his own action or that of his ministers by instituting what some people called 'committees of supervision'.[24]

A CASE-STUDY: THE HIGHER EDUCATION ACT (1968)

The study of the passing of an important law is a good way of grasping in concrete terms this permanent interaction of the government and its majority. The example of the law on higher education of November 7, 1968 shows that the discipline imposed at the final vote does not preclude the possibility of preliminary debate, which can be very lively. We must add that the above matter touched on some of the most burning political questions, those of the May 1968 crisis, the fact that the government's case was defended by a 'convert', Edgar Faure, and not by one of the first-generation gaullists. Moreover, he was publicly reproached for this during the parliamentary study days at La Baule (September 10–12, 1968) by Alexandre Sanguinetti who reminded the Minister of Education that he was 'a man of the Fourth Republic', to which the Minister replied, 'as an historian, I cannot dispute that fact. However, I feel no twinge of remorse. I find that a man of the Fourth Republic has fully understood General de Gaulle'.[25]

There was a certain tension between the Minister of Education and the U.D.R. deputies, who met together for the study days at La Baule.

The U.D.R. group set up their ad hoc working groups or 'parliamentary action groups' to examine important pressing reforms. The group dealing with 'university reform' had as its president Michel Habib-Deloncle and as chairman the rector* Capelle; the general secretary of the U.D.R., Robert Poujade, put forward the group's point of view at its full sitting, in the presence of the Prime Minister, the Minister of Education and Georges Pompidou. But André Fanton, one of the deputies for Paris, summed up the views of many of the gaullists in the following words, addressed to the Minister of Education: 'We feel that the policy that is being envisaged is very different from what we expected.' On the intervention of Georges Pompidou, the matter was finally sent back to Paris for further study by the group. The study days simply concluded with a provisional statement that was not put to the vote. On the whole, the gaullist deputies were worried about the politicization of the universities and many of them wanted some kind of selection for entry to the institutions of higher education. 'The task facing Mr Edgar Faure is a worthy one but very difficult,' declared Robert Poujade, General Secretary of the U.D.R. 'We have sometimes complicated this task, but that is what democracy is: we have debates and discussions, and this helps things to move forward.'

Some days later, on September 17th, the Minister of Education held a three-hour discussion in the Assembly with the U.D.R. deputies. He began by reminding the gaullist deputies firmly but discreetly that the action of the government depended on the will of the Elysée and not of the Palais-Bourbon: 'I will remain at my post,' he said, 'so long as I have the confidence of General de Gaulle.' Indeed, he only lost his portfolio when the General retired in May–June 1969. Before that, he altered nothing in his bill, nor did he change his opinion on selection, 'I refuse to accept malthusianism'; nor on political activity in the university, 'When people ask us for liberty, must we immediately speak in terms of refusal or limitation?'; but he gave the deputies some assurance, 'I will never allow a red flag or a black flag to be raised on a building of which I am in charge'; and, above all, he promised the deputies a full and detailed discussion, announcing that he would ask the government not to use the vote bloqué ('block vote') on the debate in the Assembly. 'The second meeting between the U.D.R. group and Mr Edgar Faure was less tense than the first,' *Le Monde* declared.[26]

The Association for a Modern University, a parallel organization of the U.D.R. led by Léo Hamon and F. G. Dreyfus, examined the proposed bill on September 28th and 29th. It was approved by the

*Translator's note: the French equivalent of the English Vice-Chancellor.

organization but subject to 'amendments' which were not mere points of detail: they were against the equal representation of staff and students on the university councils, advocating a threefold division – a third of the places to be given to professors, a third to other teachers not necessarily members of the university in question, the remaining third to the students; they were in favour of the election of the presidents of the councils for four or five years – not renewable; voting should be compulsory for staff and students alike.[27]

The day before the debate was to take place in the Assembly, the Minister of Education, who stuck to his position, was received by General de Gaulle, in the presence of the Prime Minister, Maurice Couve de Murville. The government still firmly maintained that there should be no selection and that political and trade union activities should be allowed in the university; at the same time, it rejected the compulsory vote but negotiated and finally accepted a compromise based on the compulsory constitution of a quorum for the election of student representatives.[28] Furthermore, the Minister of Education agreed to renounce his principle of equal staff-student representation by giving regular titular teachers half the seats in the council, the other half being divided amongst the other categories of teachers or university personnel and the students; the professors finally gained a 60 per cent representation in relation to the other full-time teachers. The most interesting point here is the way in which this compromise was reached: on the one hand, within the committee for cultural, family and social affairs – that is to say before a united body of the majority and opposition members – and, on the other hand, within the U.D.R. parliamentary group, in the presence of the Prime Minister and the Minister of Education. The general secretary of the U.D.R., Robert Poujade, vigorously defended the compulsory student vote; the Prime Minister politely but firmly emphasized that, since the basic aim of the bill was to introduce more democratic administrative procedures within the university, it was not right to go against the spirit of the reform by imposing participation instead of encouraging it. He called for unity in the majority and advised it to be wary of taking up positions on the subject that might appear reactionary. Roger Frey, the Minister of State responsible for co-ordinating the relations of the government with parliament, asked the Minister of Education to meet the group to discuss the details of the compromise concerning the representation of students and teachers. Meanwhile, the Républicains indépendants had pronounced their wholehearted agreement with the bill.[29]

'In negotiations such as these,' concluded the editorial of *La Nation*, 'there must be neither winner nor loser. . . . Certainly, the government has, in accordance with its responsibilities, demonstrated quite clearly the limits beyond which it cannot go without endangering the very spirit of the bill. But the government has also shown a certain understanding of the anxieties expressed by men whose loyalty cannot be questioned. The text which will be voted on is the result of collaboration between the government and the Assembly.' [30]

By 441 votes to none – the communists and six gaullist deputies including Christian Fouchet, Alexandre Sanguinetti and Raymond Triboulet had abstained – the Higher Education Bill was finally adopted, without the government having had to resort to a vote of confidence or to impose a block vote. In order to win over the majority, the problem had had to be discussed during the study days of the parliamentary group, in a specialized university movement inspired by the U.D.R., in several full meetings, in the political committee of the parliamentary group, and finally in the parliamentary committee, before the debates were held and the bill voted upon in session. General de Gaulle indirectly, the Prime Minister directly and all the leaders of the U.D.R. were involved in the matter: former ministers, educational experts, the president of the group, the general secretary.

RELATIONS WITH THE U.D.R.

Apart from the periodic meetings of the committee of the Républicains indépendants group and of certain full meetings of the group with the Prime Minister or another minister, the contacts between the *Fédération nationale des Républicains indépendants* and the government were kept to a minimum until June 1969. It was known that the F.N.R.I. had gone so far as to exclude from the meetings of the party leaders the R.I. ministers, who were thus considered as being on leave from their party. As the minority of the majority, the Républicains indépendants remained aloof in the face of a power which escaped their control even if some of them played a role therein. Obviously the same cannot be said of the U.D.R. Since February–March 1959, the ministers belonging to the gaullist movement can at the same time sit on the party executive; only one incompatibility exists, which was imposed by General de Gaulle and respected after his departure, that the general secretary of the movement cannot at the same time hold a government post. [31] A 'Stendhalian hero' was how Albin Chalandon described the general secretary of the U.D.R., as depicted by the executive committee of the movement in January 1968 which credited him with seven essential qualities: personal authority and a past closely linked with the gaullist movement, though he would not necessarily have to be a 'veteran' gaullist; an obvious willingness to widen the movement; qualities of leadership, organization and representation; a certain independence towards the different trends within the movement; good relations with the militants, the leaders, the deputies and the government, without appearing either as a rival or as a representative of the government and of the Prime Minister; an ability to be aware of the divisions in the executive committee of the movement and to take them into account; the impossibility of being a member of the government. . . .[32] Until 1967, the ministers over-whelmed the movement with their presence and their authority. Less oppressive since the reform of the statutes at Lille, this ministerial presence is nevertheless still visible. Indeed in the Fifth Republic, as the years have gone by, the rostrum of the gaullist party has gradually gathered practically all the members of the Council of Ministers. For indeed, the gaullists now have the vast majority of seats within the government – 26 out of 31 in July 1968 – and as the U.D.R. has widened its membership, it has integrated first of all some 'gaullist' leaders, who were not however members of the U.D.R., the former Prime Ministers Georges Pompidou and Maurice Couve de Murville, for example; then distinguished 'converts' such as Edgar Faure and Maurice Schumann. The representatives of the Elysée, who at one time came incognito to the U.N.R. meetings, as did Jacques Foccart, now take their place on the party rostrum. There are no longer any 'apolitical' technocrats as ministers as was the fashion in 1958: only André Malraux had been permitted not to present himself for election by universal suffrage in June 1968, all the other members of the Couve de Murville administration of July 13, 1968 were elected as deputies at this general election. Malraux left the government in June 1969.

Since then the party meetings – like those of the parliamentary group – have offered an opportunity for discussion between members of the government and leaders of the movement, who may be former ministers or even former Prime Ministers.[33] These meetings are no longer held at Matignon, as they had been in 1967 with Georges Pompidou, but at the U.D.R. headquarters, 123 rue de Lille.

THE END OF ANOMALIES?

It would seem now as if gaullism, having gained confidence from its repeated successes, had eliminated one by one the anomalies that seemed to characterize the movement in 1958, for example the anomaly of a political movement whose real leader did not wish to be associated with it, at least not publicly. General de Gaulle recognized the U.D.R. in 1967, after the Party Conference at Lille, and the members of his entourage were officially members of the party before the departure of the General in 1969.[34] Gone are the anomalies of 'technocrats' and 'apolitical' ministers, of gaullists rising to the rank of minister – even of Prime Minister – without ever having faced the nation at election time nor even having been active members of the gaullist party. Gaullism has abandoned its anti-party and anti-parliamentary tradition to conform to a more normal sequence of events: the gaullist progresses from the party to parliament and then, should the occasion arise, enters the government; moreover, those who have jumped the ladder fill in the missing rungs by becoming elected deputies and by participating in party life. Gone too is the anomaly of a purely parliamentary and governmental party: the U.D.R. machine now exists in its own right; political activism has once again become an essential element of party life. Last, but not least, the anomaly of a political movement dominated by the happy few, who became famous when they resisted defeat and the invading troops more than twenty years ago, has disappeared too: the change in personnel has taken place even at the top and a new gaullist ideal – the future of France, modernism, youth – seriously challenges the old type of hero and the traditional 'Companion'. The post gaullist era had already begun when de Gaulle was still present on the political scene.

Notes to Chapter 6

1. On Swiss television, *Le Monde*, February 25, 1969.
2. From I.F.O.P. Cf. *Sondages*, 1965, 4, pp. 47–9.
3. Press Conference, October 23, 1958, at the Hôtel Matignon.
4. Albin Chalandon, speech made at the first national council of the U.N.R., Palais d'Orsay, July 26, 1969, *U.N.R. bulletin de presse*, special number, p. 8.
5. 'Frenchwomen, Frenchmen,' he declared on television on November 7, 1962, 'on October 28th [referendum on the election of the President of the Republic by direct universal suffrage] you pronounced the final condemnation of the disastrous regime of party politics and showed your desire to see the new Republic carry on its task of progress, development and greatness. But, on November 18th and 25th, you are going to the polls to elect the deputies. Ah! May you see to it that the outcome of this second consultation is not in contradiction to the first one! Despite, in certain cases, local customs and partial views of things, may you, in selecting your deputies, confirm the choice you made regarding your destiny when you voted YES.'
6. Radio-Television broadcast, February 9, 1967. *La Nation*, special number, February 10, 1967.
7. Press Conference, November 27, 1967.
8. Press Conference, September 9, 1968.
9. Ronald Butt, *The Power of Parliament*, Constable, London, 1967, Chapter X, p. 468.
10. F. W. G. Benemy, *The Elected Monarch*, The Development of the

Power of the Prime Minister, Harvey & Co., London, 1965, Chapter VIII, p. 272.

11. In April 1962, when the Head of State replaced Michel Debré by Georges Pompidou once the Algerian problem had been settled, the central committee of the U.N.R. manifested its discontent by electing only in the *second* round the candidate put forward by the Elysée and Matignon, Louis Terrenoire, for the general secretaryship of the party (May 9, 1962). In July 1968, the disarray was even greater in the party, when Maurice Couve de Murville replaced Georges Pompidou, who was seen as the great victor of the June election.

12. Council of Ministers, January 22, 1969. It was not a denial but a qualification of a former statement necessitated by the interpretations given by the press to the declarations of Georges Pompidou. Cf. *L'Express* 916, January 27–February 2, 1969 and *La Nation*, January 23, 1969.

13. *Le Monde*, February 15, 1969 (statements on Swiss television). The idea of the subordination of the Prime Minister to the President of the Republic and not to parliament was presented to us as the cornerstone of the division of powers under the Fifth Republic, both by Michel Debré (January 20, 1965) and by Georges Pompidou (April 27, 1965).

14. Press Conference, September 9, 1968.

15. *La Nation*, January 20, 1969.

16. Cf. letter to *Le Monde*, November 4, 1965, in which Paul Reynaud reproached Pierre Mendès-France for having said that the opposition candidate in the December presidential election should, if he was elected, give the country a precise, concrete programme. It is not to the President but to the government, Paul Reynaud retorted, that the Constitution entrusts the task of governing the country.

17. Cf. Monica Charlot, *La Vie politique dans l'Angleterre d'aujourd'hui*, A. Colin, Paris, 1967, Chapters VII and XI (collection U2, No. 30).

18. *Le Figaro*, September 30, 1967.

19. 'Vers l'organisation de la majorité', editorial, *La Nation*, October 4, 1967.

20. *La Nation*, September 19, 1968, 'M. R. Mondon reçu par M. Couve de Murville'.

21. On this subject, cf. the hopes and fears of *La Nation*, editorial on 'le fait majoritaire', July 7 and 8, 1969.

22. Cf. Jean Charlot, *L'U.N.R.*, *étude du pouvoir au sein d'un parti politique*, A. Colin, Paris, 1967, pp. 178–184.

23. Interview by J. M. Royer, *Notre République* 68, January 24, 1963. It deals in particular with the preliminary debate on the Finance Law 1963 and with the discussion on the Special High Court.

24. Cf. editorial in *La Nation*, September 24, 1968.

25. *La Nation*, September 12, 1968; *Le Monde*, September 13, 1968. Edgar Faure also said, evoking in a more familiar tone his short stay in 1965 at the Ministry of Agriculture: 'It cannot be said of me that

I have not been a good friend. I have even, in the course of my public visits, suffered bad eggs on your behalf.'

26. September 19, 1968. Cf. too *La Nation*, September 18, 1968.

27. Cf. *La Nation*, October 2, 1968.

28. Quorum of 60 per cent. If this quorum cannot be constituted, the representation of the students is reduced in proportion to the difference between the actual number of participants and the 60 per cent required by the law. The first elections in 1969, after the law had been adopted, showed an average participation of approximately 55 per cent despite the boycott instructions of the principal movements of May 1968.

29. *Le Monde*, October 10, 1968.

30. 'La voix de l'unité', *La Nation*, October 9, 1968.

31. This is why Roger Frey, when he became a minister in February 1959, left the post of general secretary of the U.N.R. where he was replaced by Albin Chalandon. On the discussion at the central committee on the incompatibilities between ministerial and partisan duties. cf. Jean Charlot, *L'U.N.R.*, pp. 258–9.

32. *Le Monde*, January 11, 1968.

33. We quote Jean Charbonnel and Michel Habib-Deloncle as two of the most active party members among former ministers.

34. On the 'entourage', cf. Jean Charlot, *L'U.N.R.*, pp. 259–62.

PART THREE

PRESIDENTIAL GAULLISM

CHAPTER VII

De Gaulle

THE MAN OF STATURE

His stature surprised all those who met him for the first time and popular wit, quick to react, like the cartoonist, and to portray the famous in a word, immediately nicknamed him 'tall Charles'. 'We didn't even know that General de Gaulle was very tall,' André Malraux recalled.[1] And he was not the only Frenchman to be unaware of the fact in 1944; they knew only his voice over the waves, they still wrote his name with a single 'l', like the Gaul of their ancestors. 'The symbol enters the room,' Emmanuel d'Astier de la Vigerie recalled. 'He is even taller than we imagined him.'[2] In 1934 Paul Reynaud had also remarked that he was 'a tall lieutenant-colonel',[3] and Léon Blum two years later saw a man whose 'height, width and breadth were in a way gigantic';[4] 'a tall fellow in uniform, rather rugged', Anthony Eden noted, more prosaically.[5]

According to Léon Blum he was 'a blunt man'.[6] He was an activist, whose faith was in France and not in a party, but an activist none the less. He had the quiet assurance of those who have no doubts, the unlimited patience of the pedagogue, the superb intransigence of the man of action who firmly believes in his own judgment and vision. From 1933 to the war of 1939, in writing and in discussion, directly and indirectly, he pleaded unceasingly for the creation of a French armoured corps, the only means of checking Hitler's advance, with 'weary resignation' according to Paul Reynaud[7] and 'a suspicion . . . of disenchantment', according to Léon Blum; but weariness and disenchantment disappeared as soon as he began to make his case: 'He was hardly capable of comprehending that everyone did not embrace fully the conviction he possessed,' the leader of the Popular Front reflected.[8] Of Paul Reynaud, whose intelligence, talent and courage had struck him, de Gaulle wrote in his *Mémoires*: 'I met him, convinced him and henceforward worked with him.'[9] Of Léon Blum he noted his warmth but also his lack of authority: 'I soon realized that the president of the council, although our conversation had impressed him, would not move mountains.' [10]

The height, the uniform, the military deportment, the natural slowness of gesture, the unshakable assurance of the man made a great impression on the person with whom he conversed but kept at a respectful distance. He dominated things and people from his full height or else he retired; he did not discuss, he imposed – by his silence first of all: 'He asks no questions . . .,' remarked d'Astier; [11] 'Without a word,' Christian Pineau recounted, when speaking of his meeting with de Gaulle in London in 1942, 'he led me to an armchair, gestured to me to sit down, pushed a box full of cigars towards me, sat down himself, leant back in his chair, then looking me straight in the eyes, pronounced his first words, "Now, speak to me of France." ' [12]

'. . . In what way did he surprise me?' André Malraux wondered after his first meeting, and he replied, 'His strength first of all appeared to me in the form of his silence. . . . It was a sort of interior distance. . . . His silence was a question. . . . Despite his courtesy, one always seemed to be reporting to him.' [13] In *Le Fil de l'Epée*, de Gaulle himself said: 'Nothing heightens authority more than silence.' [14] The most important speeches of General de Gaulle – the appeal of June 18, 1940, the dramatic speeches of January 25, 1960 (the barricades in Algiers), of April 23, 1961 (the Algerian putsch), of May 30, 1968 (student and worker strikes and demonstrations in Paris and throughout France) – are all very short speeches. They last but a few minutes, just time enough to announce the decisions made and to summarize the situation in a few memorable words. Mention too must be made of the long, silent retreats in Colombey-les-deux-Eglises: 'Since everything stemming from the leader is immediately reverberated,' he wrote in *Le Fil de l'Epée*, 'he can create calm and draw attention provided he is silent . . . authority is worn away by waves of papers and floods of speeches.' [15]

Once the first astonishment had passed, some were satisfied with this haughty solitude and marvelled at it. François Mauriac was of the number and this was how he evoked the symbolic scene of the first encounter on September 12, 1944 in Paris of General de Gaulle and the guests coming from the National Resistance Committee (*Comité national de la Résistance*): '. . . How we were going to weep! De Gaulle would of course call to mind those who had been shot or tortured. What vengeance we would call forth! But this was not to be. . . . To have given one's life for France was natural, why make a fuss about it? The formation of the state, of the army, the continuation of the war, the need to force the allies to give France her rights in occupied Germany and when Germany capitulated – these were the problems. . . . An icy wind blew over us. Our deep disappointment was made of all the tears we had not shed. . . .' [16] 'I had invented many characters,' the novelist confided, 'but I had never, will you believe me, never seen a man of character really close to. Here was one . . . at last under my eyes, at once myth and flesh-and-blood, Shakespearian and contemporary, fully alive yet a part of history. . . .' [17]

The man of character was depicted by Captain de Gaulle as early as 1927 in a noble, rigorous latin style, when he addressed the students of the *Ecole Supérieure de Guerre*.[18] He is the man of storms, the leader, the man of character. A fighter who draws his strength from within himself and from events: 'Far from sheltering under the hierarchy, from seeking refuge in official texts, and by writing innumerable reports . . . he welcomes action with the pride of the master, for if he decides to intervene the affair becomes his alone; he delights in success provided he has deserved it and even if he gains no advantage from it, he accepts the responsibility of set-backs with a sort of bitter satisfaction.' He is attracted by difficulties, 'for it is in battling with them that he realizes himself. But whether he has vanquished or not, it is a matter that lies between the difficulty and himself. A jealous lover, he shares nothing that is given him, and he alone pays the price. He seeks, whatever happens, the bitter joy of being responsible'. [19] Lacking in discipline, full of pride, his superiors say, difficult, his subordinates complain; 'But when events take a serious turn, when danger looms ahead, when the fate of all calls suddenly for initiative, for a love of danger, for steadfastness, then the perspective changes and justice is rendered. A sort of ground-swell pushes forward the man of character. His advice is taken, his talents praised, his value recognized. For him, naturally, is reserved the difficult task, the major effort, the decisive mission. All he suggests is taken into consideration, all he asks granted. But he takes no advantage of this, acts handsomely when he is called on. He scarcely savours his revenge, for action absorbs him entirely.' [20] 'If de Gaulle were to be given exceptional powers – he was to say thirty years after having written these lines – to fulfil an exceptional task, at an exceptional time, this could not of course be done according to the normal procesure and ritual which are so normal that everyone is tired of them. The procedure would also need to be exceptional.' [21] De Gaulle in power, a 'new political universe' was necessary; as he confided to Louis Terrenoire three months after his return to power in June 1958: 'When I spoke to him of the rise of gaullism throughout the country,' Louis Terrenoire explains, 'he agreed,' then added, "There is, indeed, among the people a feeling of national anxiety. . . . But [the French] are absolutely unaware that France must, if she is to last, accede to a new universe." When de Gaulle is mentioned to them, they do not realize that he brings a new universe with him; they think he is assigning himself a place in some combination. There is the

Mendés-Mitterrand combination, there is therefore, they believe, the de Gaulle combination.' [22]

An aristocrat in a democracy, he forced Churchill's admiration and stimulated Roosevelt's biting sarcasm. The parliamentary world was disconcerted. 'General de Gaulle,' Jacques Dumaine noted in his *Journal* at the Liberation, 'says he has no wish to be designated as the head of the government by the Constituent Assembly. Thus he intends to take advantage of the psychological moment when they will be obliged willy-nilly to nominate him. He wants to leave himself elbow-room, and not allow himself to be bound by the platform of the *Délégation des gauches*. He intends to choose his own ministers and control the government's action'. [23] This is seen as an intolerable pretension; when de Gaulle departed on January 20, 1946, Jacques Dumaine simply remarked that 'the training of a soldier cannot be adapted to parliamentary practice'. [24]

De Gaulle as seen by himself, de Gaulle as seen by those who have approached him over the last forty years, de Gaulle as seen by his hagiographers and his biographers, and de Gaulle as seen by public opinion: these different pictures coincide to a remarkable extent, despite the different conclusions drawn from them. Authority seems to have been his essential trait, linked with energy, courage and disinterestedness. Those who voted for him in December 1965 put at the top of the qualities necessary for a President: independence from the parties and authority, whilst those who voted for François Mitterrand preferred a man nearer to the ordinary Frenchman 'and belonging to the left'. [25] 'The best known of all Frenchmen' was decidedly not an ordinary man.

FRANCE AND THE FRENCH

Was he thinking of himself when he wrote his noble tribute to Churchill: 'He seemed to me, from the beginning to the end of the dramatic events, like the great champion of a great cause, and the great performer in a great page of history'? Be that as it may, he himself played the man of character in history. He knew the weight of gestures and words. [26] He knew how to prepare his effects. [27] Thus conceived, the role of the leader eclipses all other facets of character, the leader's mask covers the man's face. 'You cannot govern with "buts",' Valéry Giscard d'Estaing will be told. Does this mean that de Gaulle knew no doubts or hesitations? Not at all. 'I have doubts,' he confided to Louis Jacquinot during the Algerian crisis, 'only fools never make mistakes.' [28] Sometimes he even publicly detailed these moments of doubt, when the road to be followed could not be clearly distinguished amid the hesitations, when the well-balanced mind was uncertain. 'Yes,' he confessed to Michel Droit on television, 'on May 29, 1968, I was tempted to withdraw. And at the same time I thought that if I left, the subversion that was threatening would gather force and sweep away the Republic. So, once more, I made up my mind.' 'You know,' he went on, 'during the last thirty years I have dealt with history and I have sometimes wondered if I should not abandon her. . . .' Then he spoke of September 1940 and the bloody clash between the French at Dakar; March 1942 and the schism brought about by the British within the Free French; January 1946 and his resignation from the presidency of the provisional government on account of the rise of the parties; 1954 and the end of the R.P.F.; December 1965 and his non-election as President on the first ballot – on this last occasion 'a wave of sadness nearly carried me away'.[29] But these confidences come *after* the events, the man of character cannot spend time on such effusions.

'Did it really move you,' Michel Droit asked him when speaking of the gaullist demonstration of May 30, 1968, 'that the French people should react in that way?' 'That goes without saying,' De Gaulle replied briefly.[30] 'Sadness', 'distress', 'anger' were evoked rarely, discreetly. In his letter to Vincent Auriol, for instance, on May 28, 1958, he declared: 'Those who, by a sectarianism which is foreign to me, may prevent me from getting the Republic out of difficulty once again while there is yet time, will shoulder a heavy responsibility. As for me, I shall have no choice, until my death, but to remain full of grief.' 'A man is a man,' he said at Cahors on May 18, 1962, 'and whatever his position, setbacks are setbacks for him, grief is grief and difficulties are difficulties. But France is France and she must be served.' On May 16, 1940, when he saw the pitiful convoys of refugees fleeing before the Germans, when he saw the army put to flight as he had warned, his whole being rose in anger. But this anger only served to reinforce his decision were it necessary: 'Ah! it's too stupid! The war has begun badly. Therefore it will have to go on. . . . What I have been able to do since then,' he said, 'was decided on that very day.' [31]

'Under an impassive, unperturbable demeanour he seemed to me,' Churchill said, 'to have a remarkable capacity for feeling pain.' [32] 'De Gaulle finds it difficult to shed a tear,' François Mauriac noted, [33] but the novelist was quick to seize 'this cry that this cold man does not hold back when, in his *Mémoires*, he comes to the epic struggle of Bir Hakeim (June 1942): "I thank the messenger, send him on his way, close the door, I am alone. Oh heart beating with emotion, sobs of pride, tears of joy!"' [34]

The whole of de Gaulle was linked to the France he loved, venerated and served as a son. He gave us the key to his feelings, his dreams, his acts, his life, in the first lines of the *Mémoires*: 'All my life,' he wrote, 'I have nurtured a precise image of France, inspired by both feeling and reason. What I have in me of sentiment naturally pictures France, like the fairy-tale princess or the madonna in the fresco paintings, as vowed to some superior, exceptional destiny. . . . If on cocasion,' he continued, 'her gestures and actions indicate mediocrity, I have the feeling of an absurd anomaly, stemming from the mistakes of the French and not from the genius of the nation. But the positive side of my mind convinces me that France is only truly herself when she is among the first, that only great tasks are liable to compensate for the leaven of dispersion that her people secretes within itself; that our country, such as it is, among others, such as they are, must if it is not to succumb to a mortal danger, aim high and stand upright. In a word, as I see it, France cannot be France without grandeur. . . .' [35]

All the elements were there – the fairy-tale princess of his infancy: 'Once upon a time,' he told the French in 1960, 'there was an old country, barded with custom and circumspection. Not long since the most peopled, the richest, the most powerful of the powerful countries it was, after great misfortune, as if shut in on itself. . . . It had little coal. It had no petrol. Its industry suffered from routine. Its agriculture was at a standstill. . . . Its population no longer increased. . . . With the doubt and bitterness that this situation inspired it with, towards itself, political, social and religious struggles did not fail to divide it. Two world wars had decimated it, ruined it, torn it asunder; many throughout the world wondered whether it would manage to pull itself together. Now this country, France, has recovered.' [36]

The madonna was there too – she who represents the image of the nation and of the Virgin, whom his mother, so he told us, venerated with a similar uncompromising passion: 'To our Lady France,' he cried one day, 'we have but one thing to say, and that is that nothing matters to us save her service. . . . We have nothing to ask of her save, perhaps, that on the day of freedom, she will deign to open to us her motherly arms that we may weep with joy, and on that day when death will come to take us away, she may bury us gently in her good and blessed ground.' [37] Now, and at the hour of our death . . . There is also in this passage at the beginning of the *Mémoires* the refusal of surrender, of mediocrity, of the withdrawal of France; the search for unity, the will to gather together all the French for a great aim which forces them to go beyond themselves, to silence their divisions; lastly he insisted on the force of circumstances, which must 'be taken as they are, for politics can only be founded on reality'.[38] The doctrine is in the likeness of the man, a universe of oppositions from which rises movement; a style in triple time, 'three-part time . . . comes as readily to him', Malraux says, 'as the horns of a dilemma to others'.[39] He condemned 'the cross-grained, the ill-tempered and the old grousers', while on the Forum in Algiers he proclaimed, 'How great, how beautiful, how generous is France.' [40] J. Touchard accurately remarks that General de Gaulle's metaphors are essentially of the sea. Apart from the typical classic images of the captain and his crew uniting their efforts to guide the boat through the tempests and between the rocks, or of the human tide sweeping down on liberated Paris, there is in the General's writings a fundamental opposition between the agitation on the surface of the water – the 'accidents', the élites – and the Olympian calm of the depths – the slow course of history, the people.[41] 'The wave is formed,' De Gaulle declared after the success of the R.P.F. in the municipal elections of October 1947. 'It will gather force and then break and when it does then the criticisms of enemies will be of no greater importance than spittle in the sea.' [42]

If on occasion he aspired to rest – for the leader becomes tired of the hair-shirt of solitude, and the melancholy which impregnates 'all that is noble' assails him [43] – General de Gaulle could not really leave the helm and would not find eternal peace aground. Who knows if his secret tragedy was not that destiny had denied him the hope of disappearing in the middle of the storm, Captain of the vessel France – after God?

THE GREAT SCHEME

No one can doubt the deep, total disinterestedness of General de Gaulle; his own interests were as nothing before the national interest. Therefore he bided his time and tried to solicit among the French a similar subordination of the individual to France. The gaullian political stage is the world, for political action and effort can only be conceived nationally. De Gaulle's every action was prompted by his belief in France as a first-ranking power in the concert of nations. An unusual view this. Foreign policy usually plays a very secondary role in the political life of countries and those political leaders who make it their chosen field are rare. Even then, they are usually idealists, seeking world peace – as Briand – or diplomats who are a failure when they try to apply their talents to other fields – as Anthony Eden, or Maurice Couve de Murville. De Gaulle was, on the contrary, a specialist gifted enough to play the part of a general practitioner. In 1967 he chose the holiday period to invite the French to reflect: 'In the normal run of things,' he told them, 'each of you, understandably, is absorbed by his personal life and by daily events, and only now and then do you take a general look at what may happen to our country. And yet everything depends on that. . . .' [44] Peace? No rose-coloured spectacles, no pious declarations of 'war on war': it must be fought for, for 'nothing, absolutely nothing, is as important to us as it is to rebuild, thanks to peace, our very substance, influence and power'.[45] Progress? It is the condition of grandeur and national independence: on the eve of the second ballot of the presidential election in 1965, when de Gaulle for the first time agreed to be interviewed on television by a journalist, he said, 'I have been credited with a phrase which I have never said and with greater reason have never thought – *"L'intendance suit"* [practical details will take care of themselves]. In fact, the French are responsible for France, but they are on earth, they have their lives to live; and for France to exist, Frenchmen have to exist. For France to be strong, the French must be prosperous.' [46] The practical details were not neglected, on the contrary, but the spirit remained that of the regimental colonel who sees to it that the food is satisfactory so that the morale of the troops does not suffer. The heart of the matter remained the strength of France and not the happiness of the French. For General de Gaulle, moreover, this distinction had little point, for his own happiness as a Frenchman stemmed from the success of France.

Consequently, everything was organized around national ambition. The gaullian vision of a President representing national unity, above ideologies, parties, interests and all that divides the French, is directly linked to the priority given to foreign affairs. The head of a state, seen from without, is the incarnation of his country in whose name he speaks and acts. Nothing must diminish his authority. The state is that which 'conditions all the rest',[47] for it is 'the guide and bulwark of the nation'. [48]

When he intervened during the crisis of May 1958, only two days after the Algerian coup, de Gaulle spoke first of the state: 'Its degradation,' he said, 'inevitably entails the estrangement of the associated peoples, the hesitation of the army in battle, the dislocation of the nation and the loss of independence.' [49]

His first care, when he came back to power, was to restore the authority of the state, just as, on August 25, 1944, when he at last entered liberated Paris he had refused to go immediately to salute the Resistance and the people of Paris at the Town Hall, but had first gone to take up his quarters at the War Ministry, rue St Dominique, and to visit the *Préfecture de police*. The government itself is conceived in terms of foreign policy. In 1945, de Gaulle provoked a crisis by refusing to the communists one of the three ministries that thirteen years later he was to refuse to Jacques Soustelle: 'They are,' he explained, 'the three levers which control foreign policy, namely: the diplomacy which expresses it, the army which upholds it, the police which backs it up.' [50] The Ministers of Foreign Affairs and of National Defence will be *his* ministers chosen primarily for their fidelity as gaullists, steeled in the Free French, and for their previous careers as technocrats rather than politicians. De Gaulle had already written in the very last pages of *Le Fil de l'Epeé*: 'There is no illustrious career in the armed forces which has not served some vast political scheme, no statesman's renown but has been enhanced by the prestige of national defence.' [51]

It is difficult to understand the misapprehension of those who imagined up until 1962 that de Gaulle had returned to power to solve the Algerian problem and that he would retire once the crisis was over. For when on June 13, 1958, he outlined publicly the policy which he considered essential: 'In the western world to which we belong, without necessarily confining ourselves to it, we must find *our* place, take *our* actions, with a view to serving at once the country and its security,' he could already foresee the objections and answered them himself when he said: 'Is all that not too much for us?' murmur those who have believed for so long that nothing can succeed, that in the end they hope that nothing will; those who have as their secret motto, that of Mephistopheles, the eloquent demon of the hopeless: 'I am the spirit that denies everything.' [52] He went on to describe the cards France held in her hand, if she managed to recover: a growing population, a renovated economy, 'new sources of energy', the Sahara, a strong army, the world awaiting recovery. In truth, fate seemed to dedicate General de Gaulle to the task of trying to obtain a great deal from limited resources; but this did not frighten the man who had known June 18, 1940, and of whom Churchill was to write, almost despite himself: 'I understood and admired, while I resented, his arrogant demeanour. Here he was – a refugee, an exile from his country under sentence of death, in a position entirely dependent upon the goodwill of the British Government, and also now of the United States. . . . He had no real foothold anywhere. Never mind; he defied all.' [53]

On September 24, 1958, only a few months after his return to power, General de Gaulle addressed a memorandum to President Eisenhower and to the British Prime Minister, Harold Macmillan, together with personal letters criticizing the inequality of the Allies within N.A.T.O. He proposed the setting up of a Western Directory, a troika comprising the United States, Great Britain and France. For the 'Realpolitik' means that in the government of the world the fact that there are some equals 'more equal than others' must be taken into account. There are the 'great powers', with a world-wide influence, and lesser powers whose sphere of influence is merely regional. The 'great powers' would decide on an equal footing their political and military strategy, including, in case of need, the recourse to atomic weapons. The 'lesser powers', through the voice of M. Fanfani, immediately protested at this distinction between the 'pillars' and the 'colonnettes' of the Alliance, and as in 1967 over the Common Market, in the Soames Affair, London and Washington did not even consider General de Gaulle's proposals. From that moment, de Gaulle gradually detached himself from N.A.T.O. – if not from the Alliance – for he considered that France must not run the risk of being drawn into war over a crisis in which she would have no part, no decision-making power and in which she might well disapprove of the attitude of the United States. In March 1959 de Gaulle took the fleet in the Mediterranean out of N.A.T.O.'s control; on November 3, 1959 – in his speech at the Military Academy – he declared: 'A country like France, should she wage war, must wage her own war. . . . Obviously, French defence might, in case of need, join with that of other countries . . . but it is absolutely vital that it should be our own defence force. . . . Were it to be otherwise . . . it would not be possible to maintain our state. . . .' De Gaulle announced that in consequence France must 'in the years to come' provide herself with a nuclear deterrent, immediately adding, 'You realize, as I do, the extent of this obligation, all that it will entail for us. From a national point of view we must be brave enough to look it in the face; the whole nation must be associated in it. . . . In the field of defence, it will be our major task in the years ahead.' [54] Less than two months before this speech, in his speech of September 16th, he had begun to settle the Algerian problem by opening the way to self-determination. He could therefore devote himself to what was for him essential, the military means of independence. One may note in passing that General de Gaulle did not wish to evade the issue as far as public opinion was concerned, even though he felt that this might lose votes. For him, there was no alternative: defence was vital and the country must be told this, whatever the political cost. Similarly, he was not deterred from being the cause of a new European crisis by the presidential election of 1965, thus reinforcing the candidature of Jean Lecanuet – who then managed to prevent de Gaulle's election on the first ballot. France's foreign policy was too serious a matter to wait upon an election. 'Hurrah for France', telegraphed de Gaulle, on February 13, 1960, to those who were responsible for the first French A-bomb explosion: 'As from this morning [France] is stronger and prouder, from the depths of my heart, I thank you. . . . The NO to Great Britain's entry into the Common Market on January 14, 1963 is closely linked to the French refusal of a multi-national atomic force under American command and Great Britain's agreement, at Nassau, to contribute its own nuclear weapons to this multi-national force and to rely for its rockets on the Americans. The third volume of the *Mémoires*, published in 1959, already defined General de Gaulle's European aim expressed later in the 'European Europe': Europe as a 'third force' between East and West, and which alone could enable France to hoist herself up to her proper rank, the first rank.

The great scheme? 'To collaborate with West and East, and contract, on one side or the other, the necessary alliances, without ever accepting any sort of dependence. . . . To bring together, politically, economically and strategically, the states bordering on the Rhine, the Alps, the Pyrénées; to make of this organization one of three planetary powers and, if necessary some day, the arbiter between the two camps: soviet and anglo-saxon.' [55] The Channel is thus a frontier which separates, and Great Britain is assimilated into the Washington block. The actions and declarations of Macmillan's and Wilson's governments did nothing, between 1963 and 1969, to shake General de Gaulle's opinion.

This is the main outline of General de Gaulle's international policy and of his defence policy. The gaullism of General de Gaulle can be summarized thus, but he was not really able to put it into practice until 1962 when the institutions had been reinforced, the Algerian problem solved. His tours of Eastern Europe and the underdeveloped countries, his condemnation of American policy in Vietnam; the severity he showed towards Great Britain, the attempt to establish a Franco-German European directory in the absence of a political European organization, at once non-integrated and more powerful, are all elements within the great scheme of the General.

It is not our task to go into details of this policy, nor to examine its outcome. Alfred Grosser in his *Politique extérieure de la Ve République* judges the results severely. On the positive side, he says, is prestige – prestige within France and without, prestige above all in the under-developed countries. 'One may wonder,' Alfred Grosser writes, 'whether prestige is not for General de Gaulle an aim in itself.' Other positive elements are the economic development of France within the Common Market and, perhaps, Franco-German reconciliation. 'But,' continues Alfred Grosser, 'the positive aspects are relatively few in comparison with the negative aspects': the destruction of a classical army – thereby weakening N.A.T.O. – in favour of a nuclear deterrent which few believe in, the refusal of a political Europe, the psychological isolation of France.[56]

In fact, the opinion one has depends essentially on whether or not one believes in the possibility of putting an end to the bi-polarization of the world today, and in the defence by each nation-state of its own interests. In his determination to restore French grandeur, General de Gaulle accentuated the importance of foreign policy in French political life. He offered the French people a 'hard' but 'beautiful' road, a 'difficult' but 'great' aim.[57] A great task – to be taken or to be left – as the General himself. 'I preserved the impression, in contact with this very tall, phlegmatic man: "Here is the Constable of France,"' [58] Churchill wrote, but he added: 'Clemenceau, with whom it was said he also compared himself, was a far wiser and more experienced statesman. But they both gave the same impression of being unconquerable

Frenchmen.' [59] Even at his funeral General de Gaulle played the part he had chosen. At Colombey-les-deux-Eglises his family, the Companions of the Liberation, the French people and the army accompanied him to his grave; at Notre-Dame de Paris the highest representatives of the French Commonwealth and of the world, of the rich and of the poor countries, came from the East and from the West to honour him. The great scheme was, for a few hours on a grey November day, a reality, perhaps a prophecy.

Notes to Chapter 7

1. André Malraux, *Antimémoires*, Gallimard, Paris, 1967, p. 124.
2. Emmanuel d'Astier de la Vigerie, *Les Grands*, De Gaulle . . . Gallimard, Paris, 1961, p. 81.
3. Paul Reynaud, *Mémoires*, Flammarion, Paris, 1960, Volume I, p. 421.
4. Léon Blum, *Œuvres*, A. Michel, Paris, Volume V, p. 115.
5. Anthony Eden, *Mémoires*, Plon, Paris, 1965, Volume III, p. 123.
6. Op. cit., p. 115.
7. Op. cit., p. 421.
8. Op. cit., p. 115.
9. Charles de Gaulle, *Mémoires de guerre*, Volume I: l'Appel, Plon, Paris, 1954 (livre de poche) p. 20.
10. Ibid., p. 29.
11. Op. cit., p. 81.
12. Christian Pineau, *La simple vérité: 1940–1945*, R. Julliard, Paris, 1960, p. 157.
13. Op. cit., p. 133.
14. Charles de Gaulle, *Le Fil de l'Epée*, Berger-Levrault, Paris, 2nd ed., 1944, pp. 67–8.
15. Ibid., p. 68.
16. François Mauriac, *De Gaulle*, B. Grasset, Paris, 1964, pp. 19–21.
17. Ibid., p. 18.
18. Three lectures – 'war activity and the Head of State', 'on character' and 'on prestige' – given in 1927 and written in *Le Fil de l'Epée* in 1932.
19. *Le Fil de l'Epée*, pp. 42–4.
20. Ibid., p. 46.
21. General de Gaulle, Press Conference, May 19, 1958.
22. Louis Terrenoire, *De Gaulle*, Témoignage pour l'histoire, A. Fayard, Paris, 1964, p. 58. The interview in which General de Gaulle made these remarks took place on March 5, 1958.
23. Jacques Dumaine, *Quai d'Orsay, 1945–1951*, Julliard, Paris, 1955, p. 31.
24. Ibid., p. 57.
25. Opinion poll of Sofres in November 1965: 'Among the following

characteristics, which do you think are those that an ideal President of the Republic should have?' 1. Close similarity to the average Frenchman: 54 per cent (voters for General de Gaulle = 49 per cent, voters for François Mitterrand = 64 per cent). 2. Independent of all political parties: 47 per cent (de G. = 50 per cent, F.M. = 38 per cent); left wing: 13 per cent (de G. = 1 per cent, F.M. = 62 per cent); right-wing: 9 per cent (de G. = 14 per cent, F.M. = 1 per cent); centrist: 19 per cent (de G. = 22 per cent, F.M. = 10 per cent). Another Sofres opinion poll, in 1964, described General de Gaulle as follows: 1. Authoritarian: 73 per cent. 2. Dynamic: 63 per cent. 3. Courageous: 61 per cent. 4. Honest: 58 per cent. 5. Able to keep up the prestige of France: 56 per cent.

26. *Le Fil de l'Epée*, p. 67.
27. Ibid., p. 66.
28. Quoted by J. R. Tournoux, *La Tragedie du General*, Plon, *Paris-Match*, Paris, 1967, p. 368. 'When, my General, will your life be freed from responsibilities, from anxieties, from torment?' Louis Jacquinot asked General de Gaulle. The latter replied: 'When I am dead.'
29. Radio-Television interview with General de Gaulle and Michel Droit at the Elysée Palace on June 7, 1968.
30. Ibid.
31. Charles de Gaulle, *Mémoires*, Volume I, pp. 42–3.
32. Winston Churchill, *The Second World War*, Volume II: *Their Finest Hour*, Book I: 'The Fall of France', p. 189.
33. François Mauriac, op. cit., p. 89.
34. Ibid., p. 124.
35. Charles de Gaulle, *Mémoires*, Volume I, p. 5.
36. Charles de Gaulle, Radio-Television broadcast, June 14, 1960.
37. Charles de Gaulle, *Mémoires*, Volume II, pp. 152–3.
38. Charles de Gaulle, Radio-Television interview, December 15, 1965.
39. André Malraux, *Antimémoires*, p. 17.
40. Charles de Gaulle, *Discours d'Alger*, June 4, 1958, and Radio-Television broadcast of July 12, 1961.
41. Cf. Jean Touchard, Lecture of 1962–3 at the Political Institute in Paris, on 'le mouvement des idées politiques dans la France, contemporaine', pp. 167–8.
42. Charles de Gaulle, Press Conference, November 12, 1947.
43. Charles de Gaulle, *Le Fil de l'Epée*, pp. 77–8.
44. Charles de Gaulle, Radio-Television broadcast, August 10, 1967.
45. Ibid.
46. Radio-Television interview with General de Gaulle, by Michel Droit, December 14, 1965.
47. Charles de Gaulle, Radio-Television broadcast, June 13, 1958.
48. Charles de Gaulle, Radio-Television broadcast, May 8, 1961.
49. Charles de Gaulle, Statement, May 15, 1958.
50. Charles de Gaulle, Radio broadcast, November 17, 1945.
51. Charles de Gaulle, *Le Fil de l'Epée*, p. 169. He uses the same words

again on November 3, 1959, at the end of his speech to the pupils of the French Military Academies.

52. Charles de Gaulle, Radio-Television broadcast, June 13, 1958.
53. Winston Churchill, *The Second World War*, Volume IV: *The Hinge of Fate*, Book II: 'Africa Redeemed', p. 611.
54. Charles de Gaulle, Speech, November 3, 1959 given to the student-officers of the Centre des Hautes Etudes militaires and of the three Ecoles de Guerre, at the Military Academy.
55. Charles de Gaulle, *Mémoires*, Plon, Paris, 1959, Volume III, pp. 179–80.
56. Alfred Grosser, *La Politique extérieure de la France*, Seuil, Paris, 1965, pp. 155 sqq. (Collection Jean Moulin).
57. Charles de Gaulle, Radio-Television broadcast, June 13, 1958.
58. Winston Churchill, *The Second World War*, Volume II: *Their Finest Hour*, Book I: 'The Fall of France', p. 189.
59. Ibid., Volume IV: *The Hinge of Fate*, Book II: 'Africa Redeemed', p. 611.

CHAPTER VIII

Pompidou

THE RISE TO POWER

'With de Gaulle – for France,' 'With France – for the French.' This subtle change in the electoral slogans illustrates and symbolizes the change in the leadership of the French state, the transformation in the political style from the heroic gaullism of de Gaulle to the more down-to-earth gaullism of Pompidou. On the eve of the presidential election, Georges Pompidou was asked the following question by Raymond Tournoux: 'If you win the election, what will be your policy in the *domaine réservé*?' * He replied, 'In my opinion there was never any *domaine réservé*. There is a tradition dating back more than a hundred years in France, which I uphold, that the President of the Republic attaches special importance to foreign policy and national defence. But how can he ignore the other areas of policy? The well-being of the French nation is important, but so is the individual Frenchman.' [1]

If the 'reserved' field of policy means the area of policy the President is particularly interested in, then for Georges Pompidou this would be education rather than national defence. 'I am the first academic to assume the highest office of the Republic,' Pompidou stated in his opening speech to parliament.[2] De Gaulle was a soldier, Pompidou a university man. Like Charles de Gaulle, he was asked whether he thought that intelligence was nothing without action. Pompidou replied, 'One can be intelligent without necessarily engaging in action,' and he immediately added, 'but if one chooses action, it is better to be intelligent as well.' [3]

His father, Léon Pompidou, taught Spanish in a boys' secondary modern school, his mother taught maths in the adjacent girls' school; Pompidou himself won the first prize in Greek translation in the national secondary school competition, the *concours général*, was eighth in the entrance examination to the *Ecole Normale Supérieure*,

* Translator's note: the field of policy reserved for the President.

was top in the national university examination, the *agrégation*, in French and Classics and holds the diploma of the Institute of Political Science. 'Apparently,' he confides, 'when I was seven or eight years old, I was asked what I wanted to do, and replied: Normale Supérieure. I didn't know what it really was then, but I was brought up with the idea of going there. And I did.' [4]

In his first important official speech as President, at Ajaccio, in the bicentenary year of the birth of Napoleon, Georges Pompidou recalled the role of scholarships in the destiny of Napoleon, who was 'a King's scholar in 1779 at the college of Autun, where he learnt French, then at the school of Brienne, where he stayed for five years, and in 1784 at the Military School in Paris'.[5] Georges Pompidou was similarly a 'state scholar'. To the French television viewers Pompidou, then Prime Minister, said in 1967, 'Where I have been perhaps the most successful, or what has given me the greatest satisfaction, is the field of education.' And he recalled that under his own government, in the space of five years alone, he had seen the erection of more institutions of Higher Education than had existed in France on his accession to the Premiership. In May 1968 this somewhat rash self-satisfaction was quoted back at him. But the events of May, far from turning against him, proved to be the final point of departure in his ultimate accession to the Presidency.

For Georges Pompidou was not for long satisfied with teaching, be it at the Lycée Henri IV. Not that he was burning with ambition. 'His appetite for the future,' writes Pierre Rouanet, 'is on a scale which befits his stature, but it is balanced by his enjoyment of the present.' [6] He knows how to wait, but he is not without desire and hates to be bored. The friendships he struck up at the Ecole Normale have served him well: it was through René Brouillet that, on October 1, 1944, he entered the cabinet of General de Gaulle, then President of the provisional government. The General was looking for 'someone who has passed the agrégation and who knows how to write. . . .' Georges Pompidou was at that time thirty-three years old. After the General's departure in 1946, Georges Pompidou was nominated Master of Petitions at the Council of State. He did not, however, leave the General. In fact he was to draw closer to him by being de Gaulle's principal private secretary during the whole R.P.F. era. When the R.P.F. disbanded in 1954, René Fillon, its treasurer, found a place for Georges Pompidou in the Rothschild Bank. Two years later he became its director-general. 'The real value of the agrégation, Pompidou said at a later date, 'goes far beyond the range of work for which successful candidates are eligible. For a person who is capable of succeeding in the agrégation will leave his mark wherever he is, and find a place somewhere, whatever his qualifications may be.' [7]

When de Gaulle returned to power, on June 1, 1958, it was obvious that he would again call on Georges Pompidou to be his principal private secretary. Through university, the grands corps, high finance and years of active discreet collaboration, Pompidou had learned his lesson and proved his worth. Only for six months would he take up office again, in the shadow of the General, now Head of the Government. In 1962 he became publicly, officially and directly second-in-command, General de Gaulle's Prime Minister. The uninitiated were surprised at this, in that the move was without precedent. According to the polls conducted by I.F.O.P., 78 per cent of the French did not know whether they were satisfied or dissatisfied. Pompidou quickly adapted himself to the new situation and turned it to his advantage, as he had done at each stage in his career. On March 14, 1965 he was elected town councillor for Cajarc, in the Lot, and in March 1967 he became deputy for his native Cantal: his career was beginning to run a 'normal' course. When in July 1968 General de Gaulle put Maurice Couve de Murville in his place, in order to keep him 'in reserve for future service', Pompidou had already been successful in three general elections – 1962, 1967 and 1968 – and had broken all the French length of Premiership records: six years, two months and twenty-five days. André Malraux addressed these words to him: 'Monsieur the deputy for Cantal, I drink to your future.' And on June 15, 1969 Georges Pompidou was elected nineteenth President of the French Republic, by direct universal suffrage, in succession to General de Gaulle.

THE COUNTRYMAN FROM THE AUVERGNE

Charcoal-grey eyebrows, thick and bushy, in the shape of an upturned V, a double chin, thinning hair crowned by a hat, a cigarette drooping from his mouth – that is how the caricaturist Faizant sees Georges Pompidou, a typical Frenchman who has 'made the grade' and still has something of his native Auvergne. For François Mauriac, in 1963 at least, he represents Raminagrobis – sharpened claws in a velvet paw. The novelist had already glimpsed the man of character in Pompidou, at a time when he was frequently and plausibly spoken of as a puppet; 'Pompidou? Why, for the last twenty years he has come promptly whenever the General has rung for him!'

He shows a certain shyness, which stems from the fact that his responsibilities were awarded on merit and not because of some birthright, a success based on qualifications and accomplishments. It is not so easy, psychologically, to tread the road from Montboudif to Paris, to rise from the lycée at Marseilles to the Hotel Matignon, then to the Elysée Palace. In front of the television cameras, he wrings his hands feverishly. But his expression always remains calm and leaves one with an impression of strength and steadfastness. He keeps his self-control, however dramatic the situation may be. His 1940 war comrades were struck by his 'remarkable physical control when faced with danger. Even if there was an enemy bombardment, he carried on with his task. He has an outstanding capacity to face up to things, once the forces start moving against him.' [8] Michel Debré, when faced with the putsch of the Algerian generals in April 1961, panicked to the point of making ridiculous statements, whereas Georges Pompidou remained unperturbed during the storm of May 1968. He told General de Gaulle and made it quite clear to the country that, come what may, he would not resign. When the Head of State left secretly for Baden-Baden on May 29th, not only leaving his Prime Minister in the dark as to his intentions but also leading him to believe that there was a possibility he might not return, Pompidou was ready for every emergency and prepared to make an on-the-spot announcement of his candidacy for the Presidency should the occasion arise.[9] For millions of Frenchmen, François Mauriac says, this represented a unique case of 'a statesman that they had seen come into being, grow and develop as it were before their very eyes, thanks to television, and who had then won the game in the worst attack the regime had ever suffered, for it was on the brink of collapse'.[10] During the last half of May 1969, when all the opinion polls predicted his defeat by Alain Poher in the second ballot of the presidential election, he reassured his supporters and reminded them that action could still shatter all the forecasts of the polls.

It is true that he enjoys a good fight. When he was Prime Minister, Michel Debré preached the public interest to the gaullists and other French citizens, whereas Georges Pompidou preferred to strike hard against the opposition leaders. But he also knows how to negotiate when necessary: this was proved when on May 25 and 26, 1968 he headed the thirty-six-hour talks, in the rue de Grenelle, with the trade union representatives of ten million strikers. He knows how to make concessions without weakening his authority. When the student demonstrations broke out, and until May 11th, he was on an official trip to Afghanistan. 'I know,' he confided six months later, 'it is only too easy to say afterwards: "This is what I would have done if I had been there." I wasn't there. On the previous Wednesday, the Minister of Education had promised in public to reopen the Sorbonne two days later. I don't think, knowing myself, that I would have made such a promise. I am certain of that. But what was done, was done. What I can guarantee is that once made, I would not have broken my promise, whatever the risks involved. And whatever the President of the Republic might have thought of these risks, I would have answered: "My General, we can't go back on our word." In circumstances such as these, decisions must be taken, not negotiated. . . .' [11] Almost as soon as he had been appointed to the Premiership in 1962 he ran the risk of General de Gaulle asking him to resign for supporting the reprieve of General Jouhaud. 'Apart from the limited exceptions laid down in the Constitution,' Pompidou declared in the National Assembly in 1964, 'none of the President's acts are valid without the second signature of the Prime Minister. And I ask you to believe me when I say that I attach just as much importance to mine as the President does to his.'

It would have been underestimating this grandson of country peasants, this son of primary school teachers, this intellectual, to have thought that he would be content with a minor role, without regard for conscience and self-respect. He confided after more than six years in government that the most difficult thing to learn was not how to speak from the platform at public meetings, nor how to appear on television, but how to show patience, perseverance and above all indifference to criticism.[12]

THE CONTINUITY AND EXPANSION OF THE INSTITUTIONS

Political continuity – from General de Gaulle to Georges Pompidou – is most evident in institutional matters. Georges Pompidou has certainly not failed to stress the fact that he possesses neither the stature nor the historical dimension of de Gaulle: 'The General knew that people would follow him,' he has declared. 'The new President will have to be able to convince the people.'[13] The style has changed, the emphasis now being placed on dialogue rather than on arbitral decision. But the exercise of power has not been fundamentally affected in so far as Georges Pompidou knows that someone has to make the final decision, and considers that this supreme responsibility lies with the President of the Republic, the only man in the country elected directly by universal suffrage. 'With a view to attracting public opinion,' he said in an article in *L'Express* in 1967, 'M. Giscard d'Estaing questions what he calls "isolated power" and demands what he calls "dialogue". He is too intelligent not to realize that a real political decision cannot please everybody and that in the last resort it depends on one man and one alone.'[14]

While he was Prime Minister, Georges Pompidou was all too aware that he was only the second-in-command. 'Under the Fifth Republic,' he wrote after six years in office, 'the Prime Minister does not bear the ultimate responsibility. This rests in the Head of State who lays down the broad lines of policy, and makes the final decisions. The Prime Minister undoubtedly shares these responsibilities when he agrees to implement a particular policy. But he has constantly to remind himself that in the last resort the ultimate decision is not in his hands. This limits his powers, but also relieves him of a certain amount of moral responsibility, all the more so since the President is General de Gaulle himself.' [15] But on his accession to the Presidency, Georges Pompidou became the commander-in-chief. During the election campaign for the Presidency, he was under heavy pressure, but he made no concessions, even to those who urged him before ballot day to reveal the identity of his eventual Prime Minister. 'We must do everything to preserve the institutions of the Fifth Republic which have given the country political strength and stability; we must preserve the role of President of the Republic elected by universal suffrage,' he declared in his programme,[16] and he counter-attacked: 'To have a leader, a majority, is apparently the road to dictatorship. A curious idea. Do we have then to provoke chaos in the National Assembly to prevent riots in the streets? The Fourth Republic, it is true, managed to have both chaos and riots.' [17] The manner in which the devaluation of the franc was decided in July 1969 by the President of the Republic with the agreement of the Prime Minister and the Minister of Finance, and was unexpectedly announced later on Wednesday August 8th in the Council of Ministers, indicates that the most important decisions are still taken by the President after consultation at the top with the few ministers involved. 'Ever since I took up my duties as Head of State,' declared the President at the close of this Cabinet meeting, 'I have considered the currency as the most important and the most pressing problem. Having reviewed all the aspects of our financial situation, I am convinced that a change in the parity of the franc is inevitable. The Prime Minister and the Minister of Finance share this conviction. . . .' [18] It is obvious that had they not shared it they would have had to comply or to resign. The centre of power is certainly the Elysée.

Even so, President Pompidou favours permanent consultation between the Executive and the Legislative. In his presidential election address he wrote, 'The character of this government must, first and foremost, be marked by its relations with parliament, both with the Senate and the National Assembly.' He believes this because first of all he thinks it is the desire of the nation – after the NO at the referendum of April 27, 1969. A less haughty style of authority will have to be adopted if a return to the previous chaos of 'assembly rule' is to be avoided. The second reason is that he is not afraid of discussion, provided that he can still have the last word if need be. De Gaulle had little patience with Assemblies and their rituals. Like a true army officer he was above all concerned with his general staff, not to mention the contempt and the rancour which had piled up during the 1930s and in particular during the tragic spring of 1940, against the politicians whose only talent, according to Malraux, 'is the art of getting around obstacles', a talent which at the same time indicates their 'outstanding inability . . . to face up to the real difficulties'.[19] 'I must confess,' said de Gaulle when the R.P.F. group split in March 1952, 'that in view of the circumstances, both of what is happening and what lies in store for us, I cannot concentrate my attention on what is happening in the hemicycle of parliament.'[20] Things are different with Georges Pompidou. He has indeed known difficult moments in the National Assembly. For instance, he will never forget the accusation made against him in September 1962 of a 'breach of honour', for having assumed the responsibility of a referendum for the election of the President by universal suffrage. The National Assembly was to vote a motion of censure against him because of this on October 4, 1962. But during his six years in office as Prime Minister, partly through necessity and partly because it was in his character to do so, he saw to it that good relations were maintained between the Executive and its majority in parliament. As soon as he became Prime Minister he tried to enlarge the majority by calling the main Christian democrat leaders into his government. However, less than a month later, de Gaulle provoked their departure when he spoke ironically of the European 'volapuk'. It was Georges Pompidou again who in 1966–7 applied himself to the task of uniting the majority in the *Comité d'action pour la Ve République* and gained the support of the *Républicains indépendants* who agreed to back unity of candidature in the first ballot of the March 1967 general election. The fact that under Pompidou relations between the majority and the government improved substantially, compared with what they had been under Michel Debré, was due to a very great extent to the personal influence of Georges Pompidou himself.[21] It is therefore not surprising that he has managed to widen the movement towards the centre, nor that he has chosen as Prime Minister Jacques Chaban-Delmas, former president of the National Assembly, who since 1958 had relentlessly asserted the claim of the Assembly for greater consideration.

The plan of Georges Pompidou, outlined during the presidential campaign and strongly confirmed in the opening statement he made at his first presidential press conference,[22] was no less than to unite all Frenchmen, from the extreme right to the extreme left, including the opposition groups as well as the majority, in a minimum of respect for the institutions and the rules which govern them. Like Napoleon, to whom he attributes the supreme merit of having known how to maintain what had been gained in the Revolution by reconciling the French, Georges Pompidou said, 'For to us, who have over the last thirty years known so many breaking points and disasters at home and abroad, the unifying aspect of Napoleon's achievements appears of particular importance and relevance today.'[23] From the new institutions of the Fifth Republic, the country has indisputably accepted the direct election of the President by universal suffrage and the establishment of a majority which guarantees the stability of the Executive. This will be maintained. On the other hand, de Gaulle's conception of a Head of State ruling without the help of intermediaries, drawing his support directly from the people, has not gained credence. General de Gaulle himself recognized that the political process of calling a referendum was less legitimate than a general election, when on May 30, 1968 he abandoned the idea of a referendum in favour of the dissolution of the National Assembly to resolve a serious national crisis. Moreover, when he tried to prove the contrary on April 27, 1969, he was defeated. Opinion polls have confirmed this analysis. The referendum has not been accepted as a regular feature in French political life and direct democracy is feared by the majority of French people. It will therefore be abandoned. In October 1962 André Malraux stated, with foresight, that 'the Fifth Republic is not merely the Fourth Republic plus de Gaulle'; for when de Gaulle made his exit, the Fourth Republic did not reappear. But the Fifth Republic after de Gaulle is not that of de Gaulle. The basic elements of the institutional transformation in France still remain, but the same cannot be said of the structure of power as conceived by de Gaulle and passionately defended by René Capitant, the most ardent supporter of de Gaulle and the strongest opponent of Pompidou, among the jurists.

EXPANSION AND CONTINUITY IN POLITICS

There is a certain significance in the fact that the first important political decision made by the new presidential team – devaluation – was of an economic and financial nature. On the other hand, the first presidential press conference given a short while before by President Pompidou had indicated no fundamental change in foreign policy. It is still too early to be able to assess the extent of political innovation or continuity in post-de Gaulle gaullism; but in any case, their main centres of interest and their estimation of what can be achieved are noticeably different. It is not that Georges Pompidou, on his accession to the Presidency, has changed his opinions but rather that he now has the power to put his policies into practice. Gone are the romantic hopes of the left-wing gaullists who had dreamed with de Gaulle of a great reconciliation between capitalism and socialism by virtue of an association of labour and capital. While he was Prime Minister, Georges Pompidou considered a referendum on this matter to be inopportune and the country had to wait for the events of May 1968 and his replacement by Maurice Couve de Murville as Premier before de Gaulle could make headway with this gaullist conception of participation – only for it to prove a failure. 'If participation means that the workers must know what is going on in their factories, just as it is in the interests of shareholders to know what is being done with their money, then I am in favour,' explained Georges Pompidou in the course of his presidential campaign. But '. . . if participation means the reintroduction of government by assembly, of what in another language is called the "soviet", then I am against it'.[24] A true liberal, he believes above all in free enterprise, in discussion and in decentralization on American lines. 'What I should like to see,' he says, 'are talks and free negotiations whereby employers and employees alike may settle the ways and means of collaboration, either by collective bargaining or by agreements in firms and professions. In the United States, great emphasis is laid in industry upon individual initiative and on the decentralization of decisions. If we were to follow this example, our own industries would be much more modern and dynamic.'[25] The role of the state is not to regulate everything but to encourage, protect, guide and humanize the efforts of men and industry, which are so vital.

In his first press conference, Pompidou went so far as to say that it was not only necessary but even desirable that French firms should increase their wealth. This is a new language in a country where people expect almost everything from the state and where wealth is always hidden because it is seen as a sign of guilt. In fact he is talking like a true British, German or American conservative, basing the wealth of the nation on the vitality of its industry, and the government's social policy on the wealth of the nation. 'The state,' he declared in *Le Figaro*, 'must define the main lines of policy relating to social progress, make the most important decisions and encourage the various social groups to discuss matters amongst themselves. But it is up to the groups themselves to determine together the conditions necessary for their co-operation.'[26] Here, we are far from de Gaulle's noble conception of a reconciliation between capital and labour. The present aim is rather an attempt to encourage understanding between the two sides, so that they may coexist within the context of a prosperous and expanding economy. The aim will be to encourage collective bargaining and 'contracts'. At the same time a more modest view is held of France's possibilities. 'Devaluation is in direct opposition to the gaullist myth,' André Malraux was to declare at the Council of Ministers on November 23, 1968. 'I am against devaluation.' And de Gaulle had refused to change the parity of the franc even though devaluation was expected. 'We must try and recover,' he declared, 'without having recourse to devaluation.'[27] Nine months later the franc was devalued by $12\frac{1}{2}$ per cent and the new Head of State, Georges Pompidou stated: 'We must base our economic power, which is the source of our social progress and the guarantee of our independence, on facts, by ascertaining the real value of the franc.' [28] The Minister of Finance went one step further when he said, 'The value of a currency is not something which is decided, but something which is observed. . . .' [29] De Gaulle had preferred a general policy of severe deflation, a sudden and prolonged halt to investments and expansion and the risk of unemployment to the humiliation resulting from a forced devaluation and the lowering of the franc, the corner-stone of France's political independence as regards the Anglo-American powers. With Georges Pompidou the economy and domestic policy once again prevail over foreign policy.

The staunch gaullists still uphold the rock of the policy of French independence regarding East-West relations. Michel Debré was relieved of the responsibility of Foreign Affairs, orientated towards a pro-European policy, but he has taken over National Defence, including the '*force de frappe*' (nuclear deterrent). It is still far too early to know whether and to what extent French policy in this field is likely to be inflected. But even if President Pompidou gives precedence to the well-being of Frenchmen over the grandeur of France in the international arena, up to now he has also taken great care to change nothing in the basic orientation of foreign policy as laid down by General de Gaulle. The nuclear deterrent? 'It costs us no more than traditional armaments, it is more effective in discouraging the attacker, it enables us to make considerable technical and industrial progress and, finally, ranks us among the major great powers,' he stated during the presidential campaign, taking up the arguments of General de Gaulle despite electoral pressure. [30] Moreover, he reminded listeners on *Europe No. 1* that 'defence always costs too much when it is not being put to use. But when it is actually needed, we sometimes regret not having devoted more money to it.' He also maintained the granting of aid to the developing countries, the policy of good relations with the East, the refusal to integrate French forces in N.A.T.O. and the major elements of General de Gaulle's Middle East policy. The only innovation is the advocation of a more active European policy. The international scene is no longer shaken by de Gaulle's thunderbolts. But even so, it cannot be said with certainty that the substance of things has greatly changed. The margin of manœuvre left to Georges Pompidou among his political friends, is exceedingly narrow in a field which, furthermore, arouses no great enthusiasm in him. After imperial grandeur we could perhaps speak of the simple but solid wisdom of Louis XVIII.

Notes to Chapter 8

1. Interview given by Raymond Tournoux, *Paris-Match*, 1045, May 17, 1969, p. 96.
2. Message from Georges Pompidou, President of the Republic, read to the National Assembly and to the Senate on Wednesday, June 25, 1969.
3. Interview by Raymond Tournoux, op. cit.
4. Quoted by Pierre Rouanet, *Pompidou*, Bernard Grasset, Paris, 1969, p. 36.
5. Text of a speech published in *Le Monde*, August 16, 1969.
6. Op. cit., p. 20.
7. Quoted by Pierre Rouanet, op. cit., pp. 47–8.
8. Ibid., p. 43.
9. On the attitude of Georges Pompidou during May 1968, see in particular Jean-Raymond Tournoux, *Le Mois de mai du Général*, Plon, Paris, 1969, p. 257 and Pierre Rouanet, op. cit., pp. 247–78.
10. Block notes of July 14, 1968, *Le Figaro littéraire*.
11. Quoted by Pierre Rouanet, op. cit., pp. 214–15.
12. *Réalités*, May 1968, p. 49.
13. Interview by Raymond Tournoux, *Paris-Match*, 1045, May 17, 1969, p. 36.
14. Interview in *L'Express*, September 4–10, 1967, p. 17.
15. *Réalités*, op. cit., p. 49.
16. *Mes dix objectifs*. (My ten aims.)
17. Speech at Villemonble, May 22, 1969.
18. *Le Monde*, August 10–11, 1969.
19. André Malraux. Speech, December 15, 1965, Palais des Sports, Paris.
20. Charles de Gaulle, Press Conference, Monday, March 10, 1952. *Le Monde*, March 12, 1952.
21. On this, see Chapter VI above.
22. Georges Pompidou, Press Conference, July 10, 1969. *Le Monde*, July 12, 1969. '. . . It is desirable,' declared the Head of State, 'and even essential that all political groups, with the exception of those whose one and only aim is revolution, should from now on direct their activity within the framework of our institutions. There will, in the future, be changes in the majority. But in no event must this call into question the régime or lead to crises in the régime . . .'
23. Georges Pompidou, Bi-centenary speech, Ajaccio, August 15, 1969. *Le Monde*, August 16, 1969.
24. Statement in *La vie Française*, May 23, 1969.
25. Statement in *Informations industrielles et commerciales*, June 2, 1969.
26. Statement in *Le Figaro*, June 12, 1969.
27. Charles de Gaulle, Radio–Television address, November 24, 1968.
28. Georges Pompidou. Statement read in the Council of Ministers, August 8, 1969.
29. Valéry Giscard d'Estaing, Radio-Television address, August 8, 1969.
30. Georges Pompidou, Radio-Television address, May 23, 1969.

1958

May 13th: *Coup d'état* at Algiers.

May 15th: Statement made by General de Gaulle declaring his willingness to assume the responsibilities of power.

June 1st: Investiture of General de Gaulle by 329 votes to 224.

June 4th–7th: General de Gaulle's first visit to Algeria.

September 24th: Memorandum from General de Gaulle to Harold Macmillan and President Eisenhower on N.A.T.O.

September 28th: Referendum on the Constitution of the Fifth Republic. The C.N.I., the M.R.P., the socialist S.F.I.O. party, the Radical Party and the gaullist associations voted YES; the *Union des forces démocratiques*, the U.D.S.R. and the Communist Party voted NO. Those voting YES won by 79.25 per cent of votes cast. All the overseas departments, with the exception of Guinea, voted YES and opted for the 'Community'.

October 1st: Creation of the U.N.R. party – *l'Union pour la nouvelle République* – which united most of the gaullist movements.

October 14th: The military ranks left the *Comités de Salut public*.

October 23rd: General de Gaulle proposed the 'paix des braves' to the Algerian rebels.

November 23rd and 30th: General election run on a single candidate, two ballot system. Success of the moderates and U.N.R. gaullists, defeat of the left, especially the communists.

December 21st: General de Gaulle elected to the Presidency of the Republic and the Community by the 81,000 selected 'presidential' voters. He obtained 78.5 per cent of the votes as against 13.1 per cent for the communist candidate and 8.4 per cent for the U.F.D. candidate.

December 28th: Devaluation of the franc, creation of the new franc, external convertibility of the franc.

1959

January 8th: Michel Debré became Prime Minister. The socialists left the majority to build a 'constructive opposition'.

April 14th: Constitution of the *Union démocratique du travail* (U.D.T.) which united the 'left-wing' gaullists.

September 16th: Speech by General de Gaulle proposing autodetermination for Algeria.

November 7th: Speech by General de Gaulle at the Military Academy and the announcement of the creation of a nuclear deterrent.

November 13th–15th: First Party Conference of the U.N.R. at Bordeaux: confrontation between the orthodox gaullists, who finally won, and the 'French Algeria' partisans.

1960

January 24th: The 'barricades' affair at Algiers. The rebels finally surrendered on February 1st.

February 5th: Jacques Soustelle expelled from the government.

February 13th: Explosion of the first French atomic bomb

April 3rd: Creation of the P.S.U. (*Parti socialiste unifié*) by the union of the new left and former socialists or mendesist radicals who, expelled from their party, had formed the Independent Socialist Party.

December 6th: After the rejection of a third motion of censure, the bill for the French nuclear deterrent was finally adopted.

1961

January 8th: Referendum on the principle of auto-determination and on the bill regarding the provisional organization of government in Algeria. The U.N.R., the M.R.P., the socialist S.F.I.O. party all voted YES; the National Group for the Unity of the Republic (*Algérie française*), the Radical Party, the P.S.U. and the Communist Party voted NO; the moderates of the C.N.I. abstained as a group. Those voting YES won by 75.26 per cent of votes cast.

January 25th:	The Servin-Casanova affair was made public by the leaders of the Communist Party.
April 22nd:	Military coup in Algiers. Enforcement of Article 16 of the Constitution. The uprising was quelled on April 25th.
June:	Peasant demonstrations followed by 'round table' discussions with the government.
September 8th:	Failure of attempted assassination of General de Gaulle at Pont-sur-Seine.
September 30th:	Suspension of the use of Article 16 (emergency powers) of the Constitution.

1962

March 18th:	Conclusion of the negotiations between France and the F.L.N. at Evian.
April 8th:	Referendum on the Evian agreements and peace in Algeria. The U.N.R., the M.R.P., the Radical Party, the Socialist Party S.F.I.O., and the Communist Party voted YES; the National Group for the Unity of the Republic and the Poujadist Movement voted NO; the P.S.U. urged its electors to spoil their ballot papers and the C.N.I. gave its electors a free vote. Those who voted YES won by 90.70 per cent of the votes cast.
April 13th:	General Jouhaud condemned to death by the Supreme Military Tribunal for his part in the putsch of April 1961 and his leading role in the O.A.S. (*Organisation de l'Armée secrète*).
April 14th:	Michel Debré, after three years and three months in office, was replaced by Georges Pompidou as Prime Minister.
April 20th:	General Salan, Head of the O.A.S., arrested.
May 15th:	Press Conference by General de Gaulle, who expressed his hostility towards European integration; the M.R.P. ministers left the Pompidou government.
August 22nd:	Unsuccessful attempt at assassination of General de Gaulle, at le Petit-Clamart.
October 4th:	The National Assembly censured the government, by 280 votes out of 480. Parliament was dissolved on October 6th by the President of the Republic.

October 28th: Referendum on the election of the President of the Republic by direct universal suffrage. Only the U.N.R. voted YES; the C.N.I., the M.R.P., the Radical Party and the Socialist Party the S.F.I.O. – united in the 'Coalition of NOES' – voted NO; the P.S.U. and the Communist Party did likewise. Those who voted YES won by 61.75 per cent of the votes cast and 46.44 per cent of the electorate.

October 30th: The *Association pour la V*e *République* launched by André Malraux.

November 9th: Guy Mollet, General Secretary of the S.F.I.O., called upon the electors to vote, on the second ballot of the general election, 'for any candidate except for a U.N.R. candidate' – which signified that, for the first time since 1947, the socialists might vote for a communist candidate.

November 18th–25th: General Election. Success of the U.N.R. and of the moderates or M.R.P. who rallied to the U.N.R. They obtained an absolute majority of seats in the National Assembly; the C.N.I. and the M.R.P. were the chief losers in this election; the S.F.I.O. and the Communist Party won some seats through mutual agreement and standing down in some constituencies.

November 27th: General de Gaulle confirmed Georges Pompidou in his office of Prime Minister.

November 28th: General de Gaulle reprieved General Jouhaud.

1963

January 14th: Press Conference by General de Gaulle, who declared that he was opposed to the entry of Great Britain into the Common Market, and to the multilateral nuclear force proposed by the United States.

March 1st–April 5th: Miners' strike.

June 13th: The National Assembly ratified the Franco-German treaty.

June 15th: France withdrew its fleet from N.A.T.O.

September 12th: Plan for economic and financial stability.

December 18th: Gaston Defferre, of the socialist S.F.I.O. party, announced he would stand for the presidential election.

1964

January 27th: France recognized Communist China.

April 17th: General de Gaulle underwent an operation at the Cochin hospital for the prostate gland.

July 11th: Death of Maurice Thorez, president of the French Communist Party.

1965

January 7th: France converted 150 million dollars into gold.

February 4th: Press Conference of General de Gaulle advocating the return to the gold-standard.

May 8th: Gaston Defferre proposed the creation of a Democratic Socialist Federation.

June 18th: Failure of the project of a Democratic Socialist Federation; On June 25th, Gaston Defferre withdrew his candidacy for the Presidency.

July 6th: The French permanent representative at the E.E.C. left Brussels. A serious crisis arose in the Common Market.

September 9th: François Mitterrand announced he would stand for the Presidency of the Republic.

September 10th: Creation of the *Fédération de la gauche démocrate et socialiste* (F.G.D.S.), composed of the S.F.I.O., the Radical Party and various clubs.

November 4th: Radio-Television speech by General de Gaulle announcing his intention to stand for the Presidency in the forthcoming election.

December 5th: First round of the presidential election. With 43.9 per cent of the votes cast General de Gaulle had to face a second round. François Mitterrand, candidate for the F.G.D.S., the P.S.U. and the Communist Party, was the other candidate to qualify for the second round. Jean Lecanuet, candidate of the C.N.I. and the M.R.P., obtained 15.7 per cent of the votes; Jean-Louis Tixier-Vignancour, a nationalist of the extreme right, obtained 5.3 per cent of the votes, Pierre Marcilhacy 1.73 per cent and Marcel Barbu 1.16 per cent.

December 9th: François Mitterrand elected, for six months, as president of the F.G.D.S.; Jean Lecanuet launched the *Centre démocrate*.

December 19th: General de Gaulle re-elected President of the Republic, by 55.2 per cent of the votes cast.

1966

January 8th: New Pompidou government after the presidential election; Valéry Giscard d'Estaing left his post as Minister of Finance to be replaced by Michel Debré; Edgar Faure entered the government as Minister of Agriculture.

January 29th: Agreement in Luxembourg by the Foreign Ministers of the Six to further the aims of the Common Market.

February 21st: Press Conference by General de Gaulle, who announced the withdrawal of France from N.A.T.O. France remained a member of the Atlantic Alliance.

May 11th: First meeting of the *Comité d'action pour la Ve République*, presided over by Georges Pompidou.

September 1st: Speech of General de Gaulle, at Pnom-Penh, on Vietnam.

December 20th: Electoral agreement between the Federation of the Left (*Fédération de la gauche démocrate et socialiste*) and the Communist Party.

1967

January 10th: Press Conference of Valéry Giscard d'Estaing (the 'YES, BUT . . .')

March 5th–12th: General Election. The U.D.Ve – grouping the gaullists and the Independent Republicans – retained by a narrow margin its majority in the National Assembly; better results than usual for the F.G.D.S. and for the Communist Party thanks to their election pacts; poor results for the centrists.

April 6th: Georges Pompidou again Prime Minister.

April 26th: The government decided to ask the National Assembly to grant it 'special powers' to make decisions in the economic and financial fields until October 31st.

June 21st: General de Gaulle condemned the beginning of hostilities by Israel on June 5th.

July 24th: General de Gaulle's speech at Montreal: 'Long live Free Quebec!' (*Vive le Québec libre!*)

August 17th: Statement by Valéry Giscard d'Estaing against the 'single-handed exercise of power'.

September 13th: The M.R.P. ceased its activities as a political party.

November 24th–26th: Fourth Party Conference of the U.N.R.-U.D.T. at Lille. Creation of the *Union des démocrates pour la Ve République*.

1968

January 19th: Robert Poujade elected general secretary of the U.D.V^e.

January 26th: New plan launched to aid the economy.

February 24th: Agreement between the F.G.D.S. and the Communist Party on a common electoral platform.

March 22nd: Birth of the 'Movement of March 22nd' at the Arts Faculty in Nanterre.

May 2nd: Following the proposal from Hanoi, the Americans and North Vietnamese agree to open peace talks in Paris, on May 10th.

May 2nd–3rd: Lectures were suspended at the Faculty of Nanterre; the Sorbonne was closed.

May 10th: Night of riots in Paris; sixty barricades in the Latin Quarter.

May 11th: Broadcast by Georges Pompidou who re-opened the Sorbonne.

May 15th: Renault factory at Cléon occupied by workers.

May 16th–20th: Strikes and factories occupied throughout France.

May 22nd: Motion of censure resisted in the National Assembly.

May 24th: Broadcast by General de Gaulle, who announced a referendum.

May 25th–27th: Negotiations between the government, employers and trade unions in the rue de Grenelle. Protocol agreement rejected by the rank and file.

May 28th: François Mitterrand declared his intention to stand as President of the Republic in the event of there being an election.

May 29th: Council of Ministers adjourned; General de Gaulle left Paris; Pierre Mendès France declared that he was ready to form a provisional government.

May 30th: Statement on the radio by General de Gaulle, who dissolved the National Assembly, kept Georges Pompidou as Prime Minister and called for the constitution of Committees for the Defence of the Republic; demonstration by gaullists from la Concorde to l'Etoile.

June 4th–6th: Return to work in many factories and firms, and in the civil service.

June 16th: The Sorbonne, occupied by the students since May 13th, was evacuated.

June 23rd–30th: General Election. Overwhelming success for the U.D.R. and the Républicains indépendants, no change for the centrists and a heavy defeat for the entire left.

July 10th: Georges Pompidou, after six years and two months in office, was replaced by Maurice Couve de Murville, as Prime Minister. General de Gaulle wrote to him: '. . . I hope sincerely that you will undertake any mission that may be entrusted you, and assume any mandate which the nation may one day give you.'

August 24th: Explosion of the first French H-bomb.

October 3rd: Alain Poher elected president of the Senate, replacing Gaston Monnerville who did not stand again for office.

October 11th: The National Assembly adopted the bill for Higher Education, by 441 votes to none.

November 2nd–3rd: The National Council of the S.F.I.O., at Clichy, demanded the replacement of the F.G.D.S. by a 'firmly socialist' party; on 7th, François Mitterrand announced to the executive committee of the F.G.D.S. that he considered himself relieved from the office of president.

November 23rd: Extraordinary meeting of the Council of Ministers: the franc would not be devalued. The government proposed a programme of measures to redress the economic situation.

1969

January 22nd: Council of Ministers. Declaration by General de Gaulle, after the statements made by Georges Pompidou at Rome regarding the possibility of his being a candidate for the Presidency: 'I have both the duty and the intention to fulfil the mandate entrusted to me to the end.'

April 27th: Referendum on regionalization and the reform of the Senate; all the parties decided to vote NO, except the U.D.R. and the majority of the Républicains indépendants; Valéry Giscard d'Estaing did not give his approval to the project. Those voting NO won by 53.1 per cent of the votes cast. General de Gaulle retired immediately from the office of President of the Republic. The president of the Senate, Alain Poher, was the interim President. The Couve de Murville government remained in office. René Capitant, Minister of Justice, resigned from the government.

June 1st: First round of the presidential election. Georges Pompidou, backed by the U.D.R., the Républicains indépendants – including Valéry Giscard d'Estaing – and part of the centrist group – Jacques Duhamel, Joseph Fontanet, René Pleven notably – came first with 44.4 per cent of the votes cast; the centrist candidate, Alain Poher, backed by the radicals too, obtained 23.3 per cent of the votes. Jacques Duclos, communist, obtained 21.2 per cent; Gaston Defferre, socialist, supported by Pierre Mendès-France, 5 per cent; Michel Rocard, P.S.U., 3.6 per cent; Louis Ducatel 1.2 per cent and Alain Krivine, trotskyist, 1 per cent of the votes cast.

June 15th: Second round of the presidential election. Georges Pompidou elected President of the Republic, by 57.5 per cent of the votes cast.

June 21st: Jacques Chaban-Delmas, president of the National Assembly since 1958, appointed Prime Minister, replacing Maurice Couve de Murville. Return of Valéry Giscard d'Estaing; departure of Edgar Faure;

entry of the centrists, René Pleven, Jacques Duhamel and Joseph Fontanet. Maurice Schumann took over the Ministry of Foreign Affairs from Michel Debré, who became Minister of Defence.

July 4th: Creation of the *Centre démocratie et progrès* by those centrists 'converted' to the majority.

July 10th: First Press Conference by Georges Pompidou at the Elysée.

August 8th: Extraordinary meeting of the Council of Ministers; the franc was devalued. Announcement of a plan to redress the economic balance.

September 17th: Statement of government policy by Jacques Chaban-Delmas approved by 369 votes to 85 in the National Assembly.

1970

November 9th: General de Gaulle died at Colombey-les-deux-Eglises. He was eighty and had just published the first volume of his *Mémoires d'Espoir* (Le Renouveau, 1958–1962) and written chapters 1 and 2 of the second volume.

INDEX

The meanings of groups of initials are given on page 11